THE DATABASE
FACTORY

THE DATABASE FACTORY

Active Database for Enterprise Computing

Stephen G. Schur

John Wiley & Sons, Inc.

New York • Chichester • Brisbane • Toronto • Singapore

Publisher: Katherine Schowalter
Senior Acquisitions Editor: Diane Cerra
Managing Editor: Jacqueline A. Martin
Composition: Kevin Shafer & Associates

Designations used by companies to distinguish their products are often claimed as trademarks. In all instances where John Wiley & Sons, Inc., is aware of a claim, the product names appear in initial capital or all capital letters. Readers, however, should contact the appropriate companies for more complete information regarding trademarks and registration.

This text is printed on acid-free paper.

This publication is designed to provide accurate and authoritative information in regard to the subject matter covered. It is sold with the understanding that the publisher is not engaged in rendering legal, accounting, or other professional service. If legal advice or other expert assistance is required, the services of a competent professional person should be sought. FROM A DECLARATION OF PRINCIPLES JOINTLY ADOPTED BY A COMMITTEE OF THE AMERICAN BAR ASSOCIATION AND A COMMITTEE OF PUBLISHERS.

Library of Congress Cataloging-in-Publication Data:
Schur, Stephen G.
        The database factory: active database for enterprise computing/ Stephen G. Schur
        p. cm.
        Includes bibliographical references.
        ISBN 0-471-55843-5. — ISBN 0-471-55844-3 (pbk.)
        1. Distributed data bases. 2. Data base design. I. Title.
QA76.9.D3S335 1994
005.75'8—dc20

Printed in the United States of America
10 9 8 7 6 5 4 3 2 1

This book is dedicated to my wife, Maxine

ABOUT THE AUTHOR

Stephen Schur is co-founder and vice-president of Productive Methods, Inc., a consulting organization headquartered in San Mateo, California. Incorporated in 1982, the company's mission is to plan, design, and implement active database information systems. Prior to forming Productive Methods, Schur designed information systems for organizations in the financial, manufacturing, and transportation sectors.

Schur's articles in the trade press popularize and explain the active database paradigm. Recognized as an industry expert, he speaks at database and strategic technology symposia. A graduate of Middlebury College, Schur received his postgraduate certificates from the University of Paris and Victoria University of Wellington.

CONTENTS

2

DIVISION OF LABOR: CLIENT/SERVER 27

3

AUTOMATING AUTOMATION: ACTIVE DATABASE 51

4

THE ASSEMBLY LINE: ACTIVE COMPONENT ASSEMBLIES 77

5

BLUEPRINTS: COMPONENT CASE DESIGN 105

6

CONCURRENT SOFTWARE ENGINEERING: SUCCESS CIRCLES   133

7

JUST-IN-TIME: STATE-BASED BEHAVIOR   159

8

MACHINE TOOLS: DATABASE AGENTS   185

9

THE DATA WAREHOUSE   209

10

THE INSTRUMENT PANEL: ACTIVE DATABASE FOR COMPETITIVE ADVANTAGE

PREFACE

A new vision of enterprise computing is now emerging, just when it is most urgently needed. Active database offers such exciting possibilities that I feel compelled to share how the active paradigm can help us to develop information systems better, faster, and at lower cost than in the past.

In information technology as in general business, the technical advances of recent years have created new challenges. The downsizing of computer hardware has led to distributed computing environments. The monolithic enterprise mainframe has yielded to a powerful but complex world of diverse client/server products. The downsizing of corporations has removed entire management layers from the organization chart. Decision-making details have been largely delegated to "empowered" staff. Middle management's reporting responsibilities have been largely delegated to software, expanding the role of database information systems. Information from the database drives corporate operations, highlighting the need for quality and relevance in database operations.

As software development evolves from a craft to an engineering discipline, the production of information needs to become as automated and standardized as the production of manufactured goods. The Database Factory approach applies the principles of modern "lean" manufacturing to information production. The benefits of this approach include

- **Low-cost information systems.** Sharable, reusable active components instead of complex, monolithic programs.
- **Rapid deployment.** Self-adjusting data-oriented applications instead of rigid, labor-intensive procedural data processing.
- **Demand-driven production.** Concurrent software engineering and business process engineering instead of dead-on-arrival application programs.

Realizing these benefits is neither automatic nor easy. Skill, discipline, and training are required for information technology professionals and managers alike. The goal of this book is to show how to plan, build, and implement active database information systems.

This book is primarily intended for software developers wishing to build active database applications. For software engineers, *The Database Factory* will ease the pain of the paradigm shift. Professionals involved in business process engineering are the secondary audience of this book. They will find here an event-driven approach to workflow integration. Technology managers responsible for migrating enterprise computing from the "glass house" to the client/server environment will find practical insights to help them in their risk-laden but necessary task.

ACKNOWLEDGMENTS

I must acknowledge the tremendous influence of Dr. E. F. Codd, the father of the relational database model, and of Taiichi Ohno and Shigeo Shingo, the fathers of the Toyota production system. My thanks go to Philip Chapnick of Miller Freeman publications who encouraged me to write this book. I would like to thank my patient editor, Diane Cerra, whose support made this project possible. I owe much to Dr. Lani Spund of Apple Computer for his guidance with the VITAL systems architecture. Thanks to Tim Negris of Oracle Corporation for applying rigor and discipline to the main concepts. I am grateful to Tarakam Peddada of Sun Microsystems for his helpful comments. I would like to thank Peter Dolan, Ray Harrison, Bill Phal, David Taylor and Karen Watterson for their insights and assistance. I am also deeply indebted to the skunkworks developers and "tiger team" participants among my consulting clients.

ACKNOWLEDGMENTS

1

DATABASE FACTORY ORIENTATION TOUR

This chapter presents the Database Factory approach to enterprise computing and explains why it is urgently needed. Corporate data is the primary resource for informed decisions, a prerequisite for competitiveness. However, despite such efforts as structured programming, CASE and 4GLs, most database applications fail to fully transform the raw data resource into the information required to support enterprise goals. The failure arises from rigid, narrow-focus application architecture, not the underlying database technology. The Database Factory approach applies the manufacturing principles of automation and standardization to software engineering. Just-in-time assembly, concurrent software engineering, successive refinement, and mistake-proofing are manufacturing principles that lend themselves to software development. For software manufacturing to be successful, three major realignments must first prepare the foundation: priority shift, paradigm shift, and technology shift.

■ 1.1 EMPOWER THE DATABASE TO EMPOWER THE WORKFORCE

During the Machine Age, the measure of power was heavy iron typified by cannon, locomotives, and rolling mills. In the Information Age, the measure of power is the depth, timeliness, and accessibility of knowledge. Communications bandwidth has become more crucial than shop floor capacity. Without the ability to communicate by telephone, an enterprise is deaf and dumb. Without access to the database, an organization is blind. Because every firm is now directly or indirectly reliant on computer software, every decision point in the enterprise is an interface point between workers and information systems. The alignment of information flows with workflows distributed throughout an organization is known as *enterprise computing*.

In an information-intensive business environment, knowledge is power. Competitiveness pivots on how effectively information systems enable management and staff to gain advantages. The single most important requirement for commercial power is the ability to transform operational data into tactical information, and ultimately into strategic knowledge. The main resource that fuels this power is the corporate database.

Imagine a clean, quiet factory working day and night to produce the one product that forms part of all other products: information. This factory, the Database Factory, is the subject of this book. Figure 1.1 shows the itinerary of a factory tour suggested by the sequence of chapters in this book.

This chapter introduces the premise of the Database Factory and explains why it is urgently needed. Chapter 2 presents a client/server primer while contrasting passive and active databases. Chapter 3 explains database server programming and event management. Chapter 4 discusses why active component architecture provides benefits similar to those of modern manufacturing technology. Chapter 5 shows how sharable and reusable code can cut costs while raising the quality of software. Chapter 6 explains how mixed teams align information systems to business workflows. Chapter 7 shows how to build self-adjusting state-based information systems. Chapter 8 explains the categories and benefits of database agents. Chapter 9 includes a proven client/server data warehouse design. Chapter 10 examines the uses of an active database to gain a competitive advantage.

The center of Figure 1.1 shows the Database Factory floor plan, which will be explained in detail throughout the remainder of this book. The active database server at the hub of factory operations incorporates its own control infrastructure and event-management infrastructure, as well as SQL execution facilities. The active client coordinates its behavior with that of the active server. Database agents synchronize the active database environment. The Data Warehouse consolidates data from the active server and older technology sources such as mainframe files for enterprise distribution. The Development Warehouse is the repository of standard components for active applications.

The Database Factory is a flexible factory. Market forces and business events determine what is produced, how it is produced, and where it is distributed. This

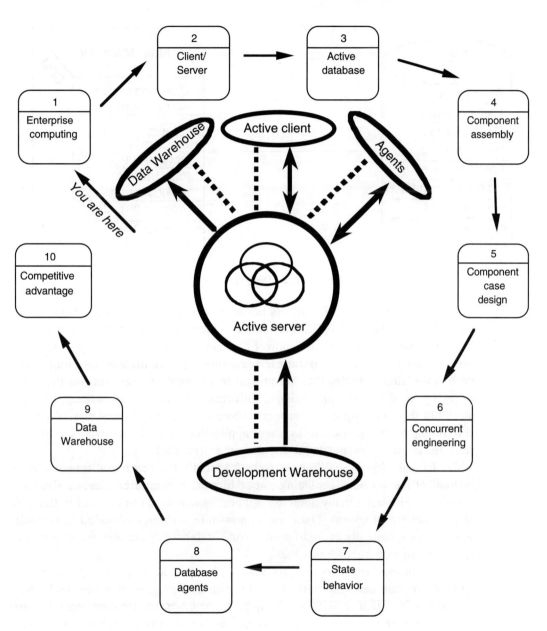

Figure 1.1 Database Factory tour

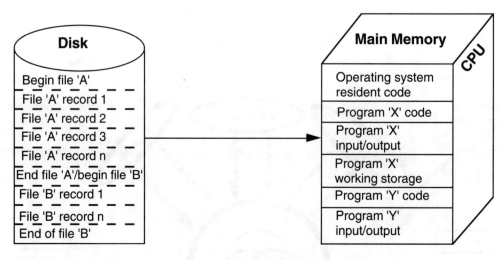

Figure 1.2 Data retrieval

factory has no bureaucratic barriers between management and staff, between the front office and the back office, between the enterprise and its trading partners.

As the nature of commercial power changes from capital-intensity to information-intensity, the role of database technology grows increasingly important. Problem-solving activities that are critical to corporate success rely on the firm's collection of database applications. Unfortunately, these database applications often fall short of supporting corporate objectives. Although they may succeed in automating routine clerical tasks, these applications have a narrow focus that prevents the coordination needed to support enterprise goals.

Predatabase *legacy applications* were frequently built as literal translations of manual office systems, replacing paper files with computer files, as shown in Figure 1.2. Similarly, many database applications continue to be built in the style of predatabase programs. Database access code is often embedded in compiler language programs. By embedding this code, database operations are subordinated to rigid procedural program logic.

Most compiler languages are procedural. They provide step-by-step instructions on how program tasks are performed. Of course, a programmer must code these instructions and that activity can be quite labor-intensive. By contrast, relational database operations are declarative. They specify operations in terms of the results of the operation by using a nonprocedural language such as *Structured Query Language* (SQL). The specific means by which those results are achieved is delegated to the database server.

Programming, testing, and refining declarative database operations is faster than programming, testing, and refining procedural program routines. In cases where procedural programming supplements the lack of procedural constructs in standard SQL, server-based procedural database programming is an alternative which offers the advantages of shared code with fast, central execution.

Because of the relatively high expense of writing and maintaining program code, procedural language applications historically have addressed the stable, core business applications that are tied to the accounting cycle. Unfortunately, because these stable applications automate cost centers and not profit centers, they often hold the least promise for commercial advantage. A company that restricts its database to clerical applications finds it difficult to compete with a business that uses a fully integrated active database. The company that uses such a database can help its planning, production, distribution, and customer service teams respond to ever-changing business conditions. This responsiveness is possible because the active database environment shown in the center of Figure 1.1 aligns workflows with data flows to synchronize operations with changing business conditions.

Whenever today's applications are designed simply to emulate those of a more stable era, database technology falls short of realizing its potential. But this need not be the case.

The corporate database contains information vital to controlling inventory, anticipating demand for products, or evaluating investment risk. However, this valuable knowledge lies latent within the mass of less-significant data. Furthermore, data that appears of little value in one context may prove crucial in another. The challenge of enterprise computing is to design for the full spectrum of constant business change.

To meet this challenge, the database structures, the data-access capabilities, and the data-distribution function must actively rather than passively model the enterprise. The "factory" operations that process data into information must automatically adjust themselves to events. Relational database-management software is fully capable of handling an active, event-driven enterprise model. Using today's software technology and an active model of the enterprise, we can make database systems as robust and flexible as real-time manufacturing systems. Only by releasing the power within the database can we hope to empower the workforce.

■ 1.2 BRIDGING THE APPLICATION GAP

Software development technology has lagged behind the impressive hardware advances of recent years. Computer hardware continues its steady improvement in price/performance, thus creating a demand for "downsized" database applications in areas previously not considered to be cost-justified. Computing and the demand for more computing pervades all sectors of the enterprise.

This rise in demand, fueled by hardware advances, exacerbates the well-known backlog between the time an information system is "ordered" or requested and the time that development work begins. The system-development backlog levies a costly premium both monetarily and qualitatively. The law of supply and demand applies to information systems in the following ways:

- **Cost.** Whenever any product is in short supply relative to demand, the market price for that product tends to be inflated.
- **Quality.** When the customer has to line up or back-order years in advance, there is less pressure for product quality than is the case when competing offerings are available for the customer to pick and choose.
- **Opportunity.** Whenever a company lacks knowledge about important business issues such as its resources, customers, bank accounts, sales, or inventory, such ignorance impairs corporate performance. A slow time-to-market cycle for information systems translates into a slow cycle time for projects and products. Workgroups become frustrated with their inability to make sound decisions and "reverse delegate" to management. Work must go on, even though it is based on poor or late information, and lost opportunity is the usual end result.

A development backlog of software forces corporate management information systems (MIS) departments into a reactive mode. Once agents of change, today's MIS managers must allocate much of their budget to maintaining their existing applications. Many of these applications were implemented years ago using proprietary operating systems and traditional programming languages. The MIS department perpetuates the backlog by maintaining these legacy applications on proprietary platforms. The closed proprietary environments provide no advantage in standardization, interoperability, or portability. Instead, legacy applications bury users in paperwork and create "islands of inefficiency."

In contrast to the costs of a proprietary platform, a proactive MIS group can achieve budget-effective results through *downsizing*, which involves porting mainframe and minicomputer applications to smaller hardware platforms such as personal computers. *Rightsizing* involves the replacement of proprietary technology (usually mainframe-based) with more compact and cost-effective platforms, which are the right size for most applications. In practice, downsizing and rightsizing are often the same. When a stable COBOL application is ported from a mainframe to

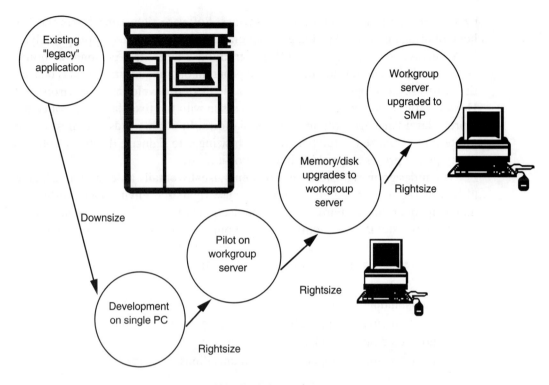

Figure 1.3 Rightsizing

a workgroup local area network (LAN), both downsizing and rightsizing have occurred.

Rightsizing introduces the idea of scalable applications. *Application scaling* means that the application performance varies linearly with the power and capacity of the platform. During initial development, for example, a proactive MIS group can cut hardware costs by rightsizing information systems on inexpensive personal computers, and then scale up the implementation platform from single-processor *reduced instruction set computer* (RISC) workstations to full-scale *symmetric multiprocessor* (SMP) configurations to meet the burgeoning needs of the application. Because hardware costs are deferred until the application delivers its benefits, the scalable hardware architecture shown in Figure 1.3 appeals to cost-conscious management.

Software rightsizing holds the promise of even more dramatic savings than hardware rightsizing, but is more difficult to achieve. Because labor costs are much higher than hardware costs in the typical MIS budget, potential labor savings are even more significant than hardware savings. Software rightsizing offers the best hope of bridging the application gap, but only if it is implemented appropriately.

Arguably, developing a COBOL program on a large, fast personal computer (PC) costs less than developing the same program on a mainframe. This is because the software developer has sole use of a dedicated development environment. However, these savings are small in comparison with the fixed labor cost of coding a procedural language program on any platform. In other words, the most appropriate way to realize the full benefit of rightsizing is to rightsize the entire software development process by making it less labor-intensive.

System design in rightsized environments usually entails at least as much complexity as the mainframe equivalent. Because rightsized environments often mix hardware, operating systems, and communications vendors, they can be more complex to administer than monolithic minicomputer or mainframe environments.

Designing a rightsized database application calls for many of the same skills as those required to design a mainframe database application, including

- Understanding the *database management system* (DBMS)
- Understanding the application logic and logical database design
- Understanding the application user interface
- Understanding the application communications interface.

In mainframe architecture, the entire application is centralized on the mainframe and the terminals are simply peripheral devices. By contrast, systems integration skills are required to make the various disparate components of a rightsized solution work well together.

In a rightsized client/server environment, the application and its data are distributed between the server machine on which the database resides and the client machines interfacing with the user. The workstations running client software often run single-user operating systems (such as MS-DOS with Microsoft Windows). Most high-performance database servers require a multiuser, multiprocess operating system such as UNIX or Windows NT. Since the client software and the server software execute on autonomous devices, the hardware most suitable for these processes may come from different vendors. Mixed-vendor systems require more skill to integrate than single-vendor implementations.

Designing server processes requires different skills from those needed to program client application software. For that matter, different skills are needed to design such diverse layers of the client application as a *graphical user interface* (GUI) and a SQL command handler. Between the client and the server is the communications network and its protocol (called *middleware*), the knowledge of which is a skill in itself.

Complexity, specialization, and division of labor are inherent characteristics of client/server database architecture. For client/server database applications to succeed, customers must be able to utilize them without first having to master or even fully understand the enabling technology. The goal is to put database users on a similar footing with automobile users. Most drivers are neither automotive engineers nor garage mechanics.

■ 1.3 FROM HAND-CRAFTED TO MANUFACTURED SOFTWARE

Software development currently is a craft. As in the case of other handicrafts, assessing the value of individual artifacts is subjective. In the absence of a more rigorous yardstick, projects are often judged by *weight*, the number of lines of program code. Sometimes projects are evaluated by *time*, that is, by the number of years of effort. Both approaches are subjective and confuse efforts with results, reward verbose COBOL programs, and encourage slow cycle time. Sometimes software is evaluated in an aesthetic framework, as though it were some kind of collectible item such as an antique farm implement. Cryptic programs that can be deciphered only by the individual who wrote them are subjectively valued as "elegant," as though convoluted or cryptic software were elegant.

Standard parts and automated manufacturing are the hallmarks of the modern Industrial Age. In practical terms, the two go together. Race cars are built by hand using custom-made parts, but are expensive and require constant maintenance. Race cars perform well on the racetrack, but we certainly would not commute to work in one.

Software manufacturing involves transferring the twin disciplines of standard parts and automated manufacture from industrial manufacturing to software development. The notion of software manufacturing is so intuitively appealing that a number of expedients have been tried during the last decade with varying degrees of success.

1.3.1 Structured Programming

Structured programming was a pioneering effort to downsize software. The main idea in structured programming is to reduce the complexity of large programs by breaking them down into smaller subprograms. This is frequently accomplished through *functional decomposition*, the breakdown of a large multipurpose program into a number of single-purpose routines. Figure 1.4 compares an unstructured and a structured program design. The unstructured monolith on the left could have

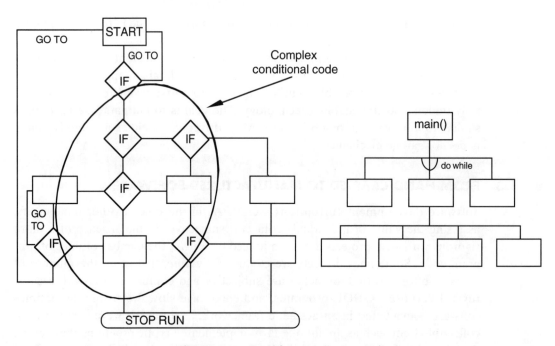

Figure 1.4 Complex versus structured

been written 20 years ago in assembly language for implementation on a mainframe having less computational power than a personal computer's Intel 80486 processor. On the right is the equivalent structured design, which is clearly easier to maintain and understand. Instead of the confusing jumble of conditional GO TO branch instructions of the monolith, the top-level routine of the structured program calls a number of single-purpose routines dedicated to specific functions.

Structured programming promotes standard coding practices. Because the standard coding remains after the original programmers depart, structured programming represents a qualitative advance over earlier *ad hoc* approaches. However, the limited scope of structured programming constrains its effectiveness. Structured programming has served well as a programming technique, but programs are only effective when they serve business needs.

Many well-programmed applications are dead-on-arrival (DOA) because they fail to meet their intended business goals. This is caused either by defective analysis or by shifts in business requirements during the development cycle. Because analysis and design come before programming, structured programming techniques are powerless to rectify design flaws. The failure of applications to meet evolving business needs is often accentuated by a design phase that has been needlessly lengthened with excessive meetings. In a volatile business environment, the longer it takes to complete a design, the less relevant that design is likely to be.

Instead of adding labor to an activity that is already labor-intensive, a better approach would be to reap the benefits of structured programming without the additional costs. One potential solution is to downsize and centralize core functionality by implementing structured programs within the database server together with the data on which these programs operate.

When a monolithic client program is replaced by a collection of server-based database programs, the required changes may be isolated in one of these small components, which can subsequently be modified without impacting other components. Furthermore, the database operations that provide the main functionality of a database program can be coded and tested by using interactive SQL, which requires much less time than that required for coding and testing embedded SQL procedural language programs.

1.3.2 CASE

Computer-aided software engineering (CASE) is intended to bring partial automation to database and process design. CASE is derived from engineering *computer-aided design* (CAD) applications. Just as an electronic engineer's productivity can be assisted by using CAD to design an integrated circuit, CASE software seeks to augment a software engineer's productivity.

CASE products are often classified as upper-CASE or lower-CASE. *Upper-CASE software* helps a software engineer draw design documents such as the entity-relationship diagram shown in Figure 1.5. *Lower-CASE software* generates code, such as the SQL commands to create tables in a database.

Automated documentation and code generation are useful capabilities, but current CASE products do not automate software design as completely as CAD software automates integrated circuit design. CASE vendors never claim that they use their own CASE product to generate itself, nor is it realistic to expect proprietary CASE products to be fully interoperable with open-systems applications. Chapter 6 examines CASE for active databases in the context of the Development Warehouse.

Structured programming attempts standardization without automation, and proprietary CASE—the type of CASE used to design traditional structured programs—results in partial automation without standardization. Since neither approach yields a complete solution, companies often despair of developing an in-house solution. As an alternative, these companies turn to commercial application packages to avoid the cost, risk, and delay of custom programming.

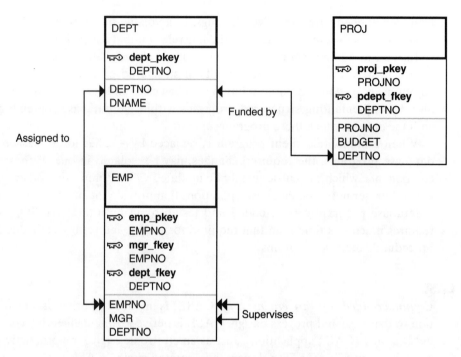

Figure 1.5 CASE design document

1.3.3 Application Packages

A *package* is an application that is sold by a vendor to perform specific functions in a given subject area, such as inventory control or accounts payable. Packages are often specific to a subject area within a vertical market, such as retail point-of-sale. The main premise of a package is that the customer need not create an individual application because it has already been written and packaged by the vendor.

The benefits of substituting packages for in-house development are

- **Rapid availability.** The customer simply installs the package, monitors results during a parallel testing period, and adjusts parameters as needed.
- **Labor displacement.** The vendor's staff creates and maintains the package. Development costs are shared among the customers of the package, each of whom usually pays less than the cost to write and maintain specific subject-area applications in-house.
- **Hand-holding.** Vendors train customer employees in the use of the package. Customers who encounter difficulties can get help from support representatives, or can work together through a user group.

The disadvantages of substituting packages for in-house development are

- **Incomplete solution.** The package is a compromise that addresses the broad requirements of a subject area. Individual customer requirements may require custom modifications of the package, but the package may or may not allow such customization. Extensive customization usually negates the labor displacement and cost-saving advantages of the package.
- **Proprietary.** Packages are often sold without their source code, so the customer has no way to audit the package, to enhance the package for a better satisfaction of business needs, or to fix any defect in the package. Essentially, the customer is at the mercy of the vendor, and consequently at risk if the vendor goes out of business.
- **Incompatibility.** In-house applications and packages from different vendors may not be fully compatible. The lines of demarcation between subject areas may be fuzzy enough that important functions are either handled redundantly, or not handled at all.

1.3.4 Fourth-Generation Languages (4GLs)

A *fourth-generation language* (4GL) creates an application in a nonprocedural manner by means of high-level commands that specify the results of an operation, not how that operation is to be performed. By contrast, a third-generation language (3GL) such as COBOL or FORTRAN uses lower-level commands to specify in great detail the procedural steps in the program. Data-manipulation languages for relational database-management systems (notably SQL) resemble 4GLs in that they are nonprocedural and operate on sets of rows, unlike the procedural record-oriented access methods of earlier database models.

The advantages of using a 4GL are

- **Faster development.** Prototyping and implementing an application using a 4GL takes less time than designing, coding, and debugging a 3GL application.
- **Consistency.** A 4GL is a program that writes programs, so it can be expected to generate the same low-level commands from high-level commands every time. The low-level commands generated for SQL access are pretested and work correctly the first time.
- **Disposability**. Because of the relatively low labor cost invested in a nonprocedural 4GL program, we can afford to swap it out when it no longer meets your business needs. Discarding and regenerating a 4GL application is often less expensive than attempting to modify it.

The principal disadvantages of 4GLs are

- **Proprietary.** Unlike compiler languages such as C++ or declarative languages such as PROLOG or even SQL, no standardization exists for 4GLs. A given 4GL may generate source code for a standard language. It may run on a variety of hardware and operating system platforms, but it is unique from any other 4GL in syntax or internal design.
- **Simplistic.** Classic 4GLs automate rote data-processing tasks. Once the user gets past the learning curve, the 4GL provides a relatively straightforward means of report generation or data-entry screen processing. The 4GL's functionality may be insufficient for more complex problems, forcing the use of a 3GL such as C or FORTRAN.

■ 1.4 SOFTWARE ASSET MANAGEMENT

To summarize, the benefits of structured programming, CASE, application packages, and 4GLs are

- **Labor displacement.** An external third party writes and ideally maintains the application programs.
- **Generality.** Development costs of a small variety of generic baseline designs are amortized over a wide user base in multiple customer sites.
- **Rapidity.** The period of uncertainty before an application is implemented is reduced by the reuse of prior work, or by the automation of new work.

Although all these benefits are clearly desirable, none of the various approaches tried during the last 25 years solves the problem of how to make software less labor-intensive and more reliable. These approaches simply are labor-saving devices for computer programmers. In reality, partial automation of conventional programming solves the wrong problem. Programming faster may be beneficial, but programming less is better by far.

The real challenge is to reduce intermediate layers of expense, delay, and distortion between the event-driven business world and its information model. Application programs comprise much of the intermediate overhead between the active enterprise and its information content. If the event-driven business environment changes faster than the programs that model it, the programs are a drag on corporate performance. Information, key facts, and measures of business performance all are to be found in the database.

Database components containing both information and the methods of operating on that information represent an asset to be managed. They hold value as a corporate resource and as the work-in-process inventory of software development. From the viewpoint of software asset management, the database is an asset to be managed, while program development and maintenance are a liability to be reduced.

Only when we maximize database assets and minimize program liabilities can we hope to develop information systems faster, better, and at a lower cost. For too long, the process model has received undue attention at the expense of the data model. Programs that embody the process model automate manual data processing business procedures. The database, which embodies the data model, automates facts, business relationships, and (in active servers) information production.

∎ 1.5 SOFTWARE MANUFACTURING CONCEPTS

Faced with the imperative of making software development work better so that the enterprise can work better, how can we approach the problem? How can a company move from handcrafted artifacts to standard, interchangeable components and automated software manufacture? One promising approach views software asset management similarly to asset management in industrial manufacturing. Consider the following useful trends in real-world manufacturing:

- Just-in-time inventory
- Flexible factory
- Concurrent engineering
- Successive refinement/quality circles
- Mistake proofing.

This book explores in detail how these approaches might apply to manufacturing software applications in a database factory. Each of these proven principles of manufacturing serves as a high-level guide toward automation and standardization of software development.

1.5.1 Just-in-Time Inventory

Whether because of or in spite of the backlog, applications are often pushed on customers who neither need nor want them. The scenario is similar to shopping at a store that has an overabundance of things we do not want or no longer want, but is chronically out of stock for those items we currently need. In commerce, low utility and high waste are symptomatic of supply-driven or push inventory. In information systems, some likely causes are

- **Long lead times required by computer programming.** Fewer or smaller programs or, ideally, none at all are much more desirable.
- **Prespecification during requirements definition.** Demand-driven rapid prototype development is preferable.
- **Freezing the design.** Since it is impossible to freeze the business environment, freezing in-process data and process models to meet an arbitrary deadline may result in a finished product that nobody wants to buy.

Just-in-time inventory means that items required to turn work-in-process into finished goods are delivered to the factory floor just in time to be included in the production run. This is also known as *demand-driven* or *pull inventory* because customer demand drives production, which in turn pulls in the inventory needed for current work-in-process. The benefits of this approach include economy of effort, less paperwork, reduced scrap inventory, lower inventory cost, and reduced storage requirement. These benefits are only realized through discipline and coordination. They require cooperation among customers, manufacturers, and suppliers.

The components of just-in-time applications work together as and when needed without the extensive setup time required by procedural programming. Just-in-time applications replace procedural programs with database programs—the collaboration of procedural and nonprocedural database operations. The goal is to minimize development cycle time, thus reducing software development cost. Just-in-time software development would contrast with the "day late and dollar short" development prevalent in past years. As with the pull inventory implementations in manufacturing, just-in-time software development requires rigorous discipline to replace rigidity with agility.

1.5.2 Flexible Factory

Flexible factory is a term for the capability of a factory to produce simultaneously a variety of different items in the same plant. Flexible factory also refers to changing the production mix without having to close down the production line for lengthy and costly setup.

For example, a flexible consumer goods factory could shift quickly from refrigerators to freezers, or produce both at the same time. Old-style automobile factories had to close the plant for a week or two while lathes and jigs were manually readjusted for the new model. Modern facilities with numerically controlled lathes and robotics perform the changeover in a matter of hours. Automobile manufacturers who continue to run their plants in the old manner cannot produce enough cars fast enough, at a low enough cost, to compete in mass markets.

The software equivalent to a flexible factory is a self-adjusting information system. This type of system is capable of quick adaptation to changing workflow and information requirements both during development and after implementation, without a lengthy pause for retooling. An active database environment where the database server responds to events by altering application behavior has virtually no retooling lag. The interface files in the "plumber's nightmare" shown on the top of Figure 1.6 would require extensive reprogramming and interface retooling whenever any of the seven applications required modification. By contrast, the message-based approach shown on the bottom of Figure 1.6 is a "developer's dream." Maintenance cost is reduced because a nonprocedural database language and integration by messages offer more flexibility than rigid program and interface file integration.

1.5.3 Concurrent Engineering

Figure 1.7 shows the traditional *waterfall* view of software projects. The cascades in the waterfall represent the following development phases:

- **Requirements definition.** Define the functions that the application is required to perform.
- **Data modeling.** Specify conceptual entities in the application, their attributes, and the relationships between them.
- **External database design.** Define logical database structures.
- **Program design.** Specify programs in the application.
- **Coding**. Write and compile the programs specified in the program design.
- **Database programming.** Create data definition, data manipulation, and database interface code.
- **Unit testing.** Test individual data-definition, data-manipulation, and application-program modules.
- **Integration testing.** Test database and programs together after they have been tested individually in unit testing.

At the close of each development phase is a pause for possible in-course corrections. Waterfall project control is intrinsically sequential, which tends to make labor-intensive software development even slower.

Given a workable methodology, substituting concurrent project control for sequential project control would be a better approach. Manufacturing companies face similar problems as they seek rapid time-to-market. The solution adopted by

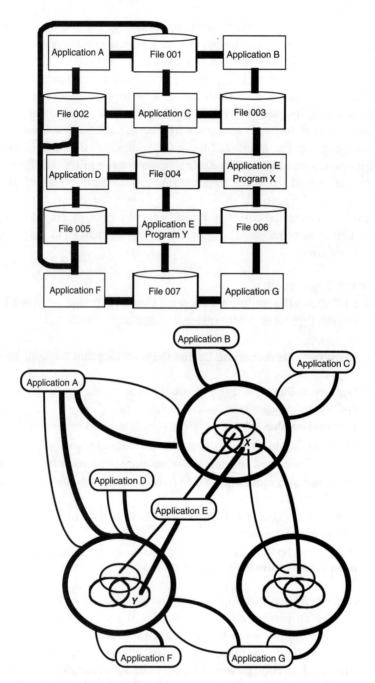

Figure 1.6 Plumber's nightmare versus developer's dream

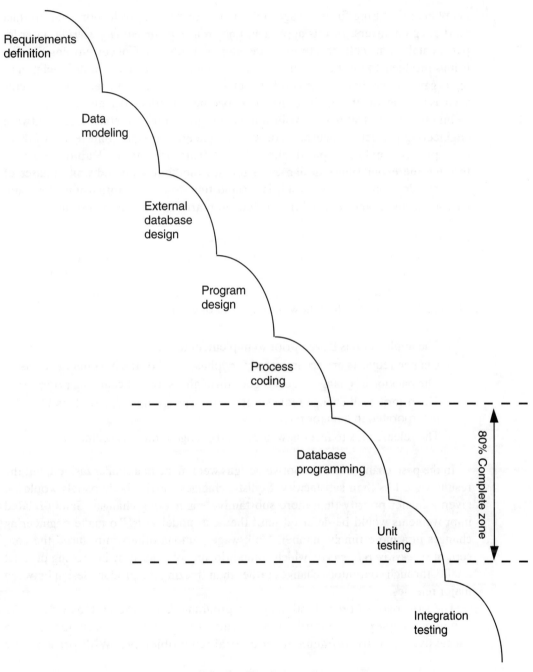

Figure 1.7 The waterfall

many manufacturing firms engages joint teams of design, production, and product marketing engineers. In this approach, known as *concurrent engineering*, interdepartmental teams collaborate in all development phases. Concurrent engineering brings products to market faster than sequential engineering methods by eliminating organizational barriers or conflicts between departments. Instead, departments such as production and engineering work together to reduce risk and waste.

Figure 1.8 illustrates the evolutionary design spiral of a concurrent software engineering project. Concurrent software engineering utilizes joint teams of database professionals and paratechnical staff from user areas. Rapid iterations through the evolutionary design cycle replace the "hurry-up-and-wait" phases of waterfall development. The result is a rapid time-to-market turnaround for database applications and reduced risk of "dead-on-arrival" information systems.

1.5.4 Successive Refinement and Success Circles

Life at work would be easier if information systems evolved in step with the business environment. Many of today's information systems lurch forward after long periods of frozen inaction, causing them to fall out of alignment with the business. This can be caused by the following sequence of events:

- The application is frozen prior to implementation.
- Change requests are accumulated for "phase two" or the next major release.
- The backlog of change requests goes through a series of changing priorities.
- The priorities of change requests are frozen, programmed, tested, and finally incorporated in a major release.
- The release fails to meet new needs and change requests accumulate.

In the past, changes to automotive designs were made in a similar fashion, but the results were less than satisfactory. Stylistic changes to trim body panels would be given a higher priority than more substantive engineering changes. Safety-related improvements would be deferred until the next model year. To make engineering changes in a more timely manner, Volkswagen among others introduced the concept of *successive refinement*, which is the principle of constantly improving product quality through continuous changes rather than freezing the product design between major releases.

The slow pace of procedural language programming in the past, as well as the daunting complexity of information systems in proprietary environments, made successive software refinement an unattainable objective. With present-day

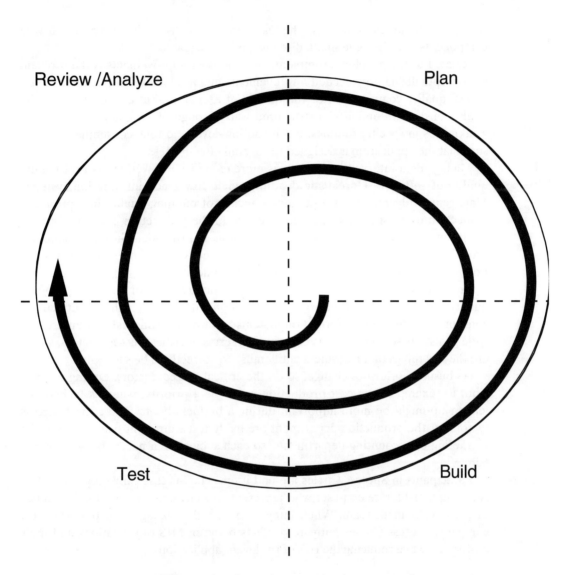

Figure 1.8 The evolutionary development spiral

methodologies and software-development tools, successive software refinement now is feasible.

The Database Factory approach discussed in this book is a form of evolutionary database development that quickly moves an information system through successive design-build-test iterations. The Database Factory is feasible because software components have become small, discrete, and manageable.

Related to the problem of implementing product improvements is the problem of conceptualizing how needed improvements might be made. Inspection and statistical quality control monitor the quality of execution, but cannot improve the quality of design. Similarly, a structured walk-through of program code can spot weaknesses in specific routines, but is too low-level and time-consuming to make sure that the application is designed for overall effectiveness.

Management intervention usually is more effective at lowering than raising the quality of software. Unrealistic deadlines yield low-grade information systems. Management decree is not a pragmatic means of building quality into products. Inspection of finished goods comes too late in the production cycle to improve quality without expensive rework. Continuous improvement in the production process improves quality in ways that policy directives and after-the-fact inspections cannot. This is a major benefit of quality circles.

In quality circles, workers meet regularly to discuss ways of improving product quality. *Success Circles* are a software development variant on the quality circles concept, used to orient information systems toward departmental and enterprise-wide goals. These goals may be expressed in terms of critical success factors, which are the few things that a business entity must do correctly to be successful.

As business priorities change, so do the critical success factors. During a recession, for example, low-cost production might be a priority, whereas technology leadership might be more important during a business boom. The critical success factors for the production department are likely to be different from those of the marketing or accounting departments, so each subject area needs its own Success Circle.

Participants in Success Circles are end-users. The Success Circle representative is a computer-literate end-user who represents the circle and is also a key member of the development team. When integrated with the management practices of a company, Success Circles mitigate conflicts between MIS organizations and their customers, while reducing the risk of irrelevant applications.

1.5.5 Mistake Proofing

Mistake proofing refers to the ability of an automated manufacturing process to prevent mistakes automatically. For example, during circuit board assembly, a defect would occur if any of the connectors of a chip fail to attach properly to the motherboard. A small break in contact might elude visual inspection, and a defective board might pass automated testing, only to develop an intermittent fault while in service. Mistake proofing replaces inspections and sampling with automated sensors that monitor the board-mounting operation. If any of the connectors fails to attach to the motherboard at the same time as the others, the board in question is immediately removed from the production line.

Mistake proofing in software development replaces programmatic operations with automatic operations. In Figure 1.5, for example, the column in the employee table called *DEPTNO* refers to a column of the same name that is the identifier of the department table. Clearly, the department number of every employee in the employee table should be a valid department number that refers to an actual department in the department table. This is known as *referential integrity*. A real-world payroll application might have hundreds of employees and dozens of departments. Each relationship must have its integrity protected in order for the application to work correctly. Without referential integrity, the company could make mistakes while processing its payroll.

The programmatic approach to referential integrity would validate the department number by performing a look-up on the department table. Although this is a simple procedure, a real-world payroll application would need many such look-up procedures—so many that one might be omitted or might contain a coding error. Despite code inspection and testing, some coding errors are likely to remain in the production applications and cause functional errors during payroll processing.

Unlike programmatic referential integrity, the mistake-proofing approach utilizes automatic database server features such as *declarative referential integrity*. With declarative referential integrity, relationships between tables are declared at the same time as the tables are created. Afterward, referential integrity is enforced by the server so mistakes are automatically prevented.

Referential integrity is only one example of mistake proofing. The state-based operations discussed in Chapter 7 and the agents discussed in Chapter 8 help build mistake proofing into active database applications.

■ 1.6 LAYING THE GROUNDWORK

The benefits of applying manufacturing principles to software development include flexibility, rapidity, and quality. If an enterprise succeeds in realizing these benefits, an overall humanizing effect on corporate culture matches the overall improvement in the bottom line. These positive results are the result of commitment, coordination, and hard work and do not come cheaply or easily. The benefits of the Database Factory can only be realized after three major realignments have taken place: priority shift, paradigm shift, and technology shift.

1.6.1 Priority Shift

When computers were bigger and more expensive than people, assigning a top priority to the hulking mainframe may have made sense. Such is the historical rationale implicit in the specification methodologies of classic software design. Computer time used to cost more than that of programmers or end-users. Getting everything correctly specified was essential prior to time-consuming programming and testing. In today's business environment, requirements do not sit still long enough to be laboriously specified. Because requirements change faster than they can be specified, the programmer has no hope of getting everything correct before development begins. The first priority must now shift to using inexpensive machines and cost-effective software components to support the best asset of the enterprise: skilled, creative, and talented individuals.

1.6.2 Paradigm Shift

For the Database Factory to make sense, the change in priorities must also be accompanied by a change in how to view information systems. As illustrated in Figure 1.9, passive subject-area applications mimic a hierarchical organization chart. Just as large, hierarchical organizations must make a concerted effort to avoid bureaucracy (or suffer in the marketplace), complex software hierarchies carry a heavy maintenance burden. As a passive computing model struggles to keep up with an event-driven enterprise, choke points develop. Interface files become difficult to synchronize. Hot spots develop in program code when procedural programs attempt the role of database servers.

The entity-relationship chart shown in Figure 1.10 illustrates typical interactions between different departments. In contrast to the hierarchical chart, the entity-relationship chart shows relationships such as

- Sales as a client of manufacturing
- Manufacturing as a client of customer service
- Sales, manufacturing, and customer service serving customers

These relationships are specific to actual workflows and interact with one another. Whenever a customer places an order, that order affects the manufacturing production plan. The shipment of product to the customer creates a customer-service relationship.

The various client and server roles within the enterprise are ratified and validated within the Success Circle framework. The result is information systems that add value and not just cost to business workflows.

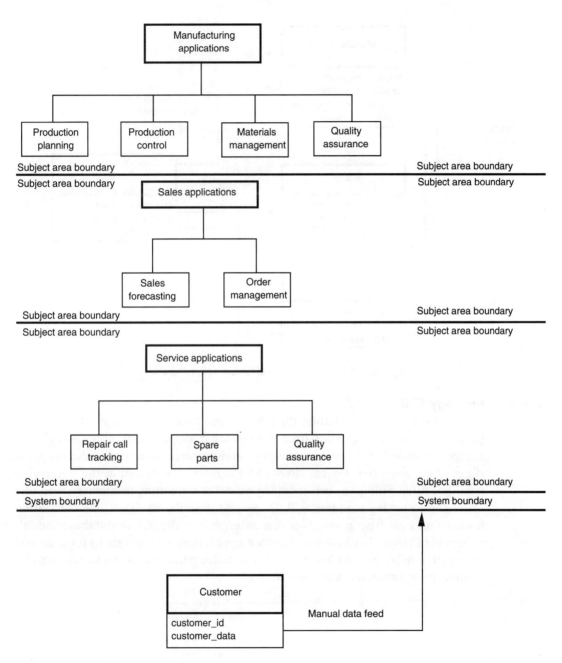

Figure 1.9 Application organization chart

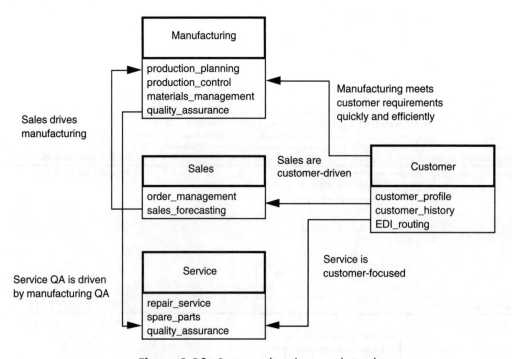

Figure 1.10 Business client/server relationships

1.6.3 Technology Shift

To build the Database Factory, the priority and paradigm shifts must be accompanied by a technology shift from a monolithic, central computing model to a component-based, distributed technology architecture. Adopting a business paradigm of collaborative logical clients and logical servers within the enterprise would be futile without a corresponding model of computing technology.

As the following chapters will define and describe in detail, the computing model that best fits an event-driven enterprise is the active database model. Component assemblies in active database applications collaborate to produce and distribute timely, relevant information. The active paradigm assists workgroups by aligning information flows and workflows.

2

DIVISION OF LABOR: CLIENT/SERVER

This chapter presents an overview of client/server database architecture, beginning with the history and evolution of this often misunderstood distributed computing model. Client/server is a message-based computing model that divides application processing between client processes and server processes. Both the client and the server processes consist of intercommunicating software layers. Client/server architecture offers the advantages of hardware/software optimization, high performance transaction processing, and interoperability.

A database server may be passive or active. Since two types of database servers (active and passive) are available, a business must be able to choose which server technology best suits its needs. Selecting the wrong database server can be severely detrimental to the success of a company. Only with a clear understanding of the advantages and disadvantages of server features, as well as their relationships with client processes, can an enterprise attain the full benefit of client/server computing.

■ 2.1 CLIENT/SERVER PRIMER

The term *client/server* refers to the cooperative relationship between two software processes connected by a communications medium. In client/server computing, one process (the *server*) acts in response to request messages from other processes (the *clients*). This type of cooperative processing was initially called the *requester-*

server model by Tandem Computer in the 1970s. Today, client/server database architecture is a prevalent software-development model.

A client/server database application distributes tasks within a communications infrastructure. Client/server database architecture balances the application workload between client processes and server processes. A database server concentrates on the database-related portions of the application to centralize data-management functionality. Client software maximizes user access by distributing the remaining application functionality. This division of functionality between clients, servers, and the communications infrastructure that integrates them is akin to division of labor in the enterprise. Each element has its own specialty and all elements work together. Whenever client/server cooperation breaks down, production grinds to a halt, just as it does when a factory suffers a blackout.

As shown in Figure 2.1, the client process manages the interface to a human user, or to some automated requester such as a financial quotation service. The server process manages the interface to an automated service provider, such as a DBMS. The internal nature of the service provider is hidden. The only way to activate the service provider is through the server, and the only way to communicate with the server is to send a message to the server's interface.

In the case of a relational-database server, the specifics of physical data access are hidden from the client software. The only way to request data services is through a data-manipulation language such as SQL, which is an American National Standards Institute (ANSI) standard language like COBOL or C. Although variations exist among different vendors' extensions, the SQL language itself is standardized. However, the way in which standard SQL is transformed into physical database operations is proprietary and unique to each vendor.

The concept of a server is not exclusive to databases. Various types of nondatabase servers include

- Factory automation, robotics, and machine vision servers
- FAX-voicemail, electronic mail, and network routing servers
- Virtual reality, simulation, and multimedia servers.

Historically, the first servers were print servers. These were designed for shared access to peripheral devices such as laser printers. The next generation was the file server, which was intended for file sharing in a LAN environment.

Because they store shared data in shared file structures, file servers often are confused with database servers. The data-access logic of a file server database is implemented in programs that execute on the individual LAN workstations, not on the server. The LAN operating system intercepts input/output (I/O) commands

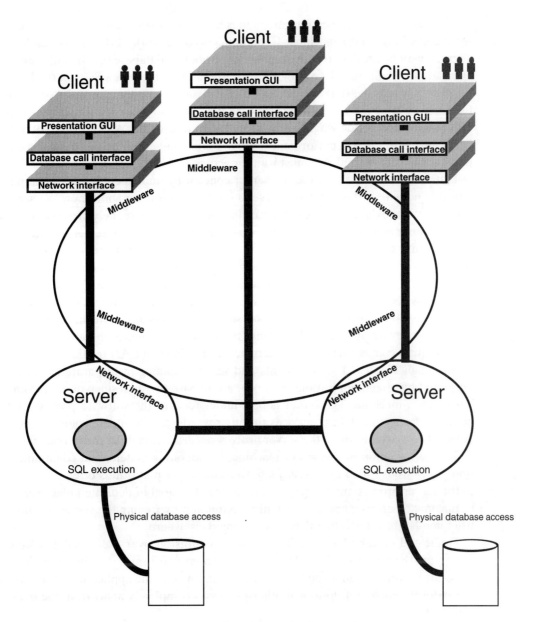

Figure 2.1 Client/server database architecture

and redirects them to the database file on the file server instead of the local workstation disk.

The network communications medium is far slower than the internal data-transfer speed of the server machine. Communications network performance tends to degrade with heavy data traffic. Joining data from two database files in a file server application is controlled by a program that executes on the user's PC, not the LAN file server where the data resides. All of the data potentially required from each file must traverse the LAN to get from the file server in order for the PC-resident program logic to decide what to include and what to exclude. While this heavy traffic is slowing the LAN performance, other users competing for the limited data-transfer capacity of the LAN must wait for access.

Database servers extend the file server concept by implementing data-manipulation logic within the database server's own execution capability, on the same computer as the data itself. A database client sends a short request message to the server. These SQL commands tell the server what service must be performed, but not how that service is to be performed. The server responds to request messages from the various client processes, which by themselves have no direct means of access to the physical database. Looking at the database servers in Figure 2.1, the client messages consist of SQL queries, and the server responses are query results or confirmation messages. The database server automatically performs operations such as retrieving or joining data. Only the data that provides the answer to the client request comes back from the server, thus minimizing LAN traffic.

Although Figure 2.1 shows clients and servers residing in disparate hardware separated by a communications network, a database server resides on a machine but is not a machine. The server is best understood as the software process that provides access to database services (in other words, an executable computer program). The machine where the server process resides is called the *server machine*.

The combination of the server machine, its operating system, and communications software is called the *server platform*. The server platform is often dedicated to the server process and the physical database. The goal of dedicated platforms is to maximize performance and minimize contention by freeing the server machine from nondatabase tasks that may be performed elsewhere.

Dedicated server platforms often lead to confusion over the concepts of the server and the server machine. However, the server platform is not always dedicated to the server. To minimize hardware costs in low-volume applications, the server platform may be set up to run other processes completely apart from the database server.

The client platform consists of the client machine, its operating system, the user interface, a database application program interface (API), and data communica-

Table 2.1 Client Platform Hardware and Software

Client Hardware	**Client Software**
Desktop computer with fast central processing unit (CPU)	Single-user operating system
Medium-capacity, medium-speed hard disk	Callable library database API
High-resolution monitor	Graphical user interface (GUI)
Mouse or trackball pointing device	Mouse driver/window manager
Network interface adapter card (NIC)	Network software (middleware)

tions hardware/software. A typical client platform might include the hardware and software summarized in Table 2.1.

The client platform is often nondedicated. In the typical case of a PC client platform (single-user, single-process operating system), other application tasks run on the PC in addition to client/server interactions with the database server.

For example, the database client in Figure 2.2 transfers data from the database server through the client API into a spreadsheet. Once the data returned by the SQL request is transferred to the spreadsheet, a financial analyst performs "what-if" analysis by using the spreadsheet software. When the analysis is complete, the financial analyst prepares a management presentation based on the spreadsheet data. The presentation is forwarded to executive management. Summary graphics from the spreadsheet representing key indicators of workgroup performance are forwarded to the appropriate departments as enclosures within "Heads up!" electronic mail transmissions.

In this example, information flows through the company's communications system from the financial analyst's PC to an executive support PC and to various workgroup PCs. These are, in a sense, the client's clients. The information includes not just data from the database, but also graphics and electronic notes from the financial analyst. The flow of database data with added value in the form of graphics, notes, and images is a kind of electronic in-basket for the recipient's work. This integration of sound, data, and graphical information with automated routing in a "paperless" environment is called a *workflow application.*

■ 2.2 CLIENT/SERVER FEATURES

Although client/server database applications appear more complex than their monolithic architecture equivalents, the features of client/server database applications potentially offer the following significant advantages:

- Hardware/software optimization

- Transaction processing performance (concurrency and multiversioning)
- Openness (portability and interoperability).

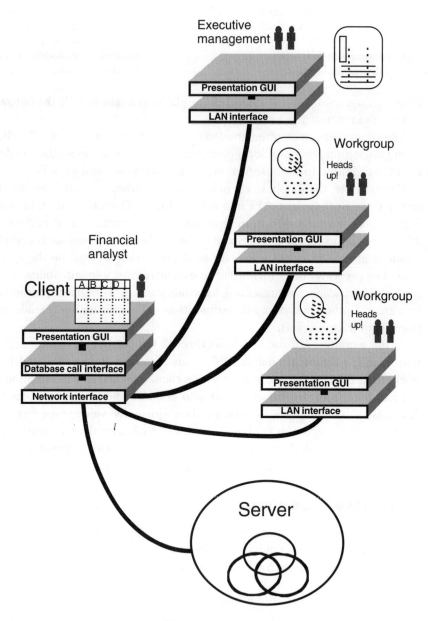

Figure 2.2 The client's clients

2.2.1 Hardware/Software Optimization

Database servers assist hardware/software optimization by centralizing data-management features while distributing other features. Data administration and security are centralized in database server functions and in database utilities. These utilities are client programs that usually execute on the server machine. They help optimize the database environment in a number of ways, including

- Monitoring performance (server speed and utilization data)
- Loading/unloading data (data transfer between database and files)
- Starting, stopping, or shutting down the database server
- Controlling database security.

Because these utilities are provided with the database server, they do not need to be programmed into application code. Because access to data is controlled by the database server, client/server database security is nearly impossible to circumvent. The SQL commands GRANT and DENY are used by the database administrator to specify the data access and to update privileges of individual users, workgroups, and logical roles.

Like security, automatic recovery from failure is centralized in the database server. During normal processing, logical units of database work (or *transactions*) either are completely applied to the database (*committed transactions*) or are completely discarded (*rolled-back transactions*). All transactions are logged. In case of a hardware failure or a power outage, the server's recovery facility restores the database to a consistent state in which transactions are committed or rolled back.

Scaling is the capability of moving a database server to a larger (or smaller) hardware configuration with a corresponding linear increase (or decrease) in database capacity or performance. Scaling makes it possible to downsize an application during initial development or re-engineering, then progressively rightsize the server machine through one or more upgrades as the application grows. Scaling defers hardware costs because, at any given stage in development or implementation, the customer only pays for the hardware resource necessary at that stage.

Horizontal scaling is the ability to incrementally upgrade an existing server machine by adding more disk space, more memory, more processors, or a faster CPU. As the hardware is upgraded, a corresponding gain is realized in database processing power and capacity.

The top portion of Figure 2.3 illustrates horizontal scaling. During initial prototype development, the server machine is a UNIX PC with 330 MB of fixed disk, 12 MB of main memory, and a 486 CPU. After two months of prototype development, the server machine is horizontally scaled up to 550 MB of disk, 16 MB of main

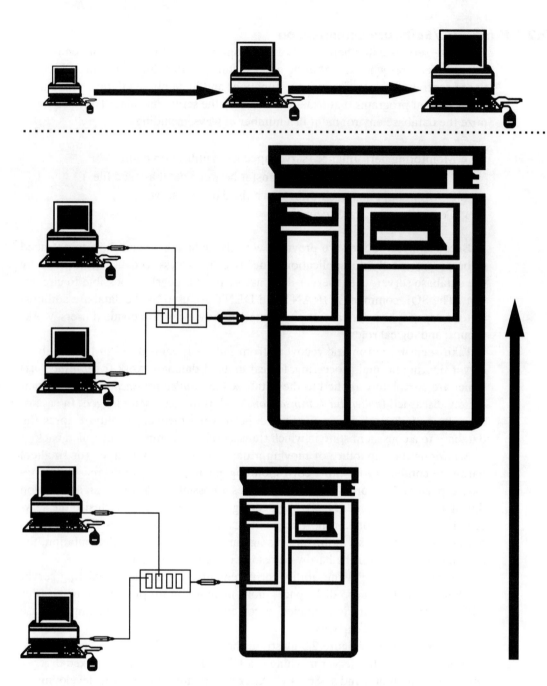

Figure 2.3 Horizontal and vertical scaling

memory, and a Pentium CPU. Following this upgrade, the server has enough capacity for high-volume concurrent usage. It can now be used to model high-volume database performance and application functionality.

Vertical scaling refers to the ability to port the database to a different and more powerful server machine with a proportional improvement in database performance. This is shown in the bottom portion of Figure 2.3.

Because DBMS software is usually priced according to the power of the server machine and the number of client connections, scaling optimizes software as well as hardware costs. A DBMS license may be purchased initially for a small development platform, then upgraded for the full-size production platform. The incremental cost of the upgrade is only incurred after the application has been developed, integration tested, and the system is rightsized.

2.2.2 Transaction Processing Performance: Concurrency and Multiversioning

Concurrency is the degree to which multiple users can simultaneously read and update the database. A database transaction is a logical unit of application work that is made up of individual database operations. For example, an inventory transfer transaction includes the operations of subtracting from source location stock count, adding to receiving location stock count, and making an entry in the inventory movement audit trail. A client/server database application achieves high concurrency by isolating the transactions of different clients.

The most widely used concurrency mechanisms are locking and multiversioning. *Locking* protects transaction integrity by preventing data-management operations by other clients from taking place until the client holding the lock has completed its current action. Because only a few database entries are locked during an update (and none at all in case of a data-retrieval request in most DBMS products), other clients have concurrent use of the remainder of the database.

Multiversioning allows clients that read data to coexist with those that update data. A database server with multiversioning (such as those provided by Interbase or Oracle) preserves the prior state of rows undergoing an update. Because data-access clients automatically retrieve prior-version data, they do not have to either lock data or wait for another client's lock to be released. The effect is consistent operations and minimal wait time.

2.2.3 Openness: Portability and Interoperability

A communications medium connects a database server and its clients. The communications hardware and software in the middle is known as middleware. Much of the complexity of client/server applications comes from middleware interfaces between the client and server portions of subject area applications.

Figure 2.4 shows the complexity resulting from poor middleware integration. In this example, data required by inventory control, finance, and sales applications is managed by Oracle, Sybase, and Informix servers. This scenario occurs frequently in an era of mergers, acquisitions, and consolidations.

In this example, three different versions of each application exist. The inventory data is split among the Oracle, Sybase, and Informix servers. The clients processing inventory data are also disjointed. For example, the Sybase client cannot access the Informix data. Even though all three versions of the inventory application have equivalent functionality, the syntax needed for the client interface makes them different. Middleware restrictions make it necessary to maintain three separate versions of each application.

By contrast, the universal interface shown in Figure 2.5 allows each client to access appropriate data from all three servers. In this example, it is no longer necessary to maintain multiple client versions of each application.

Although the various clients shown in Figure 2.5 share a common interface, sensitive data is protected from unauthorized access. The *database administrator* (DBA) has granted access privileges so that one application can read some, but not all, of the data in another application. For example, a telephone sales representative can see how many products are available in inventory, but cannot examine another employee's bonus.

■ **2.3 LAYERED CLIENTS, SERVERS, AND MIDDLEWARE**

The three main strata in client/server architecture (clients, servers, and middleware) form three disparate but integrated layers of functionality. Not only are these strata physically distributed and functionally distinct, they often are supplied by different vendors.

In one sense, the inherent stratification of client/server architecture makes it appear more complex than earlier mainframe and minicomputer architectures. However, stratification or layering actually serves to divide and conquer complexity by isolating complex integrations within each layer. For example, a database server includes sophisticated algorithms to manage transaction-processing performance, but these are hidden within the server layer. In fact, each of the three strata is logically subdivided into layered client architecture, layered server architecture, and layered middleware between clients and servers.

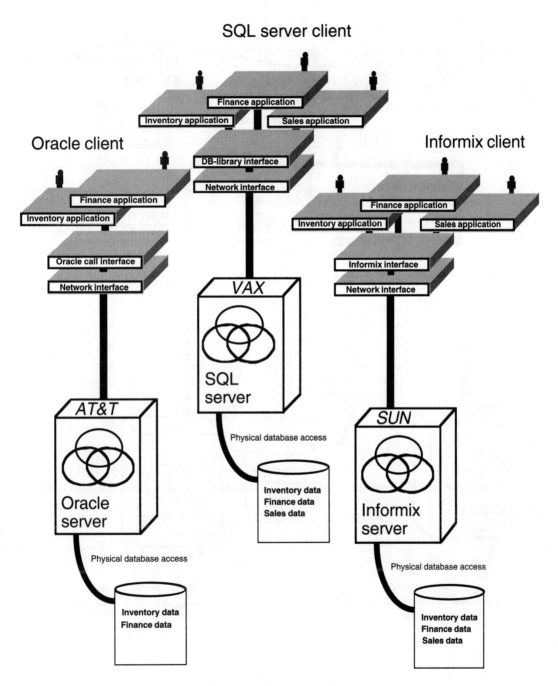

Figure 2.4 Client complexity

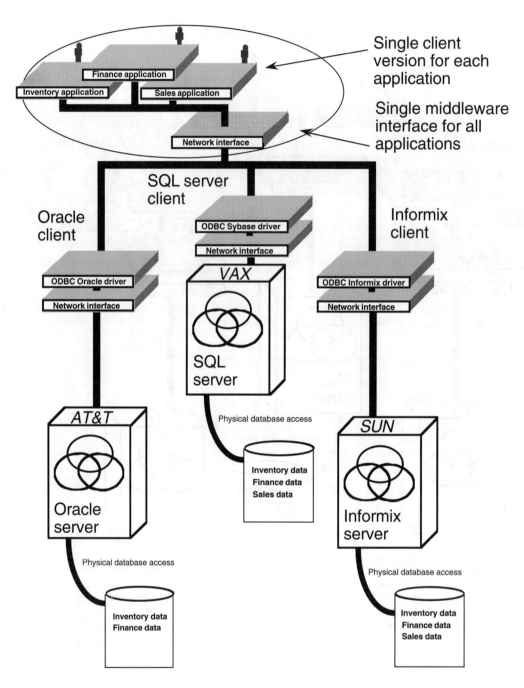

Figure 2.5 Client interface integration

2.3.1 Client Layers

A database client is logically layered. These layers consist of

- The front layer with which the user interacts
- A database API layer
- A communications-interface back layer with which middleware interacts.

Layered clients are message-driven on both sides. They pass requests from the user to the server, and pass responses from the server to the user.

Messages from the user to the server are communicated by activating the user interface. Activation is caused by some event that is meaningful to the interface. Events that are meaningful to an interface are at a lower level of abstraction than events that are meaningful to the business.

For a text-based interface, pressing the ENTER key could cause activation. A GUI might be activated by means of a mouse click or by touching an area of the screen. These low-level events are significant to a given client component in a given operational state, but not to the overall application.

Low-level events have a limited impact. They invoke the behavior specific to the corresponding event handler in the component that receives them. Whenever the user enters data, clicks a button, or selects from a menu, the behavior associated with the appropriate interface object is activated. Activating the GUI invokes the behavior associated with its interface objects. For example, clicking a button is a low-level event in the button's frame of reference. The button has methods of behavior for each low-level event to which it is sensitive. A higher-level event (for instance, an access denial by the server's security system) might alter or disable the sensitivity of the button.

The front client layer activates the middle layer whenever a database operation is requested by a front-layer method. Each SQL command is passed from the front layer to the database API in the middle layer.

The middle client layer routes and reformats messages between the outer layers. The front layer of the client interacts with the user on the outside and the database API in the middle layer. When the server returns an answer set or error message to the client, the database API in the middle layer takes the answer set from the back layer communications interface and forwards the results to the appropriate interface object in the front layer.

The *Open Systems Interconnection* (OSI) reference model is a layered set of communications protocol specifications designed to serve as implementation guidelines. The OSI model includes overlapping functionality among different layers, which might prove inefficient if literally implemented. The OSI model thus provides a guideline or conceptual roadmap, and does not correspond in every detail to typical mixed-vendor TCP/IP implementations. Just as the Applications Layer sits on top of the Presentation Layer in the OSI model, the database API is layered on top of any network-specific router/reformatter software. This layering isolates the database API from the implementation details of the network.

The back layer of the client contains network and communications interface files, drivers, and routines that integrate the client with the network.

2.3.2 Middleware Layers

Middleware is the communications network infrastructure essential to client/server integration. Like a telephone system, middleware seldom receives attention when it works properly. However, the network usually has a narrower *bandwidth* (data-carrying capacity) than the server platform, so network capacity is as important as server capacity.

Middleware enables server and client features to perform tasks that they could not accomplish by themselves. For example, Figure 2.6 shows cooperative processing between two database servers running a retail store application. A contractor shopping in a discount store would like to order four cases of lighting fixtures for delivery to a job site. When the clerk enters the order for the four cases, the server in the local distribution center detects that only two cases are in stock. It reserves the two cases and orders the other two from another distribution center. All of this processing takes places behind the scenes, and middleware makes it possible.

A server-to-server *gateway* enables the server in the local distribution center to access the database server in a remote distribution center. Middleware allows the local server to become a client of the remote server. Otherwise, to avoid losing the sale, the clerk might be forced to telephone various stores in order to locate the lighting fixtures.

Middleware can extend the range of database applications while reducing demands made on the database server. Figure 2.7 shows a repair service tracking application. Beginning when customers telephone the service center to request a repair, all details of the service call from initial dispatch to final resolution are logged on the product-support database. Service personnel enter the details of each call, including their time and any repair parts used, on a handheld notepad computer. These details are uploaded to the database server at the end of each shift.

At the support center, an operations analyst retrieves the service-call data into a spreadsheet. The spreadsheet summarizes the metrics that measure the effective-

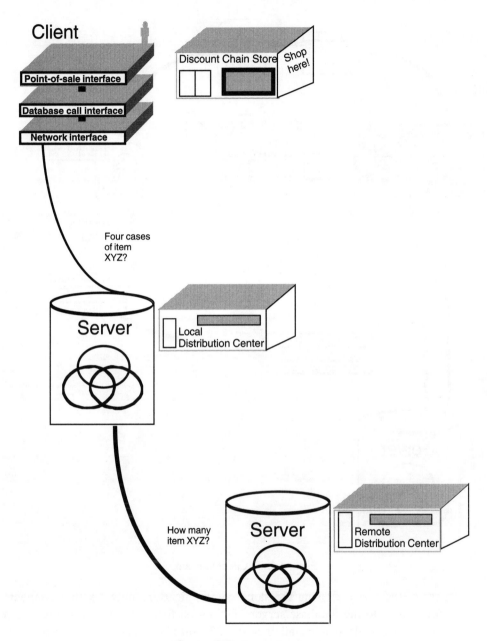

Figure 2.6 Server to server

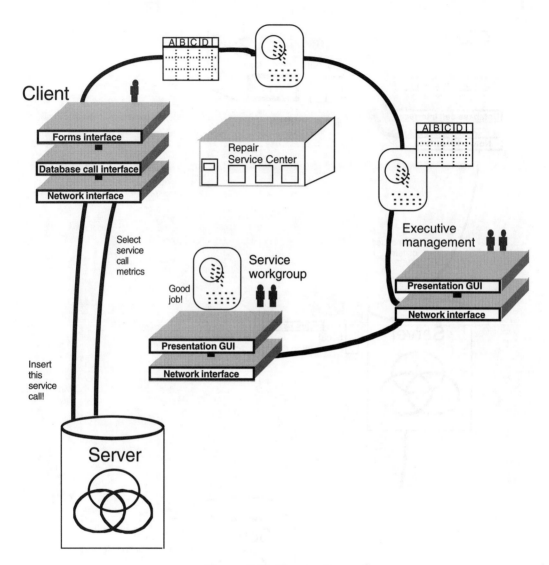

Figure 2.7 Client to client

ness of the service. Using the same communications network that connects the spreadsheet to the database server, the analyst forwards the spreadsheet to management as an electronic mail enclosure. To provide feedback to the service workgroup, the call metrics are forwarded to the workgroup with any management comments or suggestions. Middleware functionality adds workflow capability to the service tracking application while minimizing the load on the database server.

Communications protocol plays an essential part in supporting client/server database connectivity. Different vendors support the same protocol in different ways on different platforms. For example, the TCP/IP implementation on a DOS client platform may differ from the TCP/IP implemented on a UNIX server platform. However, the implementation may still achieve DOS-client-to-UNIX-server connectivity while mapping conceptually to the transport and network layers of a layered middleware model.

The *International Standards Organization* (ISO) adopted the OSI model as the X.200 protocols. From the bottom up, Table 2.2 describes the functions of each layer of the OSI model shown in Figure 2.8. Each of the six lower layers of the OSI model supports the layer immediately above it. The Applications Layer, in turn, supports client/server database applications.

Although a layered client/server database architecture is a similar concept to a layered communications architecture, they are two separate but closely related entities that happen to be implemented together in a complex integration. Because the OSI model specifies implementation guidelines for each layer of the model, the database implementation supported by the Applications Layer does not need to know the implementation details of the lower six layers. The lower layers of the communications model are implemented in the network hardware, in the back layer of the client, and in the platform layer of the server environment.

Once each of the layers has been correctly installed and tested within the framework of a methodical, systematic implementation plan, the layer above it can legitimately expect a consistent level of service.

Table 2.2 OSI Model Layer Functions

OSI Layer	Main Functions
Application	Process-to-process/virtual terminal support
Presentation	Data transformation, data formatting
Session	Establish/release session, manage interaction
Transport	Establish/release transport, transfer data
Network	Network addresses, connections, parameters
Data Link	Monitors/controls the data circuit connection
Physical	Provides the physical connection

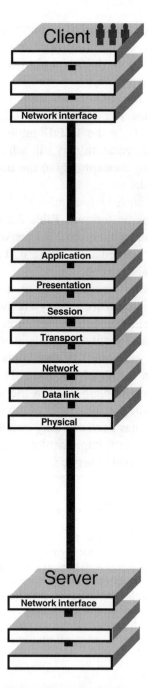

Figure 2.8 Middleware layers

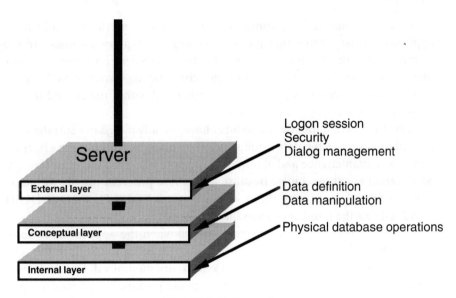

Figure 2.9 Server layers

2.3.3 Server Layers

As shown in Figure 2.9, the server environment can be viewed in the following three logical layers:

- **External layer**. This layer communicates with the middleware (front) and the conceptual layer (back). It is responsible for session, security, and dialog management.
- **Conceptual layer**. This middle layer manages SQL execution, both for data definition and for data-manipulation functions.
- **Internal layer**. This layer manages the physical resources of the database.

In the relational world, the *Data Definition Language* (DDL) and the *Data Manipulation Language* (DML) are usually the same language: SQL. While the SQL language is itself standardized, extensions to the language are vendor-specific. The approach to procedural extensions varies considerably.

Application designers face a tradeoff between putting procedural application logic in the front layer of the client or in the middle layer of the server. Database 4GL products such as Ingres 4GL, Oracle SQL*Forms, and Sybase APT run in the front layer of the client. Sybase Transact-SQL, although available to interactive SQL (isql) clients, is mainly used for server-resident stored procedures. Oracle's PL/SQL can execute in the server environment, or within SQL*Forms clients.

Building dynamic SQL commands within client methods is advisable if the application is so volatile that the data structures or query methods are subject to redefinition from moment to moment. In an application where ever-changing queries must be generated at run time, constructing dynamic SQL in the client makes sense. Dynamic SQL is usually embedded within the procedural code of a compiler-language program such as C.

Server-resident database procedures have the advantage of centralizing business procedures close to the data upon which they operate. This has the effect of simplifying code maintenance and eliminating the potential problem of different versions on different client machines. Because a database program usually includes several SQL commands, replacing these with a single EXECUTE PROCEDURE command reduces the number of messages on the network.

Database procedures are especially useful when the application logic is stable, because both the communications overhead of sending the SQL to the server, and the processing overhead of parsing its syntax, are minimized. Database procedures contribute to a robust application by providing shared application logic. When client programs have the main responsibility for application logic, each program is a potential weak link in the chain of application control. If any single client program fails, the integrity of the entire database application is compromised.

■ 2.4 ACTIVE AND PASSIVE DATABASE SERVERS

Database servers are classified as *passive servers* and *active servers*, depending on whether they perform their operations under external or internal control. Passive servers were the first of the two to be developed and are more primitive than active servers. In passive client/server implementations, the clients and the server have a master-slave relationship. A passive server is controlled by its clients, so the server is the slave of many masters. Passive database servers perform data-management operations in response to client commands, but cannot execute database programs, meaning server-resident programmed sequences of data-management operations with integrated control instructions.

Because passive servers cannot execute database programs, they cannot be programmed for self-modification of procedural operations. They cannot recognize and respond to events. In short, a passive server is the logical extension of the many clients that control it. Its sole reason for being is to service requests for the storage and retrieval of shared data. The passive server is like an improved file server enhanced with database-management features.

Data management behavior executing within a passive database server is non-persistent. Passive server SQL command execution is activated by a client request and lasts only for the duration of the current request. If the current request is replaced in the command buffer by another request, any future repetition of that initial request must go through the various stages of parsing and optimization. Because a passive server retains no persistent memory of past operations, it cannot associate a past operation with the current one, or the current operation with the next. Passive servers are incapable of consolidating sequences of data-management operations into application components.

An active database server is one that incorporates its own control logic. Active servers operate on and are operated upon by their clients, by other servers, and by their own event-management infrastructure. The SQL execution capability of active servers encompasses the data-management functionality of passive servers. However, active servers also are capable of storing and executing server-based database programs. These database programs, which are stored within the database, can be modified by other components within the client/server environment. For instance, the database programs of an active server can be both activated and modified by server-based event-management infrastructure, as well as by client requests. As explained in Chapter 3, client transactions can trigger state changes, resulting in a ripple effect that outlasts the initial client request.

In an active client/server environment, the "afterlife" of a transaction is under server control, and not under client control. Although ended from the client's viewpoint, the transaction has a ripple effect within the server by activating additional behavior (see Chapter 3).

For example, a bank permits automatic teller machine (ATM) access to overdraft accounts up to $200. A customer withdraws $200 and goes into overdraft. A stored procedure in the database completes the withdrawal transaction. The overdraft triggers a database program that levies an overdraft charge against the customer's checking account and then transfers funds from a savings account to cover the overdraft. The overdraft program alerts the ATM to check its remaining cash supply. If the ATM confirms a low-cash condition, the database server sends out an event alert.

Within the database server, the database program that is responsible for ATM maintenance has registered its interest in the low-cash event. The ATM maintenance program contains an event-handler routine for the low cash event. When the event handler is activated by an event alert, it dispatches a maintenance call to the branch where the ATM is located. The customer has completed the withdrawal and left the ATM, but the ripple effect of the transaction persists.

In contrast to a passive client, an active client is a logical extension of the server. Its purpose is to provide the interface between the server, the user, and peer clients. An active server and its clients interact in a collaborative processing rela-

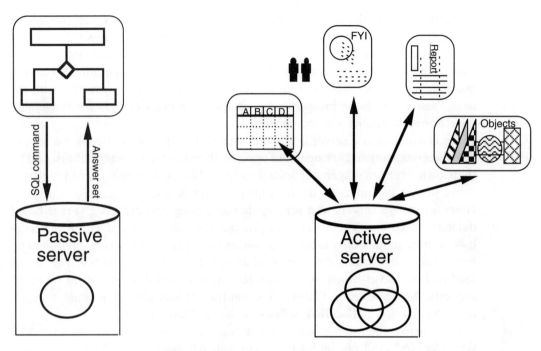

Figure 2.10 Passive and active servers

tionship, one in which the client is attuned to conditions on the server and the server responds to messages from the clients. This collaborative relationship introduces interesting possibilities that are not readily available in a master-slave relationship.

Figure 2.10 shows a passive server, an active server, and their respective clients. The passive server, whose role is confined to data-management operations, is controlled by its client. The passive client is responsible by default for the application's procedural control and event management. By contrast, the active server's database programming and event-management features unburden its clients, which become free to extend the application through specialization. The spreadsheet client and report client in Figure 2.10 summarize and present information for informed decision making. The workflow client alerts workgroups to operational changes resulting from events detected as a by-product of processing data into information.

These features add power (and potential complexity) to the client/server environment. An application may not need to avail itself of every active database feature to perform its task. For instance, a simple data-entry application may not avail itself of the features of an active server on which it is implemented. A passive application on an active server resembles a passive application on a passive server.

However, the sophisticated applications that contribute to competitive advantage benefit from active database features.

When simple applications are re-engineered for the client/server environment, active features are a cost-effective means for enhancing those applications with workflow-management features. Active features can provide the infrastructure for mistake-proof integration of office automation and management-support applications, which might otherwise be complex and prone to error.

Active features are present in most of the relational database servers commercially available today. Because database servers are one of the most highly competitive sectors of the software marketplace, vendors may be tempted to exaggerate the active database capabilities of their servers. Chapter 3 examines these active database features to promote a clear understanding of how they may be used to best advantage.

3

AUTOMATING AUTOMATION: ACTIVE DATABASE

This chapter explores the key active database concepts: database programming, event management, and self-modification. An *active database server* is defined as one that incorporates its own control infrastructure. An active server manages its own interactions with its clients and with other servers. In contrast to passive server applications in which client programs supplement the lack of functionality in the server, active applications extend the server. An active database server is capable of SQL execution, database programming, and event management. Active servers make possible component-based, self-adjusting database information systems. An active server's components may be activated by its clients, by other servers, by other server-based components, or by the server's event management infrastructure.

■ 3.1 EXTENDING DATABASE SERVERS

Although active database servers only recently have become feasible for main-stream commercial applications, the underlying paradigm is the result of 40 years of data-management evolution. The advent of active servers is the evolutionary result of ever-increasing database server capability.

3.1.1 Data Management Evolution

The *shared file management systems* of the 1960s represent the first phase in data-management evolution. IBM's VSAM and Hewlett-Packard's KSAM are examples of shared file management systems. Shared file management systems include file-access methods, file-description facilities, and storage-management utility routines. They represented an improvement over flat file applications because they standardized data access methods. However, shared file management systems have serious drawbacks in on-line transaction-processing applications with simultaneous multiuser access. In a banking application, for example, a customer may have a checking account, a savings account, and a loan account. Three different master files would have to be accessed one at a time to obtain a complete set of customer information. If the information inquiry takes place while the customer is transferring funds from a savings account to a checking account, the results may show an inaccurate intermediate status after the withdrawal from savings and before the deposit to checking. To counter drawbacks such as these, and to meet transaction processing needs, file-management systems evolved into database-management systems.

Hierarchical and network DBMSs gained pre-eminence in the 1970s. IMS from IBM and IDMS from Computer Associates are examples. These products featured mechanisms for security, data representation and concurrent multiuser access. The downside of these second-phase products is that they require advance definition of both their data structures and their access methods. Thus, they are extremely inflexible. Once the database structure (sometimes called the *schema*) has been compiled using the appropriate DDL, it is laborious to change that structure. Because data-navigation routines are copied into every application program that uses the DBMS, these programs also must be recompiled whenever the schema is altered.

The third evolutionary phase of data-management systems arrived with the advent of the relational database in the 1980s. Relational DBMS (RDBMS) products use the same language (SQL) for data definition and data manipulation. RDBMS products have the further advantage of the *relational model*, which is a paradigm based on tables and nonprocedural operations. In other words, relational products hide their physical data-manipulation routines under the wraps of SQL, which provides nonprocedural interface to the DBMS.

Within the database environment, the SQL parser and query optimizer transform SQL commands into data-management operations. When the SQL commands reach the DBMS through a communications medium such as a LAN, the DBMS environment is known as a *database server*. The main capabilities of a passive database server, such as the one shown in Figure 3.1, are SQL execution and manage-

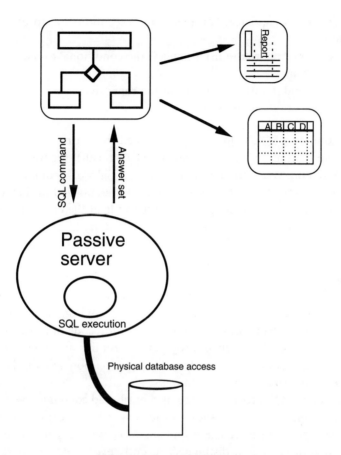

Figure 3.1 Passive server

ment of the physical database. These are important capabilities, but database applications also require execution control and persistent SQL commands. The server must be either supplemented or extended to gain full application functionality.

3.1.2 Passive Applications Supplement the Server

Passive client/server implementations supplement the server by means of client programming, usually with embedded SQL. A passive server must be supplemented to preserve the following features of a procedural program working with a shared file system:

- **Command persistence.** This means retaining a series of commands in memory or on disk.

- **Command sequence.** This means the execution of a stored sequence of commands.
- **Command alternation.** This means the conditional execution of code sequences.
- **Command iteration.** This means the repetitive, or conditional repetitive, execution of code sequences.

As soon as a SQL command is displaced from a passive server's memory, the command loses its *persistence* (capability of recall). Operating system command files containing SQL commands provide a partial workaround for SQL persistence. These commands typically are developed and debugged during an interactive session, and then saved as an operating system file at the close of the session. A command file is subsequently redirected (or *piped in*) to an interactive SQL session. The command file simulates persistence by storing SQL commands externally, but it cannot meet the need for server-based storage of core business logic.

Since standard SQL is a nonprocedural language and passive servers are limited to SQL execution, passive server applications must program the application's procedural logic outside of the server in the client environment. Embedded SQL supports persistent commands within the procedural code of the client program, hence the term *embedded*. The client program also retains its embedded SQL commands in the memory of the client machine during execution, and on the disk of the client machine between program executions.

Embedded SQL provides a type of client-based command persistence, but forces clients to ship SQL commands to the server for interpretation and execution. Because a passive server has no means of command persistence, a passive SQL application often cannot distinguish recently executed, repetitive SQL commands from one-of-a-kind *ad hoc* requests. The same resource-intensive security, validation, and optimization operations may be applied to an identical sequence of SQL commands that was submitted from another client machine just minutes earlier.

The SQL executing on an active database server can originate from within the server environment, not just from the clients. Storing SQL commands in the server provides an efficient way to achieve command persistence and repetitive execution. Stored SQL has the additional performance advantage of reducing message traffic on the communications network.

3.1.3 An Active Database Extends the Server

The SQL command execution capabilities of an active server (see Figure 3.2) are at least equal to those of a passive server for local transactions, and superior in the case of distributed transactions. For example, a passive server cannot control the

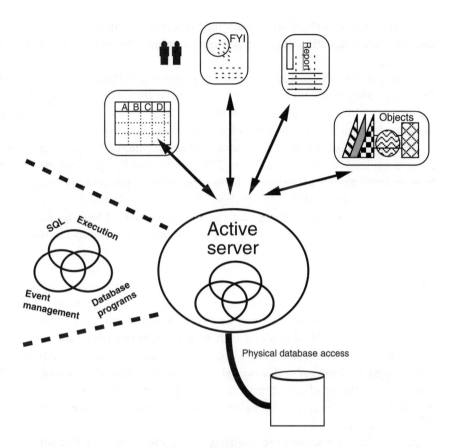

Figure 3.2 Active server

SQL operation of a *distributed update*. Distributed updates, coordinated INSERT, UPDATE, or DELETE operations on data residing on different servers, are encountered in many commercial transaction-processing applications, such as *electronic funds transfer* (EFT) and just-in-time manufacturing.

The *two-phase commit protocol* (2PC) is widely used in distributed updates to prevent incomplete updates in the event of a hardware or communications failure. In 2PC processing, multiple database servers involved in a distributed update coordinate their actions in two phases: the *prepare phase* and the *commit phase*.

Because SQL execution on a passive server is externally coordinated, passive servers involved in a distributed update cannot coordinate their own 2PC processing. Instead, a client process must poll the participating servers to coordinate 2PC activity. This programmatic task must be coded, which complicates client application programming with what is essentially a server-oriented systems programming task. By contrast, active database servers automatically coordinate their own 2PC processing.

Although the 2PC guarantees data integrity for distributed update transactions, 2PC processing may lead to slow performance. If the 2PC coordinator fails during the prepare phase, or if the network fails, database locks on the data participating in the update may limit access for a long time pending recovery.

Data replication, which is the automatic propagation of copies (or replicas) of data, is utilized as an alternative to 2PC processing by applications that do not require absolute synchronization. Data replication is particularly useful for applications that do not update data, such as the Data Warehouse discussed in Chapter 9. However, automatic data replication is an active server feature. Passive servers can only implement data replication by means of client programs in which a single client maintains connections to two or more servers. The client reads data from the database of one server and then writes it to the database of another server. The passive client is responsible for error detection and exception processing.

In contrast to command-driven passive replication, data replication in an active server environment is time-driven or event-driven. Both variants of active data replication are controlled automatically by the server infrastructure.

Application control is a central concept in active database. Active database applications are built around sets of shared behavior related to sets of shared data. Control over the production application resides within the active server, although it is partially delegated to external coordinating components (or agents, which are discussed in Chapter 8).

Passive database servers are controlled from the outside. Active servers centralize control within the server environment by database programs (that is, structured groups of database stored procedures) and by the event-management mechanisms covered later in this chapter. Although overall application control is server-based, individual data-entry or data-access operations are initiated through the client interface. However, these data-manipulation operations do not control the overall behavior of the application. From one perspective, client-initiated transaction processing may be viewed as the server's external data-manipulation behavior.

An active server manages the functionality of the core application, allowing its clients to extend and enrich the application. In Figure 3.3, for example, one client delegates its resources to the interface objects in a GUI. Another client manages an *electronic data interchange* (EDI) gateway. A third client actually is a workflow server interacting with the active server in a cooperative processing relationship. The character-based fourth client runs a downsized COBOL application, which has been upgraded from VSAM indexed files to a relational database. It retains its

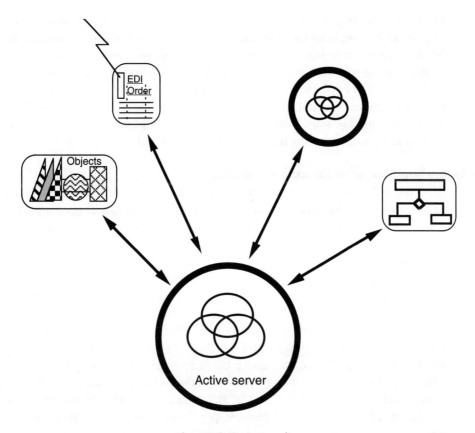

Figure 3.3 Active clients

COBOL screen-handling routines, but the core application functions are central-ized in the server. All four clients extend an application in different ways while the central portion of the application (including core business procedures) resides within the active server.

■ 3.2 DATABASE PROGRAMMING

An active database reduces application development costs by centralizing shared and reusable procedural program code with other central server-based components. Server-based procedural methods are central and accessible, so the program main-tenance effort is low in comparison with client-based embedded SQL applications.

Database programming integrates procedural logic and persistent SQL com-mands within the server environment. A database programming language must meet a number of goals to surpass client-based 3GL/4GL programming. It must be interoperable with both the SQL execution engine and the client interface. It must be message-based to operate within a client/server architecture. It should be consistent with up-to-date software engineering practice and should be fully structured with the best client-based languages. Otherwise, database programming would hold little practical advantage over client programming. Above all, a database programming language must have enough layering, component-sharing, and functionality to serve as an enabling technology for active databases.

3.2.1 Extending SQL with Execution Control

Procedural 3GL/4GL programming controls execution with such code constructs as sequence, iteration, and conditional selection (also known as *alternation*). These categories are shown in Figure 3.4. A *sequence* is simply a set of commands that are executed in their order of appearance within the source code. An *iteration* structure (for instance, a *do* loop) is a structure for repeating sequences. Conditional selection makes execution dependent on a condition or logical case. The *if-then-else* statement shown in Figure 3.4 is an example of *alternation* (conditional execution).

Passive applications embed client-based SQL in 3GL/4GL programs to supplement the lack of the flow of control structures in standard SQL. Static SQL statements are compiled into the passive client program, along with the surrounding execution control statements. Active implementations extend server-based SQL with server-based procedural control structures. These structures are stored and execute within the server environment, physically close to the data on which they operate.

By definition, vendor-specific procedural language extensions vary from the SQL standard and from one another. These include Transact-SQL from Sybase, Interbase GDML from Borland, and PL/SQL from Oracle. The PL/SQL language, which derives from the Ada language, is particularly suitable for component-based application architecture. The discussion in the following section uses PL/SQL syntax to illustrate structured database programming. On the other hand, the Ingres RDBMS features a particularly strong event-management infrastructure. The Ingres syntax is used in this chapter to describe event-management features. Note that a given active server feature may be better supported by the database server of one vendor over another.

3.2.2 Structured Database Programming

Maintainable programs are well-structured programs. The Sybase Transact-SQL procedural language extension associates related stored procedures by means of a

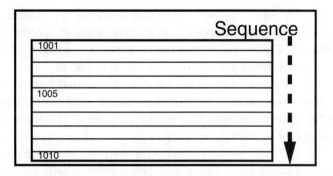

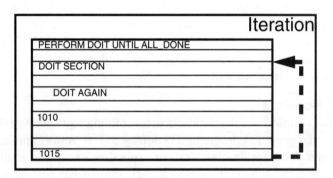

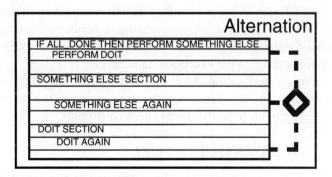

Figure 3.4 Procedural control structures

naming convention. The procedures that comprise a procedure group share the same name. Individual component procedures are distinguished by a numeric suffix. A group of Transact-SQL procedures is easier to keep synchronized than a disjointed group of stored procedures with different names.

Oracle PL/SQL procedures are structured in nested blocks. The PL/SQL structure includes two parts, a specification and a body. The PL/SQL specification defines the operational interface to the procedure. It names the procedure and declares any I/O parameters. The PL/SQL body contains the implementation details. The body consists of a declarative part, an executable part, and an optional exception-handling part. These implementation details are "private," meaning they are hidden within the database program. Only the header is public.

PL/SQL gathers logically related server-based procedural logic within a structural unit called a *package*. A package contains all the behavior appropriate to a given concept (*entity type*) in the database application. The format of a package is consistent with that of a procedure. The specification defines the calling interface and the body contains the implementation details. PL/SQL packages support the concepts of nested modularity, layering, and encapsulation. A package is the equivalent of a structured program.

3.2.3 Exception Handlers

Exception handlers are the database programming equivalent of the error-handling routines that seasoned programmers deploy to turn robust applications into bulletproof ones. The application designer specifies exception handlers for specific exceptions such as NO_DATA_FOUND. For unspecified or unexpected exceptions, PL/SQL makes provision for a generic OTHERS handler.

In a passive database application, the client is obligated to interrogate each operation to detect any exception. Embedded SQL precompiler directives (WHENEVER clauses) may conceal this, but it is evident in the generated source code. In an active application, the event-management infrastructure of the server signals the database program that a processing exception exists and control then passes automatically to the exception handler.

Note that the application designer can use declarative SQL constructs for mistake proofing to prevent exceptions from occurring in the first place. The SQL92 standard refers to these constructs as *check constraints*.

■ 3.3 RELATIONAL DATABASE INTEGRITY

The structures of a relational database—as well as the actual data values stored within those structures—imply its semantics. The main structural components of a database are its tables. In a well-structured (normalized) database, the structure of each table is based on a main concept. The identity of each entity instance (that is, each row) in each table is unique, guaranteed by a unique primary key. Each table column thus names and represents an attribute of the main concept represented by the table. For example, a *parts* table is based on the concept of parts. Its columns represent all the meaningful attributes of parts (their descriptions, quantities available, and so on). No column in the parts table represents anything that is not parts-related.

The data values in each column are members of the set of all permissible values for that column. This set of permissible values is referred to as the *domain* of the column. For example, a column named *part_source* might have its domain restricted to the values 1 (manufactured) or 2 (purchased). All values in the domain must conform to the datatype of the column, as declared when the table is created. If the *part_source* column has an integer datatype, it cannot hold a value of "m" (for manufactured) or "p" (for purchased).

In a passive database server, the datatype of a column must be a built-in datatype supplied by the DBMS vendor, such as NUMBER, CHAR, or DATE. Several relational database servers support extended (or user-defined and user-constrained) datatypes. For example, a Sybase user-defined datatype of Northern California area codes might be declared as char(3) and a Sybase rule might constrain the domain so that only the values 408, 415, 510, 707, and 916 are allowed.

Of all the permissible values possible, the set of current actual values constitutes the state of the column. The type and domain of a column determine the set of potential data values for that column. The run-time data value held by the column in a given row is further constrained by the values held by other columns. If taken in the context of the other column values in the row, a column value that is legal within the domain might cause the row to represent a logically impossible state.

The two main categories of integrity enforcement that protect an application residing on a relational database server are

- **Transaction integrity.** This category protects database operations.
- **Data integrity.** This category protects database consistency.

Transaction integrity guarantees that logically related operations are treated as a logical unit of work called a *transaction*. Each transaction must be completed in its entirety (that is, committed) or undone in its entirety (that is, rolled back). All relational database servers (as opposed to file servers) support transaction integrity as part of their SQL execution facility.

The data integrity requirement that each row in a table is uniquely identifiable by its primary key is called *entity integrity*. All RDBMS products support entity integrity.

Active servers protect entity integrity when a table is declared, as specified in the SQL92 standard. The CREATE TABLE statement declares the appropriate column(s) as the *primary key*. The primary key declaration disallows duplicates and null values, so entity integrity is protected when the table is created.

By contrast, passive servers rely on a physical index structure for entity integrity. The index is declared as unique on the primary key column(s), which means that no duplicate rows are allowed. When a row is inserted or updated, any value in the primary key that is the same as an existing value is disallowed by the index structure and causes an exception. Any rows that were inserted into the table before the index was created are not protected and may violate entity integrity.

Referential integrity, which is another category of data integrity, is the requirement for consistent key values between rows in two or more tables participating in a relationship. The value held by a column (called the *foreign key* because it is the key of another table) in one or more rows of one table refers to the primary key column of another table.

For example, the location (*loc*) column is the primary key of the location table and a foreign key column in the department (*dept*) table. If a new department row is added to the department table having NEW YORK as the value of the location column, then the primary key to which it refers must have a row whose value is NEW YORK. Referring to a nonexistent primary key value would be a violation of referential integrity.

In an active database environment, referential integrity is declared when the table is created and automatically protected thereafter as part of the database infrastructure. For example, setting up a primary key to foreign key relationship between the department (*dept*) and employee (*emp*) tables shown in Figure 1.5 would be done as follows:

```
CREATE TABLE emp (
 . . ., /* declare each column and its datatype */
 FOREIGN KEY (deptno) REFERENCES dept);
```

Referential integrity is automatically enforced from this point on. When an *emp* instance is added with a *deptno* value of 30, the *dept* table is checked to make sure that department 30 exists. Likewise, it would be impossible to remove the row in the *dept* table for department 30 while *emp* instances referencing the department remain. But what if some business imperative dictates the need to close down the department, staff and all? A foreign key declaration with a so-called *cascading delete* will delete all rows referring to a primary key when the primary key row is deleted, as shown here:

```
CREATE TABLE emp (
    ..., /* declare each column and its datatype */
    FOREIGN KEY (deptno) REFERENCES dept
            ON DELETE CASCADE);
```

These same state-based integrity constraints could be enforced procedurally in a passive database through SQL commands from the client. For example, before sending a SQL insert statement to insert an employee row into the *emp* table, a query could be performed to make increment the highest *emp_id*, to make sure that no employee already exists with the same *emp_id*. Another query could validate the *deptno*, and so on. However, while these procedural checks are taking place, another client could be assigning the same *emp_id*, or even perhaps deleting the department. Operations that are protected by server infrastructure and activated by nonprocedural CREATE TABLE commands are intrinsically stronger than operations that depend on complex, error-prone procedural code.

∎ 3.4 EVENT MANAGEMENT

Event management refers to an active server's ability to define, detect, and respond to application state transitions. Passive database servers are command-driven under external control. A passive server can only process events when they are represented as data. By comparison, active applications are equally event-driven and command-driven. Historically, event management was expensive to deploy in passive database-driven applications because the application developer had to create both the application and its event-management infrastructure.

Event management is less onerous by far with active database servers because the event-management infrastructure is supplied and supported by the database vendor. The vendor of an active database server supplies the feature set that makes database programming and event management possible, such as triggers, stored procedures, and event alerters. The RDBMS vendor is responsible for the integration of the features. The application developer is responsible for the use (or misuse) of these features in the application.

3.4.1 The Event-Management Cycle

In an active database environment, application events model the state transitions of real-world entities. Figure 3.5 illustrates an event-management cycle. A real-world financial transaction occurs that has a material effect on operations.

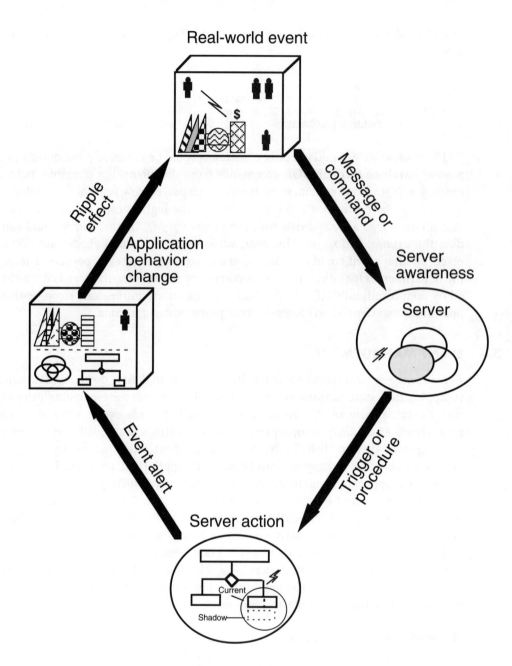

Figure 3.5 Event cycle

Transaction processing begins with data entry in the client environment. A message from the client requests the server to execute the transaction by performing data updates. These data-manipulation operations change the state of the *metadata* (data about data) in the server's control tables. The metadata state transition meets the condition specified for a previously defined event, which is promptly detected. The server takes action in response to the event.

In this example, a database program changes its activation path, effectively replacing one *database procedure* (a component within a database program) with another. The active server in this example sends *event alert* signals to its clients, which respond by changing their behaviors.

Once both server-based and client-based components have changed their behaviors, a persistent ripple effect occurs on the overall application. This reflects the impact of the original real-world event on operations and brings to a close the event-management cycle.

3.4.2 Database Triggers

Database triggers provide an interface between the server's SQL execution and event-management facilities. A database trigger is declared by a SQL CREATE TRIGGER statement, in conjunction with a triggering DML statement. The triggering statement is an INSERT, UPDATE, or DELETE command. A database trigger is set up to run before or after the associated triggering statement, and activates a database program.

Database trigger syntax is vendor-specific, which is an extension to standard SQL. Depending on the RDBMS in question, the database program is either included within the CREATE TRIGGER declaration (Sybase, Oracle) or called from it (Ingres). Incidentally, Ingres refers to triggers as *rules*.

Protecting referential integrity was an early use of database triggers. This practice was the only means available to do the job (short of procedural coding in the client environment) before the advent of the SQL92 declarative syntax discussed in the previous section. Table 3.1 summarizes the advantages and disadvantages of using triggers to protect referential integrity.

Table 3.1 Trigger Advantages and Disadvantages

Trigger Advantages	Trigger Disadvantages
Integrity protection code executes automatically	Nonstandard / vendor-specific
Trigger code is stored centrally, close to the data	Procedural and susceptible to program bugs
Barring oversight, triggers cannot be circumvented	May be inadvertently omitted or dropped

Moving referential integrity protection from procedural trigger code to declarative CREATE TABLE statements frees database triggers for event-management tasks, as shown in Figure 3.6. In this illustration, an update to a data table triggers an update to a control table. The control table has an update trigger that contains commands to alter the behavior of a database procedure. The change to the database program affects SQL execution, changing the data processing operations, changing the impact of those operations, or changing both.

3.4.3 Event-Management Features

Server event management refers to application events, or the state transitions that affect an application's behavior. Unfortunately, the term "event" also refers to low-level conditions in a graphical client interface environment (such as clicking a button on a mouse). To avoid confusion, this book uses the term *low-level events* to refer to these nonapplication events.

Event-management features are the mechanisms that define, detect, and process application events. *Event definition* is the act of naming the event. Some RDBMS products declare the event (CREATE DBEVENT is the Ingres syntax) without defining its semantics. In other implementations (notably Interbase), the event definition specifies a condition that defines the event. This defining condition is initially false (not satisfied) but becomes true as the result of a state transition.

A state transition that satisfies the defining condition marks the occurrence of the event. An event remains of interest from the time it is created to the time it is dropped (CREATE DBEVENT in Ingres). *Event detection* is the specific means by which this defining transition is made known. Automatic event detection is used by servers that define the event condition within the event creation statement. Procedural event detection uses a database trigger (or a trigger and database procedure combination) to evaluate state transitions. Once the event is detected, event processing begins.

The first step in event processing is *notification*. As shown in Figure 3.7, notification is accomplished with an event alert signal. The event alert is initiated by a command. The Ingres syntax for this command is RAISE EVENT.

The event alert is received by all components that have registered an interest in the event. (The Ingres syntax is REGISTER DBEVENT *event_handler_name*). When the event alert is received, control passes to the event handler.

Like SQL execution and database programming, event management forms part of the infrastructure of an active database server. As is true of database tables and database programs, access to event-management features is controlled by the

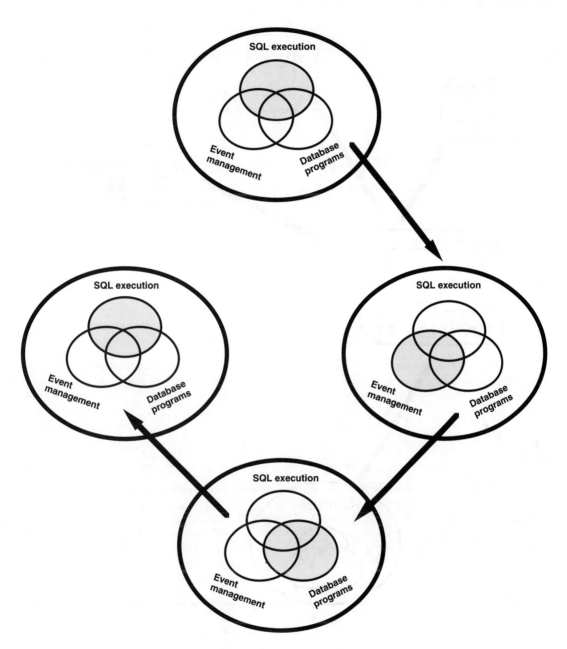

Figure 3.6 Trigger events

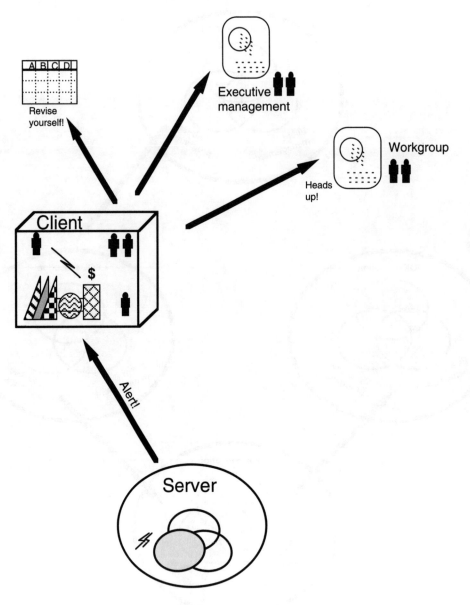

Figure 3.7 Event alert

DBA. The DBA can grant or revoke access to specific database tables. The DBA can allow or disallow the right to execute individual database programs. Similarly, the DBA grants users the right to activate events. (The Ingres syntax is GRANT RAISE ON DBEVENT *event_name.*) The right to be notified of events is also controlled by the DBA, by means of the command GRANT REGISTER ON DBEVENT *event_name.*

3.4.4 Synchronous and Asynchronous Event Notification

Event notification takes two forms: synchronous and asynchronous. Figure 3.8 shows *synchronous event notification.* The real estate workflow in this illustration requires the balance of the buyer's funds to be wired into an escrow account before it proceeds to its next state transition, conveying the title to the property. The application registers the escrow's interest in the funding event, then suspends the workflow pending the funding event. The workflow "sleeps" until the funding event takes place, when it is then awakened by an event alert.

Suspending database client operations while waiting for an event is undesirable when the client has other useful work to do. Active clients like the ones in Figure 3.9 continue processing during the time an event is pendant. A client registers for an event and continues processing. When the event occurs, all registered clients receive an event alert. This type of interaction is known as *asynchronous event notification.*

3.4.5 Simulating Asynchronous Events with RPCs

In the case of a database server with well-developed database programming functionality, but without asynchronous event capability, *remote procedure calls (RPCs)* may substitute for event alerts. To better understand event alert simulation with RPCs, consider the familiar example of withdrawing cash from an ATM. This example will use an RPC to explain how bank employees know when to load more cash into the ATM.

The commands to create the tables in this database are

```
create table accounts (
    account_id    number(4) not null,
    balance       number(11,2),
    active_acct   number(1)
);
create table atms (
```

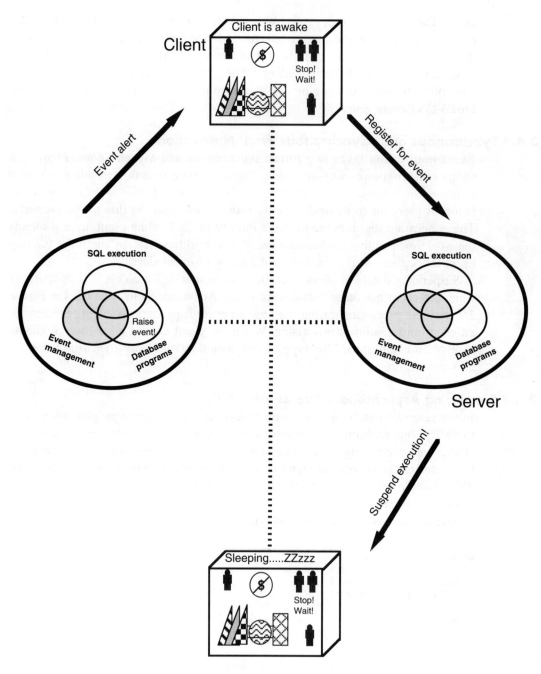

Figure 3.8 Synchronous event

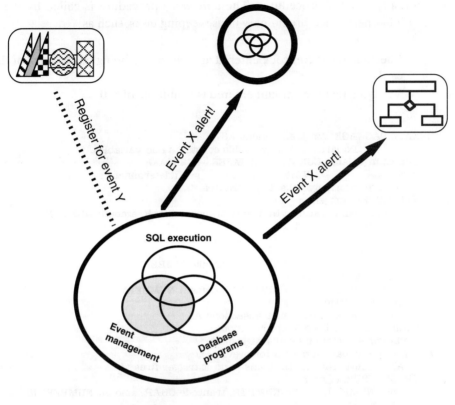

Active server

Figure 3.9 Asynchronous event

```
    atm_id        number(4) not null,
    location      char(40),
    twenties      number(3)
);
create table atm_trans (
    atm_id        number(4) not null,
    account_id    number(4) not null,
    trancode      char,
    amount        number(11,2),
    state         char(40),
    trantime      date
);
```

For simplicity, assume that the *atms* table and the *accounts* table hold data. Next, we create an *atm_transactions* package in the database. The package has four externally callable procedures. The *atm_entry* procedure is called by the ATM after it has performed preliminary housekeeping tasks, such as

- Checking the secret code entered against the encoding on the back of the card
- Verifying that the amount entered is a multiple of $20.

```
CREATE PACKAGE atm_transactions AS
        /* Declare externally visible constants and variables. */
    minimum_balance CONSTANT NUMBER   := 200.00;
    new_state           VARCHAR2(20)      := 'Indeterminate';
    /* Declare externally callable procedures. */
    PROCEDURE atm_entry
        (acct NUMBER, atm_id NUMBER, trancode CHAR, amount NUMBER);
    PROCEDURE atm_withdraw
        (acct NUMBER, atm_id NUMBER, debit NUMBER);
    PROCEDURE atm_deposit
        (acct NUMBER, atm_id NUMBER, credit NUMBER);
    PROCEDURE atm_payloan
        (acct NUMBER, atm_id NUMBER, payment NUMBER);
END atm_transactions;
CREATE PACKAGE BODY atm_transactions AS
/* Define public methods in specification. */
/* Omits implementation details regarding. */
/* deposits and loan payments for brevity. */
    /* ATM inserts row in atm_trans -> do_it trigger fires */
    PROCEDURE atm_entry
        (acct NUMBER, atm_id NUMBER, trancode CHAR, amount NUMBER) IS
        BEGIN
            INSERT INTO atm_trans
                (atm_id, account_id, trancode, amount, trantime) VALUES (atm_id,
                    acct, trancode, amount, SYSDATE);
        END atm_entry;
            /* Debit account unless exception event */
    PROCEDURE atm_withdraw
        (acct NUMBER, atm_id NUMBER, debit NUMBER) IS
        old_balance        NUMBER;
        new_balance        NUMBER;
        banknotes          NUMBER; insufficient_funds
        EXCEPTION;
        need_more_cash  EXCEPTION;
    BEGIN
        SELECT twenties * 20 INTO banknotes FROM atms
                WHERE atm_id = atm_withdraw.atm_id;
        IF banknotes < debit THEN
                RAISE need_more_cash; — an exception END IF;
        IF banknotes < (3 * minimum_balance) THEN
                feed_me(atm_id); — rpc to get more cash
```

```
        END IF;
        SELECT balance INTO old_balance FROM accounts
            WHERE account_id = acct
            FOR UPDATE;        — to lock the row
        new_balance := old_balance - debit;
         IF new_balance >= minimum_balance THEN
            UPDATE accounts SET balance = new_balance
                WHERE account_id = acct;
               new_state := 'Withdrawal applied';
        ELSE
            RAISE insufficient_funds; — an exception END IF;
    EXCEPTION
        WHEN no_data_found THEN
            new_state := 'Account number not found';
        WHEN need_more_cash THEN
            new_state := 'Supply problem';
            rpc_feed_me(atm_id); — RPC to get more cash
        WHEN insufficient_funds THEN
                new_state := 'Insufficient funds';
        WHEN OTHERS THEN
                new_state := 'Error: ' || SQLERRM;
    END atm_withdraw;
    PROCEDURE atm_deposit
      (acct NUMBER, atm_id NUMBER, credit NUMBER) IS
    BEGIN
        /* Omit — keeps example realistic, we only withdraw  */ NULL;
    END atm_deposit;
    PROCEDURE atm_payloan
      (acct NUMBER, atm_id NUMBER, payment NUMBER) IS
    BEGIN
        NULL;
            /* Omit loan payment code, we never pay on time anyhow */
    END atm_payloan;
END atm_transactions;
```

In this simplified ATM example, the exception handlers in the database program play a similar role to that of event handlers and an RPC simulates an asynchronous event alert.

Figure 3.10 illustrates how an RPC might be used to notify a remote passive server of an external event. The figure shows an active server running a real estate application. The county clerk's office uses a passive database server to store property tax data. Whenever the active server closes escrow on a property transfer, the passive server must be notified of the event that causes property tax liability to change. As shown, the active server notifies the passive server's client of the property transfer by dispatching an RPC.

Table 3.2 summarizes active server features. This table may be used as a checklist to evaluate the features of competing database servers.

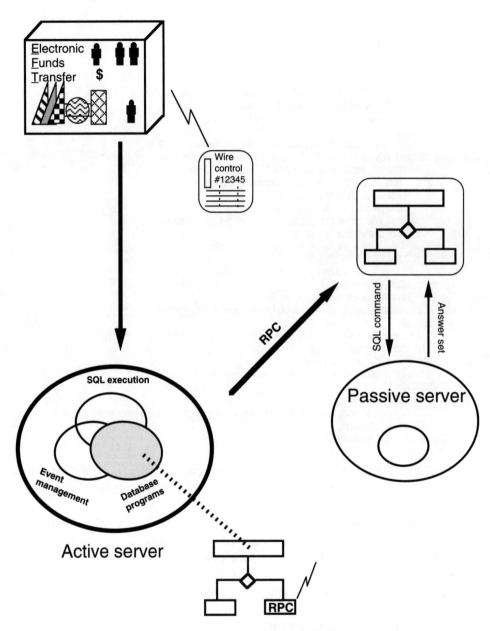

Figure 3.10 Remote procedure call

Table 3.2 Active Server Features

Category	Feature	Weight	Vendor X	Vendor Y	Vendor Z
Database programming	Stored procedures				
	Structured language				
	Nested procedures				
	Iteration control				
	Conditional execution				
	Parameters				
	Array processing				
Event management	Server triggers				
	Synchronous events				
	Asynchronous events				
	Event alerters				
Cooperative distributed database operations	Automatic 2PC				
	Event-driven replication				
	Time-based replication				

■ 3.5 APPLICATION SELF-MODIFICATION

A major benefit of constructing applications from active component assemblies is that the resulting application is capable of self-modification. An active application adjusts itself to keep pace with business events, utilizing server-based components such as database programs, triggers, and event alerters. These components are fine-grained. Because they are smaller than monolithic client programs, they are more manageable. Because they are structured and sharable, application components can be managed through the same central security facilities as all other server-based components. Because they incorporate their own control structures, server components have the power to accommodate change before they themselves must be changed.

By contrast, a passive database application is modified through changes to the client application program, since that is where control resides. Client programs are coarse-grained relative to server-based components. When part of the program requires change, the whole program must be recompiled. Because monolithic programs are complex, the risk exists that any change to part of the program will cause an unwanted side effect in another part of the program. The more complex the program, the greater the number of functions that must be tested as part of change control and the greater the likelihood of run-time functional error.

Some events are more far-reaching than others. The scope of some events is confined to a specific entity represented in the database, but other events have a wider and more persistent impact.

For narrow-scope events, the actions taken in response to an event fall within the immediate scope of a single server-based component assembly. In the ATM example presented in the previous section, most of the event-management logic was confined to the *atm_atm_transactions* package. The physical database tables, the event detection and notification mechanism, and the event handler involved in these narrow-focus events make up a logically related collection of event-processing components.

Wide-scope events have persistent side effects on the overall application. For those events that cause the application to modify its behavior, the ripple effect is managed in a variety of ways, such as

- By changing the flow of control within database programs
- By changing the behavior of database programs
- By alerting client programs so they can change their behaviors
- By updating the control tables of the application.

These self-modification mechanisms are characteristic of the active database architecture.

Self-modifying active database applications utilize the infrastructure of the database server. They require less procedural programming effort than passive applications that rely on client programs to drive operations, to check results, and to interrogate for exception conditions. However, active database applications require precision in their engineering and discipline in their construction. Self-adjusting applications need structure and order for their components to function effectively together. Chapter 4 explains how to deploy various active server features to produce powerful structured database applications.

4

THE ASSEMBLY LINE: ACTIVE COMPONENT ASSEMBLIES

Active database applications concentrate their core functionality—both structured behavior and structured data—in server-based component assemblies. Following a review of the earlier monolithic architecture, this chapter explains the server-based component types found in active database applications. As discussed in the previous chapter, these server-resident component types include database structures, database programs, server triggers, and event alerters. Component activation delegates application control to a component, performing the same function as procedural control statements in monolithic client programs. However, the component activation path is more open to change than the compiled control logic of monolithic programs. Because active database applications adjust their activation path to changing conditions, it is important to keep track of operations. Control tables in the database track the activation history of component assemblies, providing an audit trail for the application.

■ 4.1 MONOLITHIC DATABASE APPLICATIONS

Active database servers are the result of a long evolution (see Chapter 3). An examination of SQL interfaces for passive monolithic applications will place active database applications in an historical perspective.

Passive client/server applications perform data-management functions on the server, but they control these operations from monolithic client programs. This

Table 4.1 Legacy Program versus Passive Client

Legacy Program	Passive Client
Opens or closes files	Connects to or disconnects from database server
Calls for read/write operating system file services	Sends commands for server action
Processes operating system return codes	Processes database server return codes

concentration of application logic in the client environment is a throwback to pre-database legacy applications. In contrast to legacy applications, which centralize monolithic program execution in a single CPU, passive client programs distribute their application logic among multiple client machines. Instead of one central point of control, the application is controlled from multiple, distributed platforms, which creates both synchronization problems and code maintenance problems.

Procedural programming is the defining feature of a legacy application as well as the exclusive means of data access. The upper portion of Figure 4.1 illustrates the high-level structure of a legacy transaction-processing program that accesses two files.

Passive database applications follow legacy programming technology. The passive database client program shown in the lower portion of Figure 4.1 has a structure similar to the legacy program in the upper portion. Table 4.1 summarizes the (relatively minor) differences between the two sample client programs.

Passive database client programs contain both procedural code and SQL commands. Unlike database programs, passive client programs reside outside the database server. The database server interprets the embedded SQL commands in a client program, but they are completely foreign to that program. The client program considers embedded SQL commands as meaningless character string variables. Similarly, the procedural code of the client program is completely foreign and incomprehensible to the SQL execution facility of the database server.

Because passive clients and passive servers are disparate, special interface features are required to drive nonprocedural SQL operations from procedural language programs in the client environment. The next section reviews embedded SQL in order to provide an overview of these special interface features.

4.1.1 Overview of Embedded SQL Precompiler Interface

The passive client program illustrated in the lower portion of Figure 4.1 has a hierarchical structure. Once this program is activated (that is, initiated or launched) by a client-platform operating system command, it controls its own operations.

The components of this passive client program are associated physically because they are compiled and linked together to form a monolithic executable program. To the extent that the program is well-structured, these components also are logi-

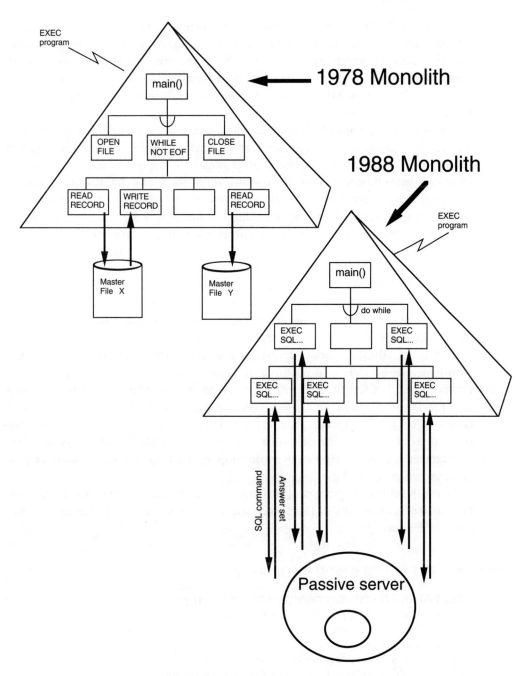

Figure 4.1 Monolithic client program

cally related. The physical relationship of belonging to the same monolithic executable code lasts throughout the life of the program. As a result of ongoing maintenance activities, which are necessary to keep the program relevant to the business, certain routines develop structural distortions as they become overburdened with secondary tasks. Meanwhile, other routines fall into disuse and eventually render themselves useless.

The logical structure of monolithic client programs is *hierarchical modularity*. Top-level routines in the program hierarchy control mid-level functions, which in turn delegate specific SQL command processing to low-level tasks. These low-level tasks call the SQL interface at the lowest level of the hierarchy. Like any application program, passive database client programs include data structures, procedural control structures, variables, and procedural commands. They also contain special-purpose, database-related code for the embedded SQL precompiler.

Embedded SQL interfaces allow compiler language programs to access relational databases. The SQL standard for embedded SQL has its origins in IBM's interface to DB2. Precompilers simplify development by permitting the application programmer to code high-level statements providing a shorthand for database interface tasks. Based on these high-level statements, the precompiler generates the low-level commands needed to control the server.

Just as a COBOL compiler translates a single COBOL source language command such as MOVE into multiple assembler commands at compile time, an embedded SQL COBOL precompiler converts high-level precompiler constructs into low-level, run-time, database-server commands embedded within the source code of a compiler language program. The DBMS vendor supplies a precompiler for various compiler languages, such as COBOL, C, FORTRAN, or Ada. Table 4.2 summarizes the specific steps in developing the C language precompiler program shown in Figure 4.2.

When the client program executes, it utilizes its linked-in embedded SQL interface to send commands to the server and pass the results back through its own internal memory.

Table 4.2 Developing a C Language Precompiler Program

Step	Work Performed to Develop Embedded SQL C Program
1	Write embedded SQL C precompiler source code.
2	Process the precompiler source code by using the vendor-supplied precompiler (such as Oracle Pro*C or Ingres esqlc).
3	Compile the C source code produced by the precompiler.
4	Link the compiled program to obtain an executable program.
5	Execute the program to control data-management operations.

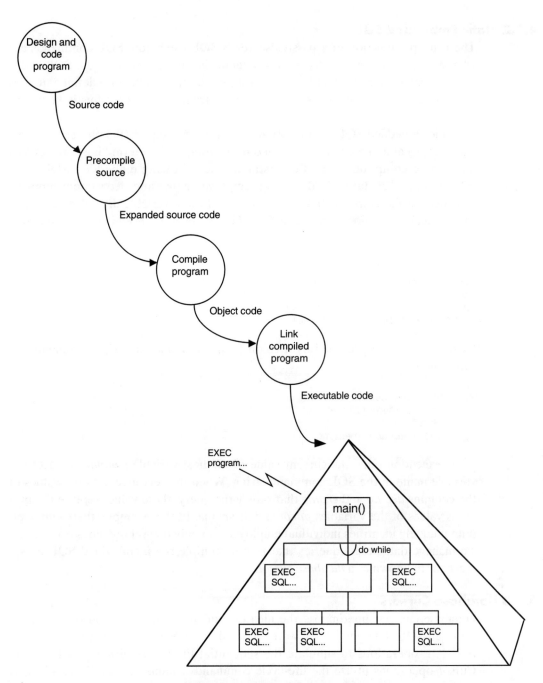

Figure 4.2 Making the monolith

4.1.2 Static Embedded SQL

The principal function of a passive server is SQL execution. SQL commands are what a passive server expects from its client. The client constructs the SQL query and processes the result that is returned from the server. When predefined queries are hard-coded as character strings in the program source code, this is known as *static SQL*.

Static embedded SQL queries often consist of a fixed part (the predefined character string) and one or more so-called *host variables*. The term "host" refers to a mainframe computer CPU. For instance, the following embedded SQL code (Oracle Pro*C syntax) will display an employee name and department number, provided a valid employee number is used. All three variable data elements must first be declared as host variables before they can be referenced in static embedded SQL.

```
EXEC SQL BEGIN DECLARE SECTION
int    pempno;      /* employee number  */
char  pname[11];   /* employee name     */
int    pdeptno;     /* department number*/
EXEC SQL END DECLARE SECTION
```

Host variables are preceded by a colon (:) within embedded SQL statements, as shown here:

```
EXEC SQL select deptno, ename
       into :pdeptno, :pname
       from emp
       where empno = :pempno;
```

At execution time, the current value of the host variable *pempno* replaces the variable name in the SQL command string. When the server returns the values of the columns *deptno* and *ename* that satisfy the query, these values replace the previous values of the variables *pdeptno* and *pname*. In this example, the *empno* column uniquely identifies individual employees, so only one set of values is returned. To manage data-access queries that return multiple rows, embedded SQL uses a mechanism known as a *database cursor*.

4.1.3 Database Cursors

Database cursors superimpose the idea of sequence and navigation on the result set of an SQL statement. They were included in the SQL language to allow multi-row SQL operations to simulate the sequential file access of a legacy program. Cursor operations utilize the life-cycle commands summarized in Table 4.3. This cycle is patterned after the legacy file operations in COBOL programs.

Table 4.3 Cursor Operation Commands

Command	Work Performed by Command
DECLARE CURSOR	Associate the cursor with an SQL command.
OPEN CURSOR	Evaluate and execute the SQL command.
FETCH	Retrieve one or more rows of the answer set.
OPEN CURSOR	Deactivate the SQL command.

For example, to retrieve employee data for a given department on an employee-by-employee basis, declare a cursor associated with a SQL statement, as shown here:

```
EXEC SQL DECLARE emp_cur CURSOR FOR
     select ename, empno, job, sal
     from emp
     where deptno = :deptno;
     FOR UPDATE OF sal;
```

The purpose of this SQL command is to update the *sal* column with an incentive bonus. The next step is to open the cursor and fetch an employee row or rows:

```
EXEC SQL OPEN emp_cur;
```

An iteration control construct such as a *do* loop can enclose the fetch statement in order to simulate a legacy program with a *do until* read loop. The Pro*C syntax is

```
EXEC SQL WHENEVER NOT FOUND STOP;
for (. . . condition)
{
EXEC SQL FETCH emp_cur INTO :ename, :empno, :job, :sal;
. . . .
```

In this application, the purpose of fetching the employee data into host variables is to display sufficient detail to verify that the correct employee has been selected before entering the bonus amount. The bonus is added to the value of the column *sal* to derive the value of *new_sal*. This update takes place before fetching the next employee row.

```
EXEC SQL update emp
         set sal = :new_sal
         WHERE CURRENT OF emp_cur;  /* restrict to current employee*/
```

When all rows have been fetched and updated, the cursor is closed.

The embedded SQL interface uses a structure within the embedded SQL program known as the *SQL communications area* (SQLCA). The SQLCA is typically copied into the C precompiler source code from a C language *include* file. The SQLCA structure contains a variable called *sqlcode* that holds the value of the result code returned after execution of an SQL command.

Most embedded SQL products follow the convention set by IBM's early database-management product Information Management System (IMS), in which a zero value indicates a successful operation. As in UNIX return codes, a negative *sqlcode* value indicates an error condition. A positive *sqlcode* value usually indicates a nonerror exception condition. For instance, a *sqlcode* of 710 from the Ingres server means that an event alert has arrived and should not be treated as an error. Instead, the embedded SQL program is supposed to respond to a *sqlcode* of 710 by retrieving the event alerter and taking the appropriate action.

4.1.4 Dynamic SQL with Descriptors

In additon to static embedded SQL commands, embedded SQL applications sometimes use *dynamic SQL* commands, which are not hard-coded into the client program. Instead, a dynamic SQL command is undefined until execution time, when it is either automatically communicated to the client program or manually entered by the user. Figure 4.3 shows the dynamic SQL interaction between an automated refinery application and a diagnostic expert system. Whenever the expert system receives a signal from the sensors, it generates SQL queries to compare data from the database with the input data from the sensors.

Dynamic SQL processing requires an interface structure called the *SQL descriptor area* (SQLDA). This structure is located in the storage of the client program. The purpose of the SQLDA structure is to describe the variables that contain dynamic data to be sent to and returned from the database. The program storage to which the SQLDA points is dynamically allocated at run time, hence the term "dynamic." The SQLDA points to so-called *bind variables*, which hold data to be sent to the database server. SELECT queries require yet another *select SQLDA*, which describes variables that hold data returned by a query.

The program structure chart in the lower part of Figure 4.3 represents the steps required for dynamic SQL operations, as summarized in Table 4.4.

In summary, the interfaces of passive-client embedded SQL (static or dynamic) act as an intermediary between procedural language routines in client programs and the nonprocedural SQL language that provides the interface to the database server.

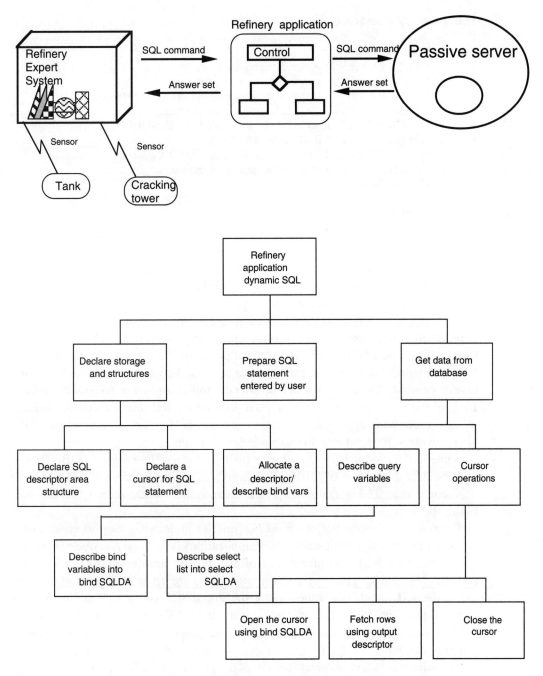

Figure 4.3 Dynamic SQL

Table 4.4 Dynamic SQL Operations

Step	Work Performed
1	DECLARE the SQL descriptor area structure.
2	PREPARE the SQL statement entered by the user.
3	DECLARE a cursor for the statement name of the SQL statement.
4	Allocate a descriptor (SQLDA instance) for the query.
5	DESCRIBE bind (input host) variables into the bind SQLDA.
6	OPEN the cursor USING the bind SQLDA.
7	DESCRIBE the SELECT list into the select SQLDA instance.
8	FETCH rows USING the output descriptor until done.
9	CLOSE the cursor.

4.1.5 Passive 4GL Clients

As passive SQL interfaces gain flexibility, they also gain programming complexity. Increased complexity usually leads to increased coding requirements at a higher programmer skill level, so flexibility in passive SQL clients tends to not come cheaply. Given the relatively high cost of procedural language coding, labor-saving alternatives have become increasingly popular.

One approach to reducing the cost of programming a client-based portion of an application is to automate code production by means of 4GLs. These nonprocedural application generators simplify client program coding in a manner similar to the precompilers discussed in the previous section. The nonprocedural 4GL commands generate lower-level procedural code and incorporate an SQL interface. Each of the main database vendors has a proprietary 4GL for character-based terminals, usually integrated with a forms generator. Vendors of standalone 4GLs also provide SQL client interfaces to relational servers.

Some 4GLs produce *query-by-forms* (QBF) or *query-by-example* (QBE) applications. The advantage of QBF/QBE interfaces is that we do not need to code SQL commands. The operator simply points and clicks on the screen, and the 4GL builds the query.

Query-by-example is useful for *ad hoc* queries in decision-support client applications. In transaction-processing client applications (where *ad hoc* queries are less commonplace), SQL commands are often preprogrammed and preparsed for faster performance. These parsed commands are stored in the client 4GL code. When the 4GL client program executes, the stored SQL commands are invoked by client trigger keystrokes. For example, hitting the TAB key to advance to the next field on the form might trigger sending a SQL query to the server to validate an account number.

The advantages and disadvantages of 4GLs are shown in Table 4.5.

Table 4.5 Advantages and Disadvantages of 4GLs

Advantages	Disadvantages
Rapid development compared with procedural coding	Proprietary; conversions are difficult
Consistent output, automatic interface generation	Most suitable for simple applications
Low labor cost because of nonprocedural coding	Generate monolithic clients

Database applications must keep pace with changes in business conditions. When SQL commands are buried deep within 4GL applications, they cannot be easily maintained in step with changes to the database structures they reference. The time and effort saved during the initial development of the 4GL application can be lost during maintenance.

To keep pace with business needs, a more expedient procedure would be to throw away a 4GL client application and entirely replace it. However, replacing monolithic client code introduces the risk of unwanted side effects in other portions of the application that were supposed to remain stable. These unintended side effects may cause functional errors in production programs, or even corrupt the database. When used for purposes other than the most straightforward reporting applications, 4GLs have the same disadvantages as other monolithic client software, including the following:

- Coding monolithic passive client applications requires a high skill level.
- Monolithic passive client applications are rigid and difficult to reprogram.
- Passive client applications are prone to error.

■ 4.2 SERVER-BASED ASSEMBLIES

Both the client and server portions of an active database application consist of *assemblies*. These assemblies are built from subassemblies, which in turn are built from one or more standard components. These components, the basic elements of active database applications, correspond to the data and process elements of passive database applications.

Unlike passive applications, active client/server applications are not completely distributed in the client environment. Instead, logically central application logic such as company-wide business procedures is centralized on the server. This frees the resources of the client machine for those logically distributed data-capture and data-access functions that involve the user. For instance, client-resident component types include the interface objects shown in Figure 4.4, as well as the behavior shown in the "scripts" of these objects.

The server-based component types include

· Database structures, which are the objects of SQL execution such as tables

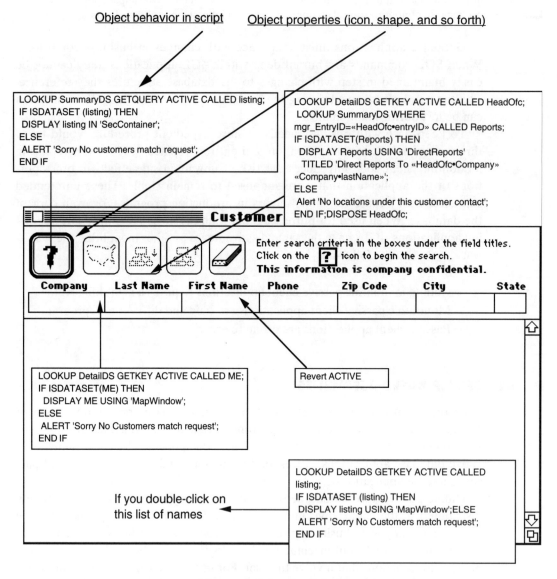

Figure 4.4 Interface objects

- Database programs, which consist of code stored and executed on the server
- Event-management components, which include triggers and event alerters.

Component subassemblies are usually (but not necessarily) prefabricated, which means they usually have been built and used in another assembly. Although most subassemblies are prefabricated, the final build of these subassemblies, which connects individual data structures, database programs, and event alerters to form a complete operational assembly, takes place only at the moment of activation. In this sense, activation resembles the assembly line of a *flexible factory*. As shown in Figure 4.5, the activation of server assemblies takes place through extended SQL commands in database programs, by event-management mechanisms, or by state changes in application data structures.

The benefits of using component assemblies for software development are

Claim	*Justification*
• No wasted coding labor	Sharable and reusable code
• No useless software assets	Self-contained components that eliminate dead code
• High reliability	Fewer lines of procedural code.

For these benefits to be achieved, each component assembly must cooperate with other assemblies to perform application work. This application design requirement is consistent with the technical requirement that all components integrate with the infrastructure of the database server. Automation facilitates coordination among component assemblies.

Automated design through CASE introduces automation early in the development cycle. The CASE approach generates components in the specific form needed for the selected RDBMS vendor's server. Certain CASE products are capable of generating syntax to create tables and database procedures in a variety of SQL dialects, notably DB2, Oracle, and Sybase.

Automated gateways provide another automated design approach. An automated gateway enables distributed applications among disparate database servers. The gateway process is programmed to understand the extended SQL dialects of different vendors and translate between them. Components are isolated within each database server and activated solely by means of SQL commands in the appropriate SQL dialect. These SQL commands are translated as necessary by a gateway utility program. Oracle, Ingres, Sybase, and Micro Decisionware currently offer database gateways.

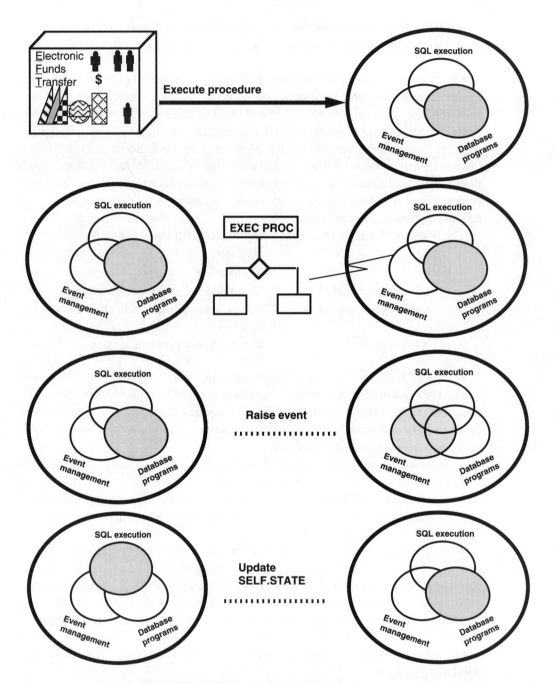

Figure 4.5 Server assembly activation

4.2.1 Data Tables and Control Tables

Active database applications encompass two categories of tables: data tables and control tables. *Data tables* are structures that contain data specific to entities in the application. *Control tables* are structures designed to hold metadata (data about data and data about behavior) spanning multiple applications. Control tables contain metadata regarding the relationships between application components, their scheduled activation sequences, their participation in workflows, and their responses to events.

Control tables extend the database catalog, which contains metadata specific to the physical database. Control tables are part of the application, and should not be confused with the vendor-supplied database catalog tables. The catalog tables, which some DBMS vendors misleadingly call the "data dictionary," are part of the RDBMS infrastructure.

4.2.2 Application Data Tables

Data table categories are the result of relational database design, which breaks down data structures into multiple tables using a design method called *normalization*. The various types of data table in an active database environment correspond to the following categories of data that they hold:

- Main tables hold data representative of real-world concepts.
- Look-up tables hold data for abstract concepts.
- Associative tables hold data for main concept relationships.
- Working tables (and temporary tables) hold current in-process data.
- History tables contain historical audit trail data.

Main tables represent the main concepts in the conceptual data model of the application. In a sales application, for example, customers and products are among the main concepts. Figure 4.6 shows the structure of the customer (main) table and the terms (look-up) table in the sales application. The customer table is a holding structure that is representative of the general concept of *Customer*. The identifier *customer_id* uniquely identifies each real-world customer in the database. The other columns in this table hold data for the attributes of customers in general, such as the customer's name, the contact telephone number, and the agreed-upon terms code. The *terms_id* code column, a foreign key in the customer table, is the primary key of the *Terms* table.

The *Terms* table holds data related to commercial terms. Unlike the real-world concept of customers, "terms" is an abstract concept. We can shake hands with customers in everyday life, but we cannot achieve eye contact with terms because

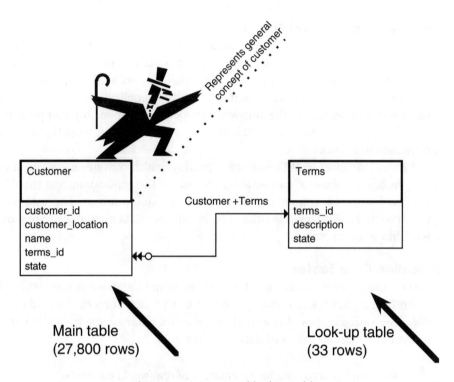

Figure 4.6 Main and look-up tables

"terms" is a commercial abstraction. Consequently, the *Terms* table is classified as a *look-up table*. In most applications, the look-up tables have fewer rows than the main tables, just as a small number of commercial abstractions are shared by many specific real-world entities.

Associative tables represent the results of relationships, meaning the interactions between main concept entities. For example, when a product is sold to a customer, it appears on an order. The order is an associative concept. It results from the relationship that associates the customer(s) and the product(s).

Working tables hold in-process data for incomplete behavior in the application. During order entry, for example, an order may be built in a pending order table. When the order is confirmed, rows are deleted from the working table and inserted in the orders table.

Temporary tables are a subtype of working table. A temporary table resembles a working table, but has a much shorter persistence (working life). Working tables retain their structure even if they lose their data. By contrast, when a temporary table loses persistence, both the data in the table and the table structure disappear. At the longest, a temporary table persists as long as the client that created it is connected to the server. Typically, a temporary table is created by a database program and only exists during the execution of that program.

History tables hold audit trail data, meaning data reflecting the past condition of an item. For example, an on-line banking application holds the current balance of demand deposit accounts in the main account table. A service charge is deducted from the account if the average balance falls below a certain level. The account history table contains daily account balances to substantiate the service charge, along with other details of past operations on the account.

4.2.3 Application Control Tables

Application control tables perform a necessary role in the application. The persistence of active assemblies—when they become active and when they become inactive—is governed by server-based application control tables. These control tables store the Bill of Operations for active assemblies and contain the schedule for time-based activation. They represent control logic, in order to keep database programs simple and flexible.

Application control tables hold metadata. The database catalog also contains metadata, but of a different type. The metadata in the catalog is specific to the physical database, while metadata in control tables concerns application components.

Just as data tables fall into various structural categories, so do control tables. The structure of each subtype of control table depends on the category of metadata it contains, and is consistent across all applications.

4.2.4 Bills of Materials and Bills of Operations

A *Bill of Materials* lists the components used in a *Component Case*, the collection of components that comprise an assembly. A Bill of Materials table includes both server-based and client-based components.

A *Bill of Operations* lists the sequence of operations for assemblies in an application workflow. The Bill of Operations is used to control the execution of database programs. In Figure 4.7, the operations list serves as a template for an audit trail. A Bill of Operations controls the sequence of operations. Database programs are executed beginning with the top-level procedure in the Bill of Operations. As they execute, the execution statistics are captured in the *Application Log*, an application table that provides an audit trail. Just as the Bill of Operations is distinct from the RDBMS catalog, the Application Log is distinct from the RDBMS log that is used to recover the physical database after a failure.

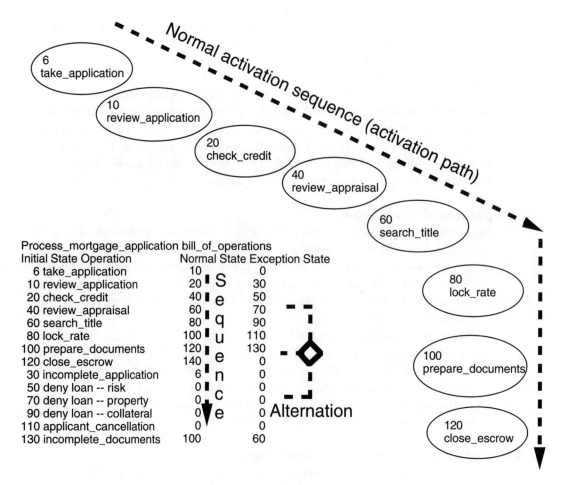

Figure 4.7 Bill of Operations

4.2.5 Schedule Tables

Schedule tables list time-sensitive operations whose schedule is known in advance. Operations that are synchronized with the accounting cycle are the most familiar scheduled operations, but many other time-sensitive operations may occur. The replenishment of bulk consumables, rotating physical inventory, and planned maintenance shutdowns are just some of the operations that might figure in the schedule of a manufacturing organization.

Like a Bill of Operations, a schedule can drive operations directly or indirectly. Figure 4.8 shows a financial services workflow that uses the direct method. In this illustration, a database program retrieves rows from the *df_schedule* table in *opera-*

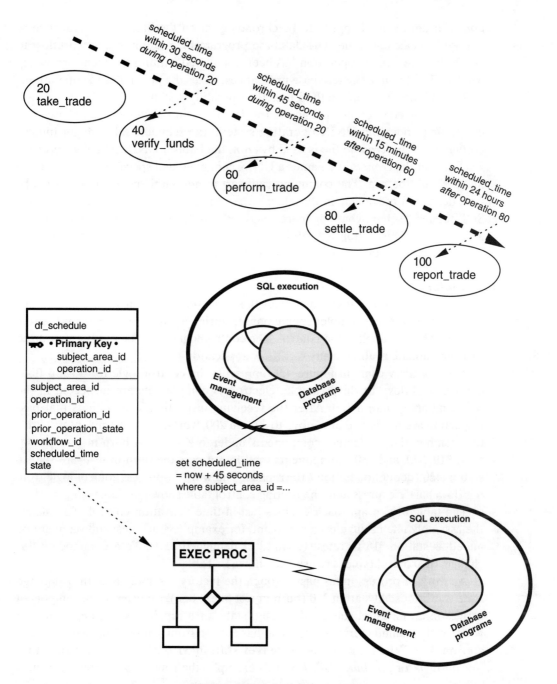

Figure 4.8 Scheduled activation

tion_id order, which happens to be chronological on the basis of interval time as opposed to calendar time. The database program then monitors the workflow to verify that the current operation has been completed within its current processing window. If it has not, the database program escalates the priority of the operation.

The indirect schedule method uses the operating system of the server platform to run scheduled operations at an appropriate time. In the case of a database server running under the UNIX operating system, the schedule table might build a *crontab* file. This *crontab* file is used by *cron*, the built-in UNIX scheduler process. Each line in the *crontab* file names a UNIX command and specifies when the command should be run. The command can start a monolithic client program of the type described previously in this chapter. Alternatively, it can start an interactive SQL session (isql in Sybase or Ingres, SQL*Plus in Oracle) with a command file as a parameter. This option is useful for performing database administration tasks, such as creating database programs, at a predetermined "quiet" time in operations.

4.2.6 Logic Tables

Logic tables store the logic to control the activation of application components. This section uses an example from a manufacturing application to explain the role of logic tables in application control. The control logic could be easily generalized to accommodate routing in any workflow application.

The workflow chart in Figure 4.9 represents the control logic for a shop floor control workflow. In this example, electronics components are inspected in the receiving area, station 100. After the receiving inspection, components that pass inspection are bar-coded and move to station 200, work-in-process inventory. Prior to assembly, the electronics components undergo a series of burn-in tests at stations 310, 320, and 330. Components that do not pass the burn-in tests are sent to station 420 (debug) or station 410 (repair). The work-in-process control logic from the flowchart is expressed in the routing control table shown in Table 4.6.

The table-driven approach enables just-in-time activation control. To balance the assembly line in the electronics plant, for example, a new test station might be added as station 315 to retest repaired or debugged parts. To accommodate this change, the control table is revised, as shown in Table 4.7.

As work-in-process items pass through the factory assembly line, they undergo state transitions. At station 310 (burn-in test phase one), for example, a component arrives in an untested state, a debugged state, or a repaired state, depending on whether the manufacturing component has arrived from station 200, station 410, or station 420. When a component leaves station 310, it is in a state of either *pre_burn_ok* or *pre_burn_failed*. In this example, the routing of an item is a func-

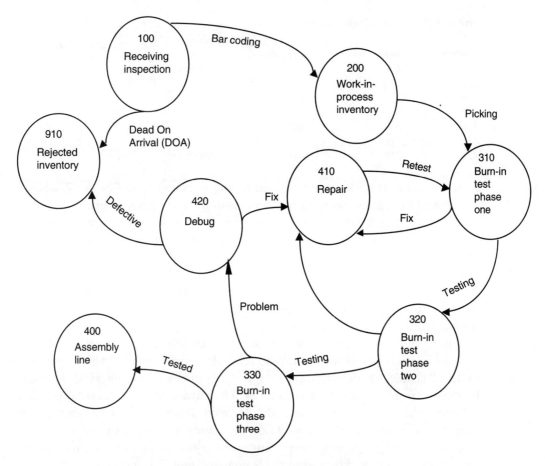

Figure 4.9 Work-in-process workflow

Table 4.6 Work-in-Process Routing Control Table

Station	norm_dest	excp_dest
100	200	910
200	310	—
310	320	410
320	330	410
330	400	420
410	310	—
420	310	910

Table 4.7 Revised Control Table

Station	norm_dest	excp_dest
100	200	910
200	310	—
310	320	410
315	320	410
320	330	410
410	310	—
420	310	910

tion of its state. This idea of state-based routing is examined in Chapter 7, where it is extended from manufacturing components to software components.

The state of each individual item in the work-in-process inventory is explicitly represented in this example in the *wip_data* main table by the *state* column, as shown in Table 4.8.

Every possible state for an item is defined in another control table called the *state table*. A state table might also describe the substates of a state (for example, nonpersistent/persistent, normal/exception) as well as the state itself (inactive/active), as shown in Table 4.9.

The set of possible states is similar to a domain column, or the set of valid values that it is permissible for an entry to take. However, domains (where supported by the RDBMS vendor) pertain to specific columns in the physical database. Domains are relatively static structures. They are created, associated (in their entirety) with columns, and eventually dropped. Rows in the state table may be activated or deactivated during workflow processing to vary the routing logic.

Unless a *work_in_process* component is in a rejected state, an exception state in the manufacturing workflow example is nonpersistent. For instance, a component that is currently in state 50 (*repaired*, a normal state) must have previously been in at least one nonpersistent exception state. A cumulative exception count is maintained in the *wip_data* table to support ISO 9000 "birth-to-death" quality control tracking. The detailed incident history of the component is stored in a history table.

Table 4.8 wip_data Main Table

component_id	Description	Station	excp_hist	state
c4035439509	cpu_board	310	0	10
c4325788934	circuit_board	310	4	50
c4057432587	circuit_board	310	1	40
c4059867587	asic_board	320	0	21
c4794370457	asic_board	410	1	22

Table 4.9 State Table

state_id	Description	excp	persist	state
10	inspected	0	0	1
15	rejected	1	1	1
20	untested	0	0	1
30	preburn_ok	0	0	1
35	preburn_fail	1	0	1
40	debugged	0	0	1
50	repaired	0	0	1
55	burn_ok	0	0	1
60	reserved	0	0	1
70	assembled	0	1	1

This example of real-world quality control tracking could be modified to handle quality control for software components used in the Database Factory assembly line. Software components are checked out of the component inventory of the *Development Warehouse*, a special-purpose database for software development. Any components altered by the developer while they are checked out of the Development Warehouse change state from *certified* to *modified*. These *modified* components undergo preassembly unit testing before they regain their certified state. The test, debug, and repair history of all components is maintained in *Total Quality Management* (TQM) tables in the Development Warehouse.

■ 4.3 APPLICATION BEHAVIOR IN DATABASE PROGRAMS

Database programs vary from single-purpose user-defined functions to multiprogram packages containing the behavior of entire classes of entities.

The work-in-process inventory routing workflow from the previous section can be managed by the following PL/SQL function (a small database program routine):

```
FUNCTION next_station
(curr_station IN INT, excp IN BOOLEAN) RETURN INT IS
norm_station INT;
excp_station INT;
BEGIN
    SELECT norm_dest, excp_dest INTO norm_station, excp_station
        FROM route_cntl where station = curr_station;
    IF excp THEN RETURN excp_station ELSE RETURN norm_station;
END next_station;
```

The *next_station* function is likely to be called from within a database program, as shown here:

```
.....
next_dest := next_station(curr_station, excp);
.....
```

For active servers, database programs are the means of centralizing procedural behavior. Logically central, nonprocedural behavior also can be centralized in the server environment for shared use by application components. This shared behavior is implemented in declarative constructs such as

- Exception handlers (automatic redirection of control)
- Datatypes/rules (declarative data-value constraint enforcement)
- Integrity (declarative entity/referential integrity).

4.3.1 Exception Handlers

Exception handlers automate application control by providing a declarative, server-based mechanism for switching control from the application "mainline" to the exception handler.

Server-based exception handling has the benefit of storing and executing exception handling close to the data. Because client-based exception handling executes in a different environment than the database server, the following extra processing steps must take place:

- The error code (that is, a negative value of sqlcode) must be communicated to the client.
- The client application must interrogate the SQLCA.
- The client procedural logic must evaluate the exception condition.
- The client procedural statements must alter the application flow of control.

Procedural code is more complex than nonprocedural code and, therefore, more prone to error. Because client-based exception handling code is stored redundantly on each client machine, a greater risk of administrative error results from maintaining multiple code copies than from the control of a single, concise, server-based component.

Returning to the manufacturing routing example to show how server-based exception handling works, production inventory items are bar-coded at station 100 for "birth-to-death" component tracking. After an the item is bar-coded, the *wip_data* table should have a row for the item as identified by its bar-coded *component_id*. Whenever the item arrives at a workcenter station, its *wip_data* row is updated. If the *wip_data* entry is not found, the likely cause is a bar-code scanning error and the appropriate action is to repeat the scan. The server automatically raises a NO_DATA_FOUND exception, and control is automatically passed to an exception handler in the *arrive_station* procedure, as shown here:

```
PROCEDURE arrive_station
/* update location and state of item */
(component_id CHAR (11), curr_station INT, arr_state CHAR (4)) IS
BEGIN
    SELECT ..... FOR UPDATE OF station
        do_update_station(component_id, curr_station , arr_state);
    EXCEPTION
        WHEN NO_DATA_FOUND THEN
                alertmsg := 'Bar-code error — scan again';
                raise_alert (alertmsg);
END arrive_station;
```

4.3.2 Datatypes and Rules

Data typing includes both type checking and null value checking. This form of declarative behavior, often taken for granted by application designers, avoids procedural testing for missing or illogical values. By contrast, a COBOL program may need to check the type, as shown here:

```
....
WORKING-STORAGE SECTION.
77 Foo Picture X.
....
CHECK-FOO.
IF FOO IS NOT NUMERIC
    DISPLAY "ERROR 58 — FOO MUST BE IN RANGE 0-9"
    GO TO ERROR-EXIT.
```

Procedural language code (such as the following line of dBASE code) must use a procedural *if-then-else* statement because it has no declarative concept of null:

```
....
IF Foo <> " " ....
....
```

Server-based declarative rules provide application-specific declarative behavior. For example, items in the manufacturing routing example can only be in states 10 through 99. However, the *state* column conforms to the *state_id* column in the state table, which can hold a four-digit integer. A check constraint to restrict the state range is declared by the application developer when the table is created and automatically enforced at run-time. For example,

```
CREATE TABLE wip_data
     (component_id  CHAR (11) UNIQUE KEY,
         description    CHAR (13),
         station        NUMBER(4) CONSTRAINT sta_fkey
                        REFERENCES
                        routing,
         state_id       NUMBER(4),
         excp_hist      NUMBER(2),
         CONSTRAINT  state_val CHECK(state_id BETWEEN 10 AND 99));
```

4.3.3 Integrity Constraints

Integrity constraints protect entity integrity and referential integrity, as illustrated by the key icons in Figure 1.5. The workflow example includes a UNIQUE KEY constraint on the *wip_data* table to enforce entity integrity. The constraint declaration is part of the nonprocedural CREATE TABLE statement, so it is automatically associated with the table from inception. The constraint is part of the server's SQL execution infrastructure and is enforced automatically by the RDBMS. The result is that no more than one row in the *wip_data* table can ever have the same *component_id* value. Each inventory item in the workflow has a unique identifier and can only be in one place and one state at once.

Referential integrity requires that a station referred to in the *wip_data* table actually must exist in the routing table. Otherwise, *wip_data* would be unreliable. The constraint named *sta_fkey* works in tandem with the PRIMARY KEY declaration on the station column in the routing table to declare referential integrity. Once declared, the database server automatically enforces referential integrity.

4.3.4 Event Activation

Active server assemblies are activated either by means of commands or in response to events. Commands are the familiar SQL statements that initiate data-manipulation operations. The EXECUTE PROCEDURE statement that activates a database program is also a type of command. An event-management construct gains control as a result of a state change within the database. The two categories of activation construct are server triggers and event alerters.

Server triggers provide an automatic interface between the SQL execution and event-management functionality of the database server. Triggers encompass or invoke further SQL or procedural operations. Because triggers potentially have a wide-ranging ripple effect, it is often desirable either to limit the scope of database

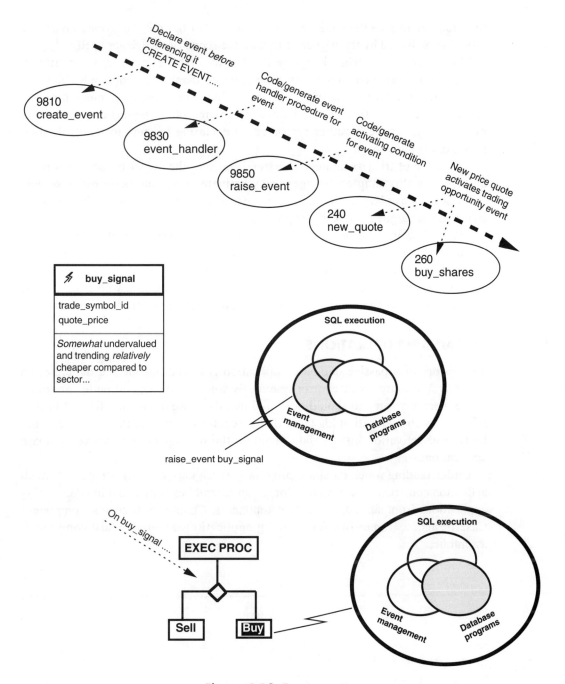

Figure 4.10 Event activation

wide-ranging ripple effect, it is often desirable either to limit the scope of database programs activated by the trigger or to limit the scope of the trigger itself.

The scope of the trigger can be limited by making execution-conditional changes to a specific column within a table, rather than to any column in the table. A conditional restriction on trigger execution limits its scope by homing in on significant changes and filtering out immaterial changes. In designing an active application, trigger scope is futher restricted by declaring triggers for control tables rather than main tables.

The scope of triggers and events extends beyond the server-based components discussed in this chapter. Triggers may activate components on other servers through database RPCs, although performance considerations and administrative concerns may argue against this approach.

Event alerts may be sent to clients and remote servers, as well as local server components. An event alert activates an event handler in the receiver, which can assemble an application workflow just in time to take advantage of a business opportunity. In Figure 4.10, a new quotation trigger associated with a SQL *insert* statement results in a *buy_signal* event. This event activates a trading workflow.

■ 4.4 EXPLAINABLE OPERATIONS

The history of a passive database application is stored outside the database, on paper or in a source-code control system. By contrast, the activation history of an active assembly can and should be stored in a database audit trail. Recent history is stored in an application log table that is regularly archived. Performance, reliability, and activation history data facilitate the management of active database applications.

Understanding which database programs, which database structures, and which activation constructs are available for use in assemblies is essential in constructing applications from shared, reusable components. Chapter 5 discusses Component Case design, a framework for building applications from standard component assemblies.

5

BLUEPRINTS: COMPONENT CASE DESIGN

An active database application is only as effective as its components, which must be designed for assembly/disassembly. It is necessary to integrate client and server components so that they work well together, or they will not get the job done. It is much easier and more reliable to connect prefabricated component subassemblies (Component Cases), compared to the effort required to build these subassemblies from scratch.

After reviewing the background of designing for shared data, this chapter introduces the Component Case approach to client/server design. Component Case kits are subassemblies built from standard components. It applies an automated design (CASE) method to the client and server components of the application. The components in a Component Case work together in a goal-directed manner. Metadata "traffic lights" show effectiveness at attaining the goal.

■ 5.1   FROM RIGID AUTHORITARIANISM TO DESKTOP ANARCHY

Programs in the past "owned" data. Shared data access was initially accomplished by the manual process of circulating hardcopy reports. Next came COBOL programs with shared file access methods, such as IBM's Index Sequential Access Method (ISAM). Whenever changes in the business led to new information needs, a new program or application had to be designed, programmed, tested, and implemented. Whenever a file structure or access method required modification, the whole database was shut down and converted to the new physical format and the COBOL programs were recompiled. Under these circumstances

- Revising shared data formats was a high-overhead activity.
- Rigorous specification preceded all program changes.
- Change requests were prioritized, filed, and forgotten.
- End-users became dissatisfied with the MIS backlog.

Figure 5.1 illustrates programmatic file access. The program in the center monolith was specified by techniques, data, and process modeling. The data model depicted by an Entity-Relationship diagram at the top of the illustration is disjointed from the process model represented by the program structure diagram inside the monolith. At best, the data model can generate file-description libraries that are copied into the program source code.

The process model governs the actual file-management operations. Procedural code within each program directly manipulates physical data files, so data quality is only as good as the weakest program. In Figure 5.1, the routine that updates the project master file neglects to validate the department number (by reading the department file), so nothing prevents projects from being associated with nonexistent departments.

5.1.1 The Desktop Revolution

In the desktop revolution of the mid-1980s, desktop computers (PCs) with large-capacity, fixed disks became available and affordable. These low-cost PCs were linked to file servers by LANs. Individual workgroups could develop and control their own information systems. Departmental computers for marketing support, cost accounting, or service dispatching could be paid for out of the office equipment budget. Spreadsheet programs such as Lotus 1-2-3 and application generators such as dBASE enabled rapid application development without compiler language programming. Spreadsheet, word processing, and file-maintenance applications were integrated by exporting and importing ASCII files. Suddenly, every workgroup became its own data center.

After the initial euphoria dissipated, a realization set in that the desktop revolution had created isolated "islands of information" in the company. Individual workgroup applications that were created to meet narrow departmental needs lacked any ability to work coherently with applications from the next department. Information systems based on spreadsheets or BASIC programs and flat files had no means of protecting data integrity. In the rush of downsized applications, the

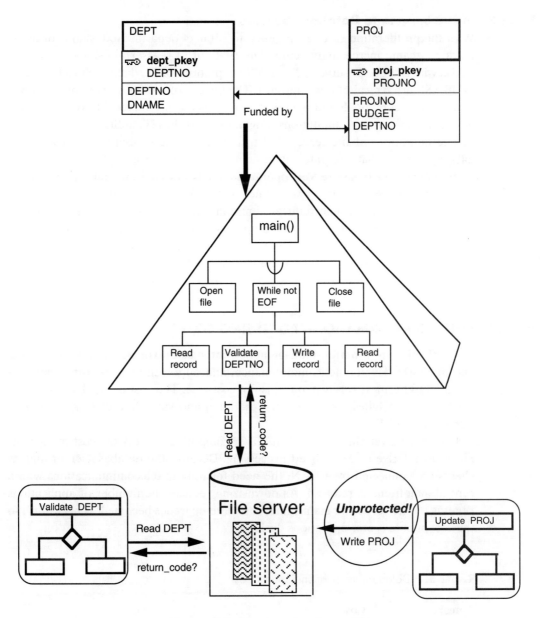

Figure 5.1 Nonshared and monolithic

controls and security features of the mainframe environment were foregone. Desktop anarchy had set in.

5.1.2 From File Servers to Database Servers

With the proliferation of PCs, the need to connect departmental islands of information became increasingly acute. The first cut at reasserting shared data was LANs with shared file servers. The LAN adaptations of PC database products such as dBASE are typical of this approach. The benefit of the file server approach was that a single copy of shared data was stored on the file server. However, performance and concurrency limitations weighed against these benefits.

The limitations of file servers led to the next stage in shared-data evolution: database servers that integrate database management with specialized communications software. Database servers operate in a network environment under a multiuser, multiprocess operating system such as UNIX. They minimize data traffic on the corporate LAN, which reduces communications costs. Database servers are increasingly implemented on "beefed up" versions of the same low-cost hardware used for client workstations. With core functions such as data management centralized on the server, the client machines can devote their resources to the processing demands of GUIs, spreadsheets, and paperless workflows.

■ 5.2 CUTTING INFORMATION-PROCESSING COSTS

Cost-effective information-management strategies maximize shared data access and minimize development, maintenance, and opportunity costs. Information is essential to business survival, but it is not cost-free. The cost of database information systems includes, among others, the fixed and variable cost factors summarized in Table 5.1.

Considering variable costs, client/server computing reduces the cost of communications relative to centralized processing. Because the database server and its clients are connected by a LAN, the need for remote telecommunications with a central mainframe is reduced. As downsizing reduces the number of applications running on the corporate mainframe, hardware upgrades become less necessary, so the cost of data center operations declines.

Table 5.1 Database Information Systems Cost

Category	Cost
Fixed	Hardware and DBMS software acquisition cost
Fixed	Telecommunications acquisition and installation cost
Variable	Telecommunications and data center operations cost
Variable	Training, coding, and code-maintenance labor cost
Variable	Output distribution, analysis, and manual processing labor cost

The remaining costs of building and operating database information systems are labor-related. Application development and software maintenance, two labor-intensive areas, consume a large chunk of the typical information-management budget. Added to these costs are the labor costs of retraining staff and reprogramming applications for the client/server environment.

Running a business on partially automated paper and verbal workflows is an ongoing high cost. Labor-intensive workflows often go unaddressed when the client/server migration is approached as a technology conversion exercise without addressing business process re-engineering. The foregone opportunity cost of not re-engineering paper workflows is substantial. Containing information processing labor costs—including the high cost of manual systems—presents the greatest opportunity for achieving cost-effectiveness.

5.2.1 Cost-Containment Strategies

An effective cost-containment plan meets the goals listed in Table 5.2. Clearly, not all cost-containment plans attain their goals. When all other factors are equal, success pivots on having the right resources (including the right technology) and the right approach.

5.2.2 Minimizing Wasted Effort

Far from streamlining operations, narrow-focus applications give rise to manual-processing islands of inefficiency. Instead of a data life cycle shaped by events and marked by state transitions, a bias develops toward procedural programs that, in the course of time, distort business procedures. Instead of a single point of data entry—the initial event that gives birth to a data item—printed data exits one application, only to be manually re-entered into another. Instead of producing information, applications produce paper to be distributed, re-entered, filed, and ignored.

Business processes, which could never receive such impressive quantities of paper without automated data processing, create their own manual processing demands. A company's entire information technology development budget is often lower than the clerical cost of processing its data processing output. The output

Table 5.2 Cost-Containment Goals

Goal	Means
Minimize wasted effort	Eliminate "islands of inefficiency"
Minimize procedural code	Keep code small and declarative
Reduce task complexity	Keep operations simple
Maximize software assets	Share and recycle standard components
Minimize integration cost	Keep like things together; avoid component anarchy

distribution, report analysis, and document-management costs resulting from partial automation are augmented by the cost of telephone calls required to explain legacy information systems that do such a poor job of explaining themselves.

Brute-force automation is not a valid remedy for islands of inefficiency. Voicemail messaging makes it possible for frustrated users to leave messages for the help desk, but does not reduce their frustration. Beepers make it possible to summon support staff at any hour, but do nothing to prevent a mission-critical system crash. If microfiche reports require further manual processing, migrating paper output to microfiche saves nothing more than storage space. The ability to annotate paper reports is lost, so microfiche can actually be a step backward.

Client/server re-engineering without business process re-engineering carries two major costs: the one-time cost of inappropriate development and the much larger recurring cost of manual processing to build paper bridges between islands of inefficiency. When software development efforts focus on minimizing waste, the ongoing cost of manual processing decreases.

5.2.3 Reducing Complexity

Software development costs include the labor cost to produce a database application (including training) and the cost of rework to make the application work correctly. A large, monolithic application takes longer to produce than one based on shared, recycled components, so the development labor cost is higher. The rework scope of monolithic applications is spread throughout large programs, so the cost of rework is higher than that associated with component-based applications whose in-course corrections are isolated to small components.

Design changes within the lead time of development are a well-known dilemma in all product development, not just software development. Business requirements rarely stand still. If it takes two years from the time of the project launch until the product roll-out, technology evolution and market forces will dictate changes to the product design under development. The longer it takes to develop the application, the less relevant the results are likely to be. Whenever the time-to-market is excessive, a product's success in the marketplace is at risk.

This "moving target" dilemma applies to all products, but the risk is particularly high for complex products such as information systems. It follows that the risk of failure is lower when the information system under development is less complex. Development risk also declines when the software resembles a manufactured product built from standard, shared components. Putting together small prefabricated components is faster than coding one-of-a-kind monolithic programs.

A client-based or server-based component is simpler than a monolithic program, with fewer lines of procedural code to test and debug. Functionality is better

Table 5.3 SQL versus COBOL Code

SQL Code	COBOL Code

CREATE TABLE DEPT /*DECLARATIVE code*/
  (DEPTNO NUMBER(2) PRIMARY KEY,
  DNAME CHAR(14) NOT NULL);
	IDENTIFICATION DIVISION.
	PROGRAM-ID: PROCEDURAL.
	...
	DATA DIVISION.
	FILE SECTION.
	FD DEPT-MASTER.
	01 DEPT-REC.
	  05 DEPTNO PICTURE 99 DISPLAY.
	  05 DNAME PICTURE X(14).
	...
	PROCEDURE DIVISION.
	....
	DCA-VALIDATE-DEPT.
	  IF DNAME = "" OR ALL " " THEN GO
	    TO ERROR-PROC. ....
	....
	GOBACK.

isolated in single-function components than multifunction monolithic programs, so the cost of in-course corrections is lower. Declarative SQL code is more concise than procedural C or COBOL code because the code specifies outcomes, rather than the details of how those outcomes are achieved. A set of active database components contains relatively more nonprocedural SQL code and less procedural code than the equivalent monolithic client program, and, therefore, has a smaller code size. As an example, Table 5.3 compares a SQL data definition statement with the equivalent COBOL code.

The COBOL procedural code is clearly more verbose than the SQL code. The design assumption is that the procedural code is omniscient, capable of anticipating and preempting any and all data-entry errors involving department numbers. Of course, the probability of coding errors makes it unrealistic to expect such reliability on the part of procedural code.

5.2.4 Sharing and Structuring Components

Shared data was the original benefit of database servers, but active servers add declarative integrity protection. Centralizing data-integrity code on the database server is an essential step in rightsizing the application. However, the data is still vulnerable to corruption so long as the protection mechanism relies on procedural coding.

Figure 5.2 illustrates a client/server version of the same application shown in Figure 5.1. The data has been migrated from a file server to the database server for better data sharing. Procedural data-access methods have been replaced by non-procedural SQL commands. Monolithic programs have been replaced by client interface objects. Integrity protection has been centralized in shared code—for instance, server triggers that have been declared on the project table to maintain referential integrity on the *deptno* column. However, triggers are the wrong component for the job of protecting data integrity, so this design is not well-structured. As Figure 5.2 shows, the trigger that once protected the *dept* table has been dropped, so a department could be deleted with projects still referring to it. This data-integrity violation could be costly in a real-world application involving customers and their account balances. It is not always enough to share and reuse server-based components. Server-based components must be well-structured and appropriate to the task. In this example, it was not sufficient to migrate applications to the client/server environment.

Figure 5.3 shows the same application as Figure 5.2. In Figure 5.3, however, database integrity is protected by the table structures themselves, rather than event-management components such as triggers. This well-structured application takes advantage of mistake-proofing mechanisms in the server infrastructure. The integrity-protection mechanisms are built-in and cannot become detached. They are automatic rather than programmatic, so they cannot conceal bugs. Best of all, they free the application's server triggers to perform event management, the task for which they are most appropriate.

In comparison to externally controlled passive components, active components are more capable of varying their behavior in response to events. Because active components are concise and self-contained, they can be developed in less time than is required to program both a master program and its slave subroutines. Because active components are event-driven, the impact of changes within lead time is often isolated within a specific event handler. An event handler is a specialized addition to a standard prefabricated component. The new code is isolated within the event handler, and the recycled code is untouched.

5.2.5 Reducing Task Complexity

Database programming resembles manufacturing. Complex assembly sequences are broken down into standard discrete tasks. In manufacturing, these tasks are assigned standard labor costs. The costed task list for an assembly kit is known as its *Bill of Labor*.

Classic software maintenance costs are estimated on a time basis because monolithic applications are too complex to permit standard labor costs. The number of

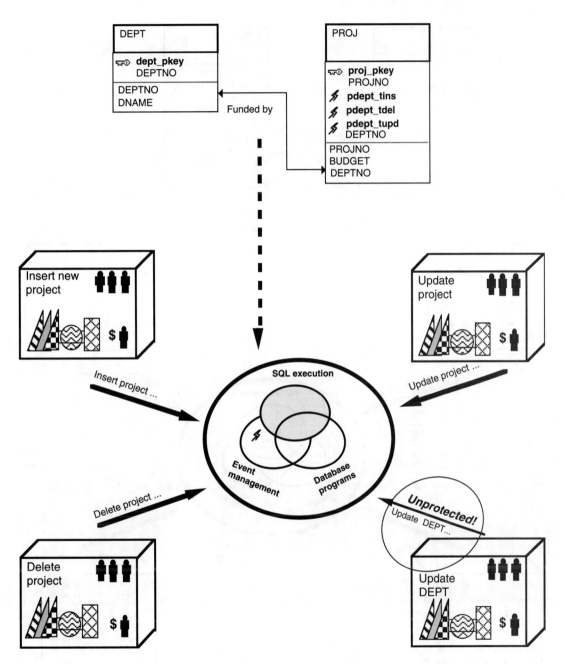

Figure 5.2 Central but unstructured

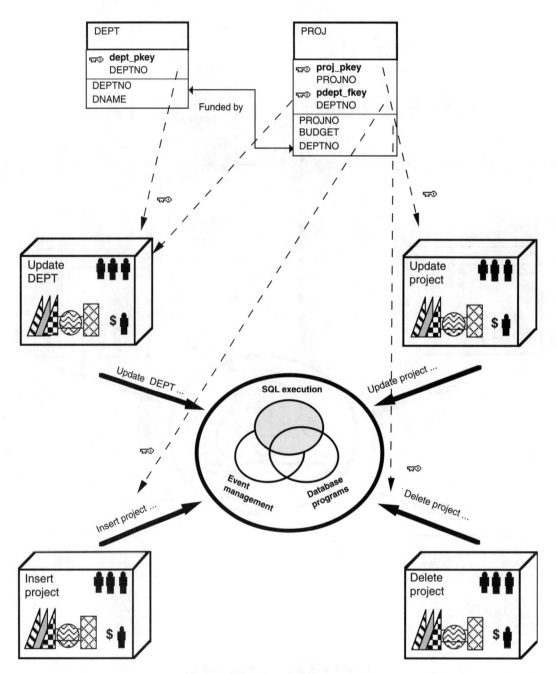

Figure 5.3 Shared and structured

logical interactions possible in a large program is so great that it becomes difficult to estimate the time required to code and debug changes. By contrast, it is relatively straightforward to estimate and test modifications to small components. It is also straightforward to monitor the actual cost of modifications and maintain quality control statistics in the database.

Figure 5.4 shows the standard labor cost of some interface items, as stored in the Development Warehouse, a special-purpose database containing component kits of source code, metadata, and documentation. The interface items in the illustration are presented to developers in a "Warehouse Catalog" user interface. Based on empirical metrics from pilot applications, standard components (both client-based and server-based) have standard labor costs. These are used to build a kit table, which provides cost comparisons for applications under development.

As standard components are reused in multiple development projects, the standard costs are adjusted based on the actual component usage experience. The repair history of each component is stored in the Development Warehouse. The TQM table is updated whenever a component is modified because of a service request. The TQM and Bill of Labor tables provide empirical data for such software quality metrics as

- Ratio of rework effort to development effort
- Ratio of standard to actual development labor
- Mean time to failure/mean time to repair
- Defects by component category/defects by subject area.

In industrial manufacturing, machine tools and industrial robots are machines that make machines. Repetitive tasks are automated by using programmable equipment to ensure consistent results. The software development equivalent of machine tools is CASE. Although it is a topic that merits an entire book, CASE might be viewed—however simplistically—as a software environment in which programs write programs.

Upper-CASE (design automation) is often used as a laborsaving device for programmers documenting subject-area applications. However, the documentation is not always kept current with modifications. Upper-CASE documentation is sometimes generated at such a high level of abstraction that it lends itself to subjective interpretation. Upper-CASE is best used to model basic tasks that perform the same business function in the same way across all subject areas in the enterprise.

Lower-CASE (code generation) products often are deployed to increase the code production rate of mainframe development efforts. Because monolithic appli-

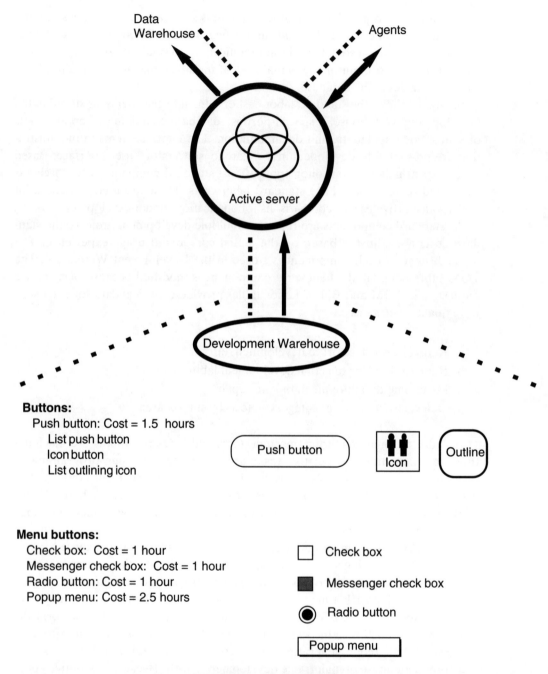

Figure 5.4 Standard labor cost

cations are coarse-grained in comparison to client/server components, the result is automation without standardization. Lower-CASE is most beneficial when it automates the production of standard information system components. Lower-CASE component production integrated with upper-CASE workflow design is automation with standardization.

The term *Component Case* connotes the idea of automated software engineering along with the idea of component assembly. Figure 5.5 shows how CASE software and the Development Warehouse are used to automate and standardize client/server configuration management. A developer has checked out version 2.1 of a Component Case from the Development Warehouse. The Component Case has been enhanced with exception handlers for financial transactions. When the Component Case is checked back into the Development Warehouse as version 2.2, the time that the developer has charged to the enhancements and the testing history is entered in the database. The enhanced version of the Component Case is automatically distributed to all client machines subscribing to the application.

A Component Case is a shared, reusable assembly of standard components that supports a shared business function. A Component Case decomposes into its components, just as a table in a relational database decomposes into its columns. However, a Component Case normally is utilized in its entirety as a prefabricated assembly supporting a distinct business function throughout the client/server environment.

5.2.6 Minimizing Integration Cost

Some of the potential risks in client/server applications are disorganization, structural defects, and misallocation of resources. The same divide-and-conquer approach that reduces the development cost of client/server applications can increase the cost of deployment. Client/server environments distribute data and behavior among multiple machines linked by a communications network. The client, server, and middleware elements are architecturally layered, so a client/server environment is a complex integration.

Active client/server database applications include an even greater variety of components than passive ones, including

- Database structures
- Database programs
- Client programs
- Client interface objects
- Triggers and event alerters.

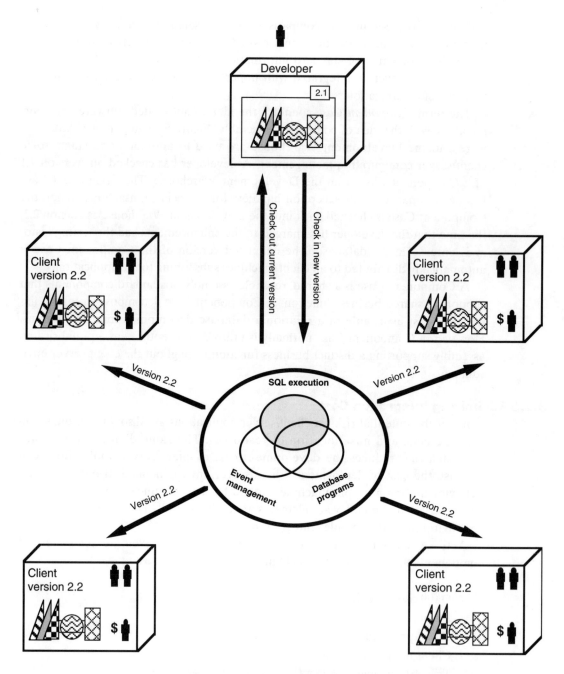

Figure 5.5 CASE standardization

Table 5.4 Partial Automation versus Component Case

Function	Partial Automation	Component Case
Data	Files, computer reports, paper documents	Database tables, interface objects, document images
Process	Computer programs, manual processing	Database programs, client behavior, triggers
Workflow	Memos, meetings, telephone calls, manual procedures	Event alerters, state transitions, voicemail, routing

Without attention to structure and order, the complexity of maintaining a multiplicity of client and server components easily can get out of hand. In extreme cases, the result is a hodgepodge of undocumented applications and elements scattered indiscriminately on various client and server platforms.

Inventory control is essential to *manufacturing resource planning* (MRP). Successful companies in every field keep track of their inventory. Banks that hope to remain successful keep track of their loan portfolios, their account balances, and their investments. Successful data administrators group logically related client and server components in a Development Warehouse, an organized, centrally stored structure, complete with version control, documentation, and security mechanisms.

Table 5.4 summarizes points of comparison between semimanual workflows and those built with a Component Case approach.

■ 5.3 COMPONENT CASES AS STANDARD ASSEMBLIES

Modern manufacturing builds products from subassemblies of standard interchangeable parts. For example, an automobile is comprised of a drive train and a body. These assemblies are, in turn, comprised of subassemblies. The drive train is made up of the engine, transmission, drive shaft, and differential. These are documented in the Bill of Materials of the subassembly, which is in turn included in the Bill of Materials of the automobile.

An automobile may be equipped with a four-speed manual transmission or an optional five-speed manual transmission, but the clutch assembly is the same in both cases. Station wagon models have lower gear ratios in the differential than passenger cars, but the rest of the drive train could be identical. In short, most of the parts in one model of an automobile are common to other models built by the same manufacturer on the same base platform.

Like manufacturing subassemblies, software subassemblies in a Component Case are modular and interchangeable groupings of standard parts. The Database

Factory equivalent of a manufacturing Bill of Materials is a Component Case kit. A Component Case kit is the working model representation of a business function. Each kit is an assembly built from client components and server components. As shown in Figure 5.6, the specific elements of a Component Case assembly are

- Database structures (tables, properties, rules)
- Database programs (procedural statements, SQL statements)
- Database event management (triggers, event alerters)
- Interface objects (properties, scripts, event handlers, menus)
- On-line documentation (metrics, demonstrations, diagrams).

Component Case elements are sharable and reusable. For instance, many assemblies share the same data tables and many applications share the same control tables.

Database main tables represent shared concepts. Each main table represents the category of conceptual knowledge that is identified by its name and key. A *parts* table, for instance, is the containing structure that represents the concept of parts. Each row in the *parts* table represents the inventory details of the physical parts identified by a given part number. The operations permitted on the *parts* table are those in the Component Case that deal with the concept of parts.

The scope of a Component Case is a business function (set of business procedures). A single Component Case may be shared by many departments. Multiple instances of the same Component Case may be used as a template, specialized in slightly different versions in different areas of a company.

For instance, inventory movements take place in several areas of a manufacturing company. When component parts move from materials inventory to the production line, they must be transferred to work-in-process inventory. When a product is built, the components in its Bill of Materials must be removed from work-in-process inventory, and the finished product itself must be entered into finished-goods inventory. When the product is sold, it must be removed from finished-goods inventory.

Each of these state transformations uses a variation on a standard inventory transfer method. However, a finished product is in a different state than the raw materials that go into its production. Because the inventory changes state, the inventory transfer behavior is always not identical.

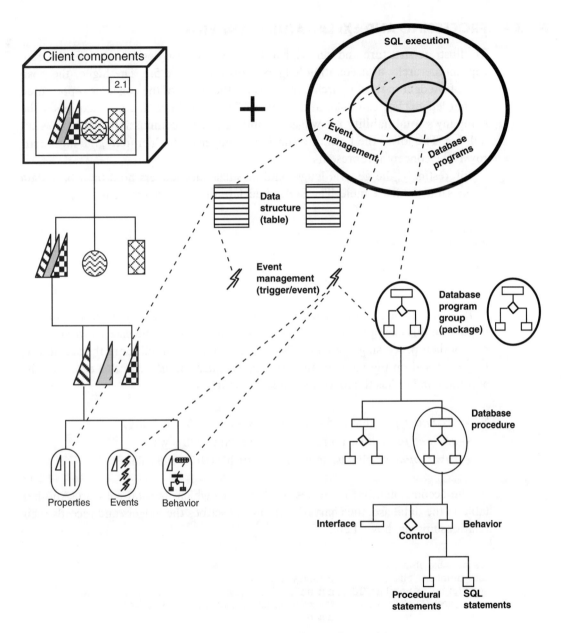

Figure 5.6 Component Case subassemblies

■ 5.4 PROCESSING AND EXPLANATORY BEHAVIOR

To illustrate structure and behavior in Component Case design, consider the conceptual hierarchy of accounting ledgers shown in Figure 5.7. The higher the position of a ledger in this hierarchy, the broader the scope of the concepts represented in that ledger. For example, in the general ledger a single line item expresses the company's total liability for wages, including salary, commissions, and tax withholding. The lower the level of a subsidiary ledger in the hierarchy, the more narrow is the concept it represents.

Interestingly, the general ledger and its subsidiary ledgers hold their base data in the same database table. The SQL to declare this table structure is

```
create table acct_entries (
acct_number   char(9)      primary key,
entry_date    datetime     not null,/*official time of entry*/
amount        money        not null,  /*individual transaction amount*/
state         int          not null);
```

Business transactions in which money changes hands have an accounting impact. In this example, these transactions make entries in the *acct_entries* table as part of their processing behavior. These entries are accounted for in the accounting ledgers based on the value of the primary key, *acct_number*. In this example, the account number has the following three elements:

- *account_type* (that is, 5 = income, 6 = expense, 7 = liability)
- *account_id* (that is, a three-digit code such as 440 = wages)
- *subaccount_id* (that is, another code such as 010 = net salary).

The account number identifies the ledger to which its total rolls up. Another table in the database, the chart of accounts, describes the ledgers and records their relationships, as shown here:

```
create table chart_acct (
acct_number   char(9)       primary key,
description   varchar(36)   not null,
rollup_acct   char(9),      /*acct to which this acct is subsidiary*/
state         int           not null);
```

For instance, the general ledger wages account has a subsidiary ledger, the payroll ledger. The general ledger and its subsidiary ledgers are associated by account number. The subsidiary ledger entries have the same *account_id* as a general

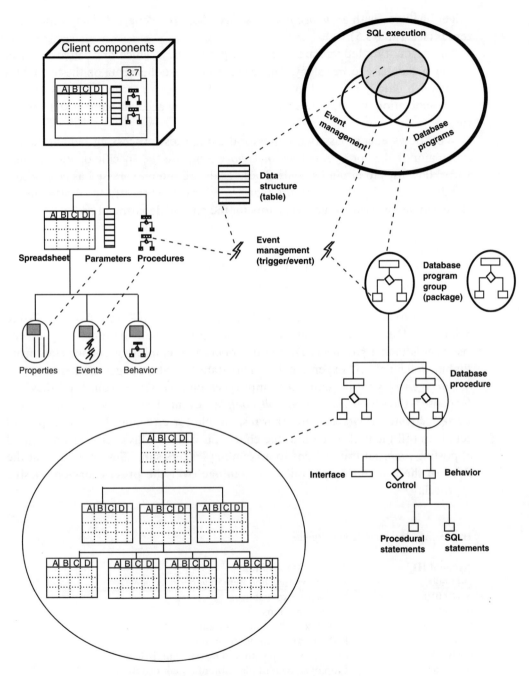

Figure 5.7 Reusable subassemblies

ledger line item, with a *subaccount_id* suffix where the general ledger account has zeroes (see Table 5.5).

The accounting ledgers are *virtual table structures*, which are called *views* in relational database terminology. The ledger views base their data on the two tables from which data is accessed, but not updated. These are termed the *base tables*. The combination of data retrieval and summation by account number defines the view.

Workflows encompass two behavioral categories: processing behaviors and explanatory behaviors. *Processing behaviors* comprise the specific operations that a workflow uses to attain its goals. These goals are often expressed as *critical success factors* (CSFs), the behaviors that are critical to successful goal attainment. For example, the critical success factors for the payroll department are

- To pay employees in a timely, accurate manner
- To withhold tax and employee benefit contributions
- To issue quarterly and annual payroll tax returns.

In order to be successful, the payroll department must perform these processing behaviors. During processing, certain operations have a financial impact, for instance, issuing a paycheck. During this operation, employees change state from "liability/eligible" to "expense/paid." This state transition triggers insertions into the *acct_entries* table. Once all employees change state from "liability" to "expense," the server raises a *payroll_complete* event. The *payroll_complete* event alerter activates a database program responsible for directing the current payroll details to roll themselves up into the chart of accounts. This event-driven method of posting financial transactions to accounting ledgers simplifies operations at the close of the accounting period, an advantage over the process-driven passive approach.

Table 5.5 Ledger Account Numbers

Account ID	Account Description
6-440-000	Wages expense line item in general ledger
6-440-010	Net salary expense
6-440-020	Net commissions
6-440-030	State tax withholding on salary
6-440-040	Federal tax withholding on salary
6-440-050	Federal backup withholding on commissions
6-440-060	Employee benefit plan voluntary contributions

Explanatory behaviors are the means of demonstrating that CSFs are being attained. These behaviors are specific to the objectives of a workflow. They incorporate shared data and shared behavior (database programs). In the payroll example, the explanatory behavior consists of

- General ledger and subsidiary payroll ledger
- Electronic images of time sheets, pay slips, and tax deposit coupons
- The ability to "drill down" to the supporting base data.

In this example, the explanatory behavior demonstrates that the payroll ran correctly and was correctly reported.

The Payroll Department Component Case is an assembly within the larger subject area of financial accounting applications. The payroll ledger is a specialized view of the general ledger. Individual views such as this payroll ledger share many structural and behavioral components with other subsidiary ledgers. All of these ledger views are based on the same shared table structure. They all share the same roll-up behavior. The payroll ledger's bottom line rolls up to a line item in the general ledger, as do the bottom lines of all other subsidiary ledgers.

Database programs are the means of implementing shared behavior in a Component Case. The payroll database programs are comparable to manufacturing operations on subassemblies that share common parts.

Consider an automobile manufactured with either a manual transmission or an optional automatic transmission. The methods of manufacturing the two types of transmissions clearly differ, but the operations involved in assembling the drive train differ much less.

Similarly, the workflow operations that create the entries of the individual subsidiary ledgers differ, but the operations on the completed ledgers do not. The Federal tax withholding requirements are the same in all states, but the state withholding requirements vary. The explanatory behavior hides this complexity behind the abstraction of the accounting ledger views. However, drilling down deeper into the explanatory behavior will explain (in all its bureaucratic complexity) and even repeat the state tax computation behavior.

▪ 5.5 ACTIVE DOCUMENTATION

An evolving Component Case is an active mini-application. As a software engineering project evolves, the documentation must keep pace. Passive data modeling diagrams do not drive the database design, but rather are driven by it. A Component

Case is stored in and retrieved from the Development Warehouse database, where metadata entries and control tables are available for queries and reports.

An *Entity Relationship* (ER) diagram can be considered as a type of graphical report based on metadata. As the metadata changes, so should the contents of its report, the ER diagram. Component Case design adds value to ER analysis by giving a precise definition to the meaning of relationships and associations. In classic ER analysis, relationships are identified and categorized by function and cardinality (for example, "one payroll department pays many employees"), but not defined in terms of quantifiable behavior. This is because workflow relationships are defined through behavior, which is by convention part of the process model and excluded from the data model. Traditional application design defines behavior (and therefore relationships) in terms of passive client procedures.

Relationships in active database design are a type of cooperative behavior possible among given rows in a given state. The relationship is activated by data operations that cause the rows representing the logical client and logical server of the workflow to change to a compatible state. As illustrated in Figure 5.8, the logical client that is responsible for the workflow defines the meaning of the relationship.

In relational design, relationships that create facts are called *associations*. The result of a join on relational database tables is another table, the *result set*. Associations are relationships whose behavior creates persistent result sets. In ER diagrams, these result sets are represented as *associative entities*. For example, the relationship of salesperson to customer yields an associative entity: the order. The *order* table of Figure 5.8 results from the association of salesperson and customer. The state of an order depends on the behavior of the association. For example, an order's state might be "forecast order," "tentative order," or "confirmed order."

The relationships between entities represented in a Component Case are revised whenever a new version of the Component Case is stored. The revised metadata is available for retrieval into the graphical client environment to redraw ER diagrams and other technical documentation. This automated documentation is more responsive to the rapid design changes typical of spiral development than manual inputs to CASE or project control software.

■ 5.6 BUSINESS OBJECTIVES AND COMPONENT CASE TRAFFIC LIGHTS

Business objectives must be measurable to be valid, since the only way to know whether the objectives have been attained is through performance measures. Performance measures are based on factual indicators, suitable for data storage within database structures. The condition (metastate) of a performance indicator is the aggregate state of its row values. In Figure 5.9, the majority of the subsidiary

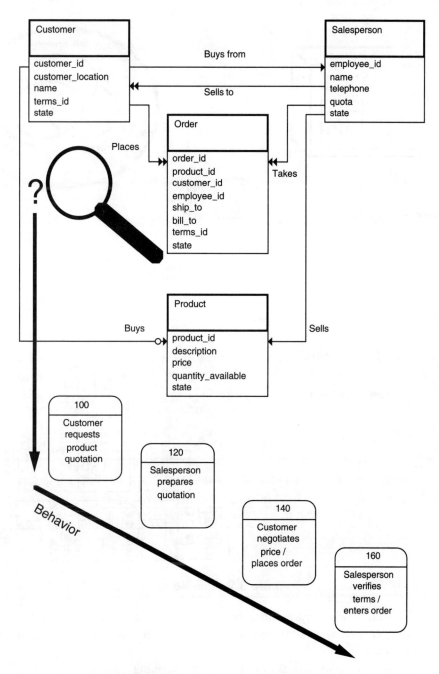

Figure 5.8 Meaningful relationships

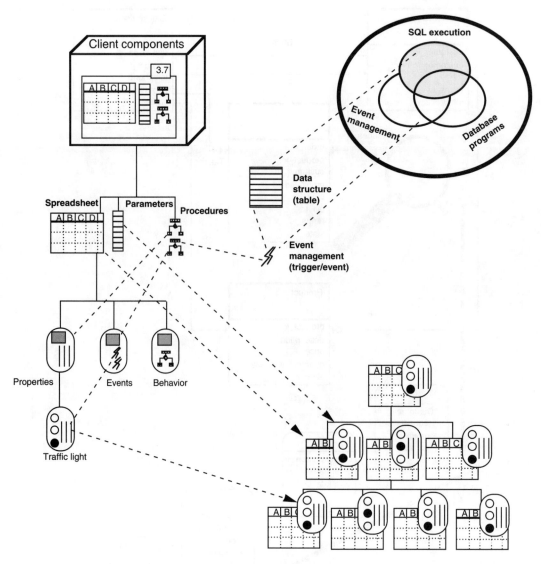

Figure 5.9 Traffic lights

ledger traffic lights representing budget-effective performance are in "green" state, so the general ledger's "traffic light" is green at the time of the "accounting period close" event.

A workgroup attains its objectives by performing a set of workflow behaviors in a correct and timely manner. These workflows are synonymous with the attainment methods for the critical success factors of the workgroup. As workflows perform operations, they mark their result states to facilitate explanatory behavior. If the preponderance of the behaviors are done right and on time, the result metastate for the workgroup is a green traffic light.

■ 5.7 GOAL-DIRECTED BEHAVIOR

A Component Case is goal-directed. The software components within a workflow collaborate to get the job done. The database server is the headquarters for this goal-directed behavior. Database main table structures represent the main concepts of the workflow. The data in those structures changes state in response to the operations of database programs. Each transitional state change marks a step toward the attainment of the goal, culminating in a finished state. It is thus possible to track the performance of workflow components toward business goals.

During execution, the behavior of each workflow is a separate activation path through the Component Case. The activation path consists of

- An outcome, expressed as a target result state
- One or more database programs performing operations on the data
- Eligible data in a compatible state for each workflow step
- A command or message to activate the database program.
- A client interface to initiate commands/display results.

Normally, the workflow passes control along the activation path stored in the Bill of Operations, processing data and routing document images. However, at any point on the activation path, exceptions may occur. When an exception occurs, it is trapped by the appropriate exception handler. Exceptions are tracked in the audit trail. Any exception without a corresponding handler indicates the failure of one or more components.

The identification of defective components in the activation path is straightforward. The Bill of Operations (among other metadata tables) is used to identify precisely which component (or components) was involved in the exception. To debug these components, the standard test data for the operation is compared with the actual data that caused the exception. This facilitates the fine-tuning steps shown in Figure 5.10.

- Isolate exceptions
- Identify the responsible components

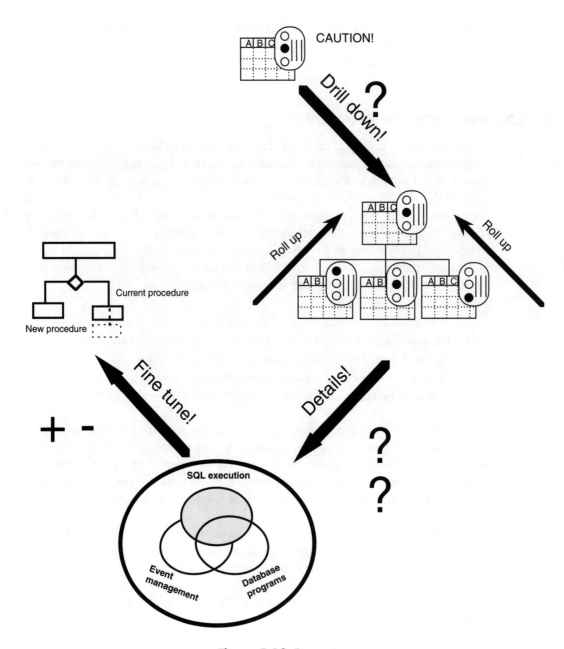

Figure 5.10 Fine-tuning

- Update the standard test data to test the exception
- Debug and rerun the operation using the modified components
- Retest all Component Cases using the modified components.

As components undergo continuous improvement, the number and severity of exceptions tends to decrease as the Component Case gets better at its job.

The monitoring of behavior relative to goals is a key design activity. If the goals are misunderstood, or if the behavior is ill-directed, the information system will drift off-target. During early development, the new design is likely to be off-target. It would be unrealistic to expect new components to act in harmony from the beginning.

A measure of project management effectiveness is how rapidly the workflow's behavior and its goals converge. When the nontechnical staff who are responsible for specifying the workflow's goals work closely with those who are responsible for programming its behavior, convergence occurs faster. Chapter 6 examines concurrent software engineering with Success Circles, a means of increasing the quality and minimizing the time-to-market of active database applications.

6

CONCURRENT SOFTWARE ENGINEERING: SUCCESS CIRCLES

This chapter discusses the Success Circles approach to concurrent software engineering, which addresses such perennial software development problems as:

- Misalignment of data/process flows to business workflows
- Misalignment of information systems to business needs
- Wrongsizing—partial/unmonitored automation.

Success Circles are an evolutionary development technique with the goal of raising application quality while reducing the risk of misalignment.

Success Circles provide a framework for collaborative software development. Success Circle representatives align the evolving application's evolution with workgroup goals and business workflows, while technical staff combat software wrongsizing with technology benchmarks. The Success Circles approach identifies logical clients and servers, defining interdepartmental workflows in terms of roles, relationships, and responsibilities. Success Circle participants use a graphical interface to the Development Warehouse database. The usage, quality assurance history, and service log of all components is maintained in the Development Warehouse.

■ 6.1 PROBLEM ONE: WRONGSIZING

The time-honored software development practice of isolating the development environment from the production environment applies to client/server development efforts. For example, a retail store chain plans to migrate its core applications from a mainframe running IBM's DB2 to a client/server environment. Client/server applications have a distributed architecture that is fundamentally different from monolithic mainframe applications. In this example, the current production platform would not be a good choice for new development. However, the current mainframe applications for the retail chain are mission-critical, which means that the business cannot run without them. For this reason, the company is tempted to enhance the mainframe applications. The inherently distributed nature of the retail chain's operations pushes development of information systems in the opposite direction, toward client/server database. How can this contradiction be resolved without "wrongsizing" new development and without disrupting mission-critical applications?

6.1.1 The Solution: Evolutionary Development

Few products arrive on the scene with no lineage, and software is no exception. Software engineering usually involves re-engineering. A successful evolutionary re-engineering process spirals through several plan-build-test iterations before culminating in implementation. The system is reviewed at each iteration of the spiral between the test and plan phases. The advantages of the evolutionary approach include

- **Prioritization of effort.** Obtain the "big wins" first.
- **Risk reduction.** Frequent reviews reduce misunderstandings.
- **Cost reduction.** Cut down on expensive rework.

In the case of the retail store migration, trying to migrate all the DB2 core applications simultaneously (or "mass migration") would be a costly and risky endeavor. On the other hand, a lengthy sequential migration plan in which each application must be completely converted before work starts on the next is even more costly. A sequential migration plan would delay the savings from rightsizing and would make it hard to resist pressures to enhance mission-critical DB2 applications on the mainframe. Between the costly extremes of mass migration and sequential migration is the middle-ground solution provided by evolutionary collaborative development.

Instead of attempting to migrate all the core applications at once, the migration effort is phased and prioritized. Using a pilot application approach, the most straightforward core application might be migrated first. Another approach would choose the pilot application from the area with the greatest backlog of enhance-

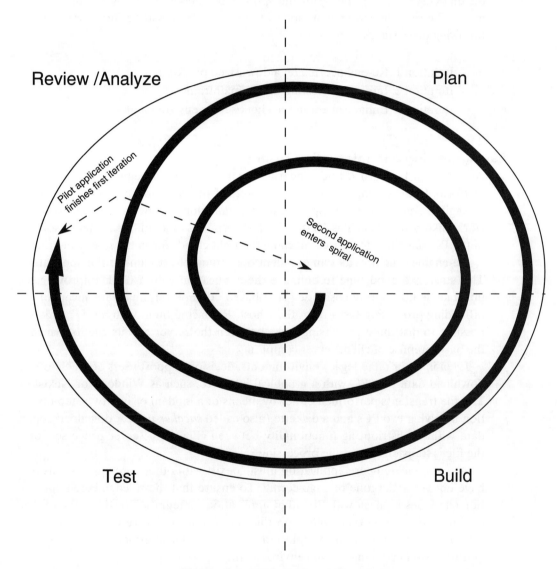

Figure 6.1 Interleaved re-engineering

ment requests. Regardless of the selection criteria for the pilot application, as soon as it has undergone the first of its plan-build-test iterations, a second application enters the spiral. This approach is shown in Figure 6.1.

An evolutionary development spiral should not be confused with an endlessly drifting curve. Each iteration of the spiral represents a distinct stage of development. The re-engineering evolution of the retail store could be summarized in the following three stages:

- Iteration 1: Re-engineering on a downsized platform
- Iteration 2: Integration testing on the mainframe
- Iteration 3: Enhancement in the client/server environment.

6.1.2 Re-engineering and Integration Testing

As shown in Figure 6.2, re-engineering a core application begins on a downsized platform. In the example of the retail store, the first stage of this evolution entails re-engineering a DB2 core application on a standalone PC by using a desktop DB2 work-alike product such as XDB. The fast response time and dedicated resources of the PC make the downsized machine the right choice for initial re-engineering.

Re-engineering provides an excellent opportunity to streamline the application. This stage is a good time to enhance the application with a GUI. Improving the interface is not merely cosmetic. Text-based "dumb" terminals are incapable of offloading processing tasks from their host. Replacing them with a GUI makes it possible to distribute processing tasks between the server and its clients, which is the basic premise of client/server computing.

Even in mainframe legacy environments, decision-support users often choose to download data to a PC with a graphical interface, such as Windows or Nextstep. The file transfer is performed either by means of a modem or in a two-step operation involving two PCs and a diskette (also called *sneaker-net*). A download copies data without distributing functionality between client and server processes; only the file is transferred, not the processing.

A re-engineered core application must coexist with other core applications that have not yet undergone re-engineering. To ensure that the re-engineered application continues to mesh with the other applications, integration testing—the second evolutionary stage—takes place on the mainframe. If the re-engineering stage included a GUI migration to replace a text-based user interface, this also is integration-tested in the mainframe environment.

Figure 6.3 illustrates an integration-testing environment that uses a LAN gateway to connect a re-engineered interface with DB2 mainframe applications. Both

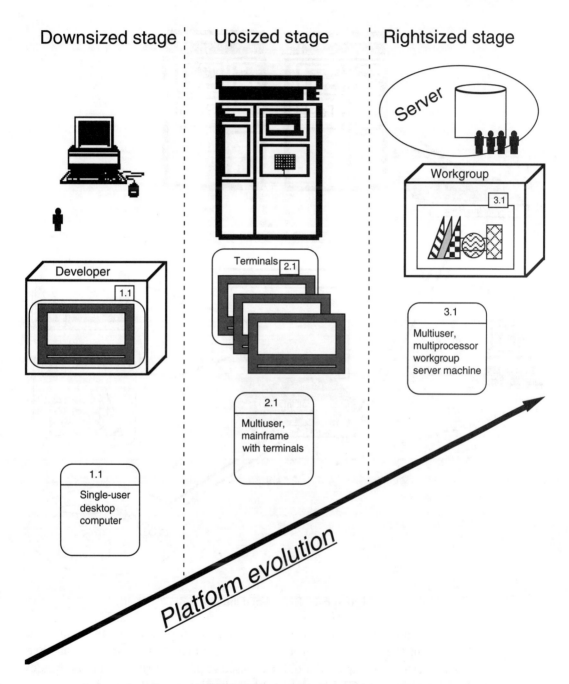

Figure 6.2 Evolutionary stages

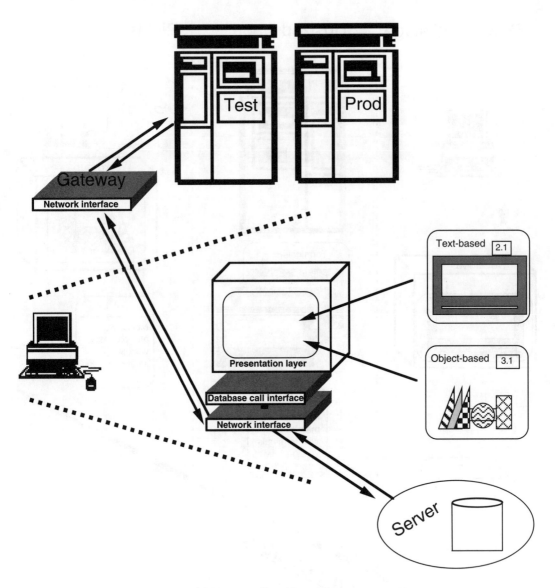

Figure 6.3 The old and the new

old and re-engineered core applications coexist in a test partition on the mainframe, isolated from the mainframe production environment. The Presentation Layer allows the tester to compare the old text-based application running in one window with the re-engineered GUI version of the application in another window.

As an alternative without multiple windows, two PCs can be placed side-by-side on the LAN in order to compare the GUI with the old text-based terminal interface. A LAN bridge connects the development PCs with a workgroup server to provide a smooth transition to the next stage of evolutionary development, rightsizing.

6.1.3 Rightsized Workgroup Servers

Once a re-engineered application has been integration-tested in the mainframe environment, it is ready for rightsizing. As shown in Figure 6.4, the data-management code of the application is migrated from the mainframe to a development server. In this manner, the evolving application is isolated from both the past and the future production platforms as rightsizing and enhancement proceed.

The development database server is a smaller computer than the production database server. For instance, a beefed-up version of the same PCs used as client machines might be adequate to run a scalable, multiuser RDBMS such as XDB that functions as a DB2 work-alike for mainframe compatibility. During this stage, a workgroup version of the single-user DBMS software used in the downsized stage is sufficient. The ultimate choice of database server could depend on requirements that only surface later in the evolutionary process.

In the rightsizing stage, the application scope is rightsized along with the hardware and the database server. The evolving application is integrated with decision-support and workflow-management software to add value to the textual data. The enhancements to the pilot application can serve as a benchmark for evaluating database servers. Such a benchmark should be based on how well competing products support an actual business process that has been integrated with a workflow application, as opposed to a selection based on some theoretical industry standard benchmark, or one that is biased by the strength of one vendor's marketing effort.

Upon completion of this rightsizing stage, the server-based components of the application are ported to a larger, scaled-up machine. This machine provides a platform for the initial production database server. The development and production servers, as well as the gateway to legacy applications on the mainframe, have different *interconnect protocol* (IP) addresses on the network, so client machines can connect either to the server or to the mainframe.

Network integration makes for smooth transitions between evolutionary stages, but the very interoperability that makes this possible also increases middleware complexity. A complex network environment can be more vulnerable to failure than a simple one. A network that is adequate for client/server development may not have enough bandwidth (capacity) nor transmission speed to support the demands of full-volume production. The risk of a post-implementation middleware

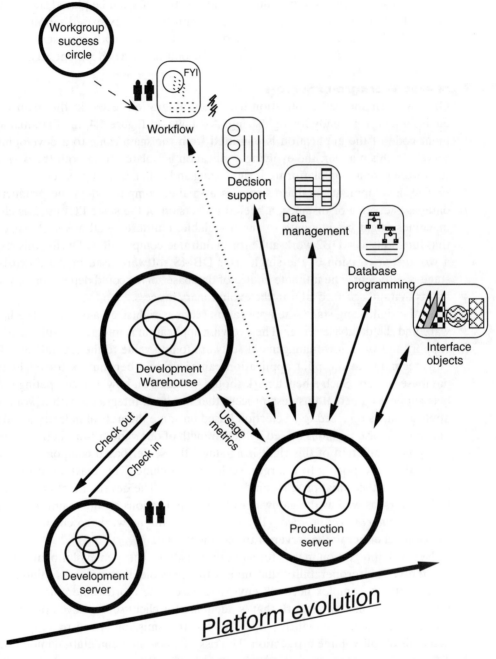

Figure 6.4 Rightsizing and adding value

disappointment is reduced by conducting a technology evaluation in parallel with application re-engineering.

6.1.4 Technology Evaluation

The purpose of a technology evaluation is to stress-test the client/server environment. Client/server database applications are only as good as the middleware infrastructure that supports message traffic. Subtle incompatibilities among network communications hardware, software, protocols, or network address assignments can and will cause client/server implementations to fail. These considerations are purely technical. They do not directly relate to the definition of application requirements, but they cannot be ignored.

Because the communications infrastructure is not application-specific, it can undergo evaluation at the same time as application re-engineering. The technology evaluation is useful for benchmarking competing communications products, hardware, and software alike. The result of the technology benchmarking effort is a standard, stress-tested environment for client/server development. This standard environment provides a scalable *starter kit*. As development unfolds, the starter kit scales up with more server resources and scales out with more client connections.

■ 6.2 PROBLEM TWO: MISALIGNMENT OF INFORMATION SYSTEMS WITH BUSINESS NEEDS

Factories that produce unwanted, unnecessary goods soon go out of business. The "concept car" designs showcased at auto shows often cannot be manufactured and cannot benefit the average motorist. Database applications that do not work, that do not meet business requirements, or that hinder business objectives similarly cannot be much help to an enterprise.

6.2.1 The Solution: Concurrent Software Engineering

In manufacturing industries, concurrent engineering is a way of designing products by using joint teams of design, production, and product-marketing engineers. The team collaborates throughout all product-development phases, thus preventing gaps and misunderstandings between functional areas. The result is that products are built to meet market demands while being engineered for ease of assembly and ease of maintenance. *Concurrent software engineering* is the concept of applying the principles of concurrent engineering to software development.

Concurrent software engineering uses joint teams of technical and paratechnical (that is, computer-literate nonprogrammer) staff in all re-engineering stages. The premise underlying concurrent software engineering is that technicians understand the technology and businessmen understand the business. The familiar problems that result from technicians second-guessing business requirements are avoided by the joint team, which is referred to here as a Success Circle.

Participants in a Success Circle develop the design. Technical participants help end-users jump the hurdles of client/server design. Paratechnical end-users help the technicians understand business goals and workflows. Success Circles differ in this regard from the early Joint Application Development (JAD) approach. In JAD teams as in traditional development, the end-users specify their requirements and the technical participants program the application. By contrast, the technical facilitators of Success Circles do not create new programs from scratch. Instead, they help the end-users put components together with minor code refinements.

Concurrent software engineering leverages time as well as talents. The elimination of misunderstandings also avoids costly rework. Because fewer "us-versus-them turf disputes" occur at review time, relatively less time is wasted at meetings. The design keeps moving forward toward the final result.

Hardware resources, such as the database server starter kit, also are leveraged. Whenever a stage three design evolves into a finished application, the development server and its database software become available for another workgroup's application, which entered the evolutionary spiral at a later time.

Database administrators and other technical staff can participate concurrently in multiple Success Circles. These "scarce technical resources" also can support production applications at the same time as they gain job enrichment on development projects. The technical facilitators are able to spread themselves thin because the Success Circle representatives (who better understand the business requirements) are using Component Case design to flush out the specific details of the application.

Do Success Circle representatives need to be experienced programmers or experienced managers? Do they need an MIS background? The answer is "no" on both counts. The profile of a Success Circle representative is

- A good communicator who speaks for the Success Circle constituency
- A creative person who is the author of new or modified Component Cases
- A PC "power user" who is an ace at using a spreadsheet or word processor
- A team player who changes a Component Case to match a group consensus
- A respected person who is a "quick study" and eligible for promotion within the company.

People skills and business savvy are the main qualifications for a Success Circle representative. Computer science courses and database experience are a plus, but are not as strong a requirement as common sense or motivation.

6.2.2 Success Circles and the Organization

Success Circles are the organizational framework to keep evolving applications aligned with business objectives. Success Circles orient development toward workflows that support departmental objectives. These workgroup objectives merge to flow into broad goals of the company.

The broad goals of the enterprise tend to be more abstract and, at the same time, more stable than the feeder objectives. Some typical broad goals might be

- To maintain at least 27% market share
- To produce at least 8% return on shareholder's equity.

Divisional and departmental feeder objectives must be met to attain the broad enterprise goals. Feeder objectives vary according to the different missions of various business units. *Workgroup CSFs* are the set of behaviors a workgroup must do and do well to meet its objectives. These behaviors vary from department to department. Departmental CSFs may form part of workflows that cross department lines. However, a company normally has a workgroup primarily responsible for attainment of CSF objectives, and that workgroup is the logical client of the workflow.

As business priorities change in response to changing business conditions, the CSFs of a company also change. During periods of high demand, for example, the top priority for wholesale distribution is to carry enough product in inventory to not lose sales and ultimately market share. During a downturn, the priority shifts to maintaining sufficient cash to assure a return on shareholder's equity, so it becomes important not to tie up capital in excess inventory.

As objectives change, the performance indicators that measure the degree of attainment for those objectives also must change. Future performance indicators most likely are derived from current data elements in the workflows for which the workgroup holds responsibility. The designation of new performance indicators can be and should be a simple change of data-access methods, provided that the workflow metrics have been designed into the database. The retrieval and display methods of the key indicators should be available in one or more Component Cases. Specializing the Component Case to the specific workgroup is a job for the Success Circle.

Success Circles relate to the management structure of a company—but only loosely. Department managers are responsible for the department's performance, and so these managers retain oversight with regard to requirements. However, management involvement at review is normally limited to avoid "micro managing" the Success Circle. If two Success Circles have divergent views regarding their requirements, the representatives from each Success Circle get together to work out a solution.

The re-engineering effort is based on workgroup feeder objectives. If departmental objectives already have been included in re-engineered workflows for which a workgroup is the logical client, then the Success Circle representatives from that workgroup should find it relatively easy to reconcile their designs to support the workflows.

In large organizations, representatives from each Success Circle form a *coordinating Success Circle* (as shown in Figure 6.5) to harmonize requirements and designs among Success Circles. Just as departmental management has oversight over individual Success Circles, corporate management reviews the results of the coordinating circle. This management review is directed toward refining the evolving design to best meet changing business objectives, but not to supervise the day-to-day operations of Success Circles.

6.2.3 Logical Client/Server Relationships

The client/server model can be generalized beyond the database to business workflows. In the course of re-engineering, Success Circles identify manual processing relationships in which one workgroup provides a service to another. In these relationships, the workgroup responsible for the workflow is the logical client, and a workgroup providing a supporting service is a logical server. The service in question is some action accompanied by a paper document in the manual system. In the re-engineered workflow, the paper document is replaced by its scanned image. In contrast to the manual process, the document image is not necessarily routed in the automated system. However, it is always available for reference from any workgroup destination in the workflow.

In a given relationship, a workgroup takes on the logical role of a client or of a server. In some other relationship, the roles might be reversed. For example, in a relationship called *ship_sold_product,* the sales department is the client of the distribution department. In this relationship, when a sale is made, the distribution department ships the product and sends a copy of the shipper to the sales department to confirm the shipment. In the *receive_returned_product* relationship, on the other hand, the distribution department is the client of the sales department. When a customer returns a product, the distribution department calls the sales

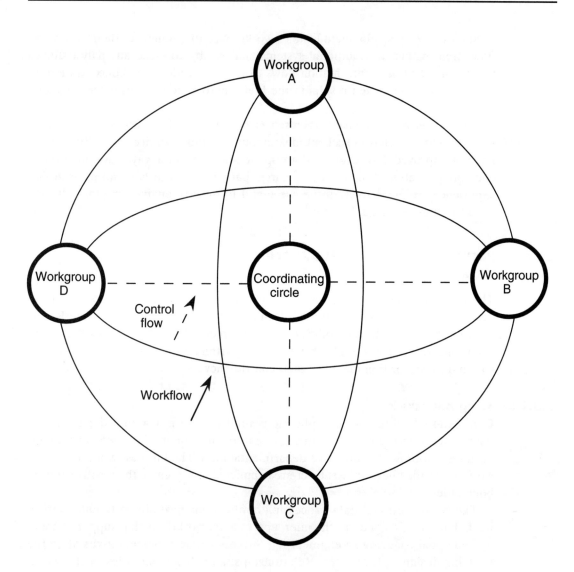

Figure 6.5 Success Circles

department to verify the *returned merchandise authorization* (RMA) number. In most companies today, shipping and receiving are no longer handled by verbal communication and manual systems. However, the underlying logical relationship holds true in the automated workflow.

Success Circle development enables workgroups to re-engineer their own workflows from within. In traditional systems analysis, by contrast, an analyst studies workgroups and their information flows from the outside. Over-concentration on the existing system often results in the literal automation of obsolescent manual systems.

The workgroup participants themselves are quite familiar with the services they provide, and often have excellent ideas about how those services might be streamlined or improved. However, workgroup members do not always have any experience in application design. Success Circle participants who have no prior design experience are more likely to be successful in their re-engineering tasks if they have a framework to guide them.

■ 6.3 PROBLEM THREE: DATA FLOW AND WORKFLOW MISALIGNMENT

The *R3 method* provides Success Circles with a framework for Component Case design. The three "R's" in the R3 framework stand for Success Circle Roles, Relationships, and Responsibilities. In the R3 method, Success Circles define the client and server roles applicable to the departments or other business entities within the organization that form their constituency.

6.3.1 Crossing Boundaries

Conventional subject-area applications tend to stay put within departmental boundaries. Because the departments of an organization are interdependent, their business workflows tend to cross departmental lines. The business workflows draw workgroups together, while subject-area applications segregate them with arbitrary boundaries.

These conventional data-processing applications partially automate clerical work, but are misaligned to the interdepartmental workflows that support company-wide goals. During re-engineering, Success Circle representatives align the evolving design to the Roles, Relationships, and Responsibilities of the workgroups they represent.

For any workflow, a workgroup plays the role of a logical client or a logical server. The designation of logical client or logical server is distinct from any client/server hardware within the department. Most workgroups fulfill both roles by acting as a client in some relationships and a server in others. In each relationship, one workgroup takes the role of server and another workgroup takes the role of client. In another relationship, the logical roles may be reversed.

Binary relationships between logical clients and logical servers are represented in an ER diagram. Figure 6.6 shows an ER diagram with two relationships between Materials Management and the Shop Floor. The Shop Floor is the client of Materials Management in the *supply_parts* relationship (represented in the figure by a "c" for "client" next to the Shop Floor rectangle). In the *deliver_assemblies* relationship, the roles are reversed (represented by the "s" for "server" next to the Shop Floor rectangle). Inasmuch as the arrow always points toward the client, the letters are redundant.

For each relationship, the server role within the relationship has one or more sets of responsibilities. For example, the *supply_parts* relationship figures in the following three different workflows:

- Supply low-level parts
- Supply subassemblies
- Supply bulk materials.

Each workflow calls for a slightly different collection of software components. These components could be exactly the same as those used in another workflow already under development (that is, a sharing of the same Component Case). The components may vary slightly, so as to form a specialized version of the Component Case.

For example, the "supply low-level parts" and "supply subassemblies" workflows are very similar in the manufacturing example. The difference between these two workflows is that the low-level parts in a subassembly change state when they are assembled but remain in parts inventory. After the end-item assembly passes quality assurance, the parts within the assembly are accounted for. Once accounted for, they are removed from parts inventory.

In this example, the Materials Management Success Circle would work with the Shop Floor Success Circle to decide whether to combine both workflows within a single Component Case. The Success Circle having the logical client role is responsible for specifying the behavior of the workflow. The Success Circle with the role of logical server specifies the specific components through which the required result is obtained.

Division of labor between logical clients and servers helps keep evolving designs well-grounded. Each Success Circle's efforts must balance with those of others, and this can be verified in a type of double-entry workflow accounting. For each relationship, a client role and a server role must exist. Otherwise the relationship is either invalid or incompletely specified.

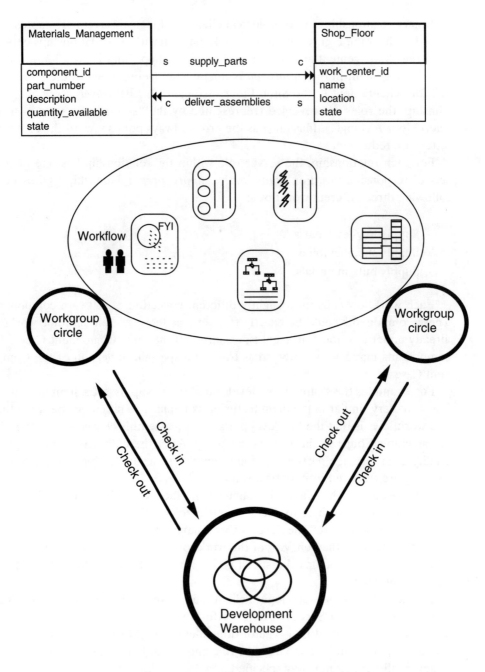

Figure 6.6 Logical client/server relationship

Reciprocity in logical client/server relationships extends to the various responsibilities within the relationship. Each behavior in the workflow that carries out the relationship is initiated by the logical client. The result state of each step is available to the client. The logical server(s) on the workflow must have behaviors to fulfill their responsibilities. They must have the means of explaining their behavior, minimally by returning the result states of their operations. The cross-referencing of logical client requests to server behavior for each step validates the evolving workflow design.

6.3.2 The Solution: The R3 Bottom-Up Approach

A Success Circle approaches re-engineering in the following two ways:

- Bottom-up Component Case design
- Top-down R3 validation.

While engaged in bottom-up design, members of a Success Circle refine those Component Cases that have proven satisfactory in other workflows and other Success Circles. A Component Case (see Chapter 5) is a set of recyclable, sharable components that work well together. Some of these components, such as interface objects, are client components, while others, such as database programs, are server-based.

Shared workflows cross departmental lines. Different Success Circles are responsible for the logical client and logical server roles in these workflows. The possibility exists that the various workflow steps do not mesh perfectly, and this is where top-down R3 validation proves useful.

Throughout the bottom-up activity, the steps in a workflow are built from components. As the revised Component Cases are saved, entries are made in an R3 table in the Development Warehouse database. The format of such a table (SQL-Server syntax) is as follows:

```
CREATE TABLE r3
    (circle_id        char(6),
     role             char(1),      /* c/s */
     relationship     varchar(26),
     responsibility   varchar(26),
     state            int )
```

The R3 table could be maintained in a spreadsheet or on index cards, but its data would not be sharable.

Table 6.1 State of Completion

State	Description
05	Start of project planning
10	Start of bottom-up design
20	End of bottom-up design
30	Start of top-down design
40	End of top-down design
50	End of test
60	End of post-test changes
70	Overall consensus/management review
80	Second iteration project plan
90	Start of second iteration bottom-up design

During R3 validation, every behavior for which each logical server is responsible in each workflow relationship is checked for consistency. For each possible result state of the relationship, a workflow step causes a transition into that state. For each result state, the logical client must have an appropriate means of recognizing that state and then behaving accordingly. Correct alignment is seldom the case at the start of R3 validation, but is always true at the end of the activity.

In R3, Success Circles attain consensus regarding functionality and completeness. Incomplete functionality distinguishes an evolving design from a completed design. An evolving application invariably lacks the features and behavior of the finished application. Just what functionality is expected of a given design at a given state of completion? How many cycles through the evolutionary spiral are expected? Since no two projects are exactly the same, these questions provoke stimulating discussions in a coordinating Success Circle.

The R3 table is a state table for projects. The early states of completion for a small project might be those shown in Table 6.1. A larger project might have a greater number of activities within each iteration of the spiral, requiring a greater variety of potential states.

Concurrent software engineering provides a process for reaching consensus on how best to align business workflows with automated workflows. The client Success Circle is responsible for articulating the required outcomes for each workflow step. The server Success Circles must agree that the client has requested services that it can design.

Occasionally, workgroups seek tight control of semiautomated procedures and show an unwillingness to re-engineer narrow-focus applications. In cases where consensus eludes the Success Circle representatives, they can refer the problem to the coordinating circle. More often, the client and server circles agree on workflow alignment, but existing Component Cases are insufficient. In this event, technical facilitators help the Success Circles to create new components or to specialize existing ones.

■ 6.4 THE DEVELOPMENT WAREHOUSE

Throughout this book, the term Data Warehouse refers to a database application whose main activity is information storage and retrieval, rather than *on-line transaction processing* (OLTP). By contrast, the term Database Factory refers to an application whose main activity is information production.

A Development Warehouse is the database from which Component Cases are retrieved for further development. It provides Success Circle members with prefabricated Component Cases from workflows that have been built, validated, and ratified by other Success Circles. These examples are checked out of the Development Warehouse. They are refined and tested on the starter kit development server. After review and validation, the modified Component Case is checked back in as a new version.

6.4.1 Development Warehouse Objectives

The goal of the Development Warehouse is to support concurrent software engineering. To be useful to both technical facilitators and Success Circle representatives, a Development Warehouse needs its own application infrastructure and graphical *visual programming interface.*

The specific details of the Development Warehouse infrastructure depend somewhat on the choice of database server. For example, a Development Warehouse utilizing the Interbase server might store an ER diagram as a database *binary large object* (blob), and use a blob filter to transfer the ER diagram to and from a CASE package. On the other hand, a Sybase Development Warehouse might store the ER diagram as a column of the datatype image within the R3 table.

6.4.2 Development Warehouse Metadata

The Development Warehouse is structured to handle metadata, including

- Data concerning server components
- Data concerning client components
- Quality assurance, usage, and modification history metadata
- On-line documentation, listings, and diagrams.

Other server metadata categories include the source code scripts for

- Creating the physical database
- Creating application tables in the database
- Creating triggers and database programs
- Creating application control table entries.

In conventional development, source code scripts are stored outside the database environment, often in the private account of the DBA. The rationale for keeping database source code outside the database is to restrict shared access, thus protecting production applications. However, when the production environment is isolated from the development environment, shared access during development cannot harm production applications. Technical facilitators need to change application tables, to add columns, or to change datatypes. Success Circle representatives need the ability to modify the behavior of database programs. They need to do this frequently, rapidly, and without unnecessary constraints. When the development server is on a different server platform than the production server, changes to structures and programs in the development database do not impact the production system.

Designing with active database components entails both new control table entries and changes to existing control tables, including

- Bills of Materials entries (the components of a Component Case)
- Bills of Operations entries (the sequence of data-processing operations)
- State definition entries (transitional stages toward the goal of the operations).

An application Bill of Materials lists the components of each Component Case, just as a manufacturing Bill of Materials lists the components of a manufactured product. Manufacturing Bills of Material typically span multiple levels of subassembly from the finished product to the discrete part. For simplicity, we should restrict Component Case Bills of Material to a single level of detail so they can be represented in a single table, such as the following:

```
CREATE TABLE comp_case
    (comp_case_id      char(8),
     description       varchar(26),  /*describes purpose */
     component_name    varchar(26),
     component_type    char(6),      /*e.g., database table*/
     version           float,
     state             int )         /*of the component*/
```

A manufacturing Bill of Operations lists the sequence of operations performed on an assembly line. A Bill of Operations control table lists the sequence of state transitions in the path toward the goal of the workflow. Each entry in a Bill of Operations lists an operational step in the path, whether for a normal state or for an exception state.

Each *normal state* change marks a transitional step toward the goal of the workflow. The state after a final transition from a transient to a persistent normal state marks the goal. An *exception state* represents either a detour on the path toward the goal, or some final state short of the goal. The definition and description of these states is maintained in a *state table*.

6.4.3 Development Warehouse Showroom

The metadata stored in a Development Warehouse includes Bill of Materials entries for client-based components and client "scripts." The term script refers to the source code specifying the behavior of client components such as buttons, input boxes, spreadsheet objects and the like.

Within the limits of the "blob" (binary datatype) support offered by the database server, the Development Warehouse might also store the standard versions of client workflows and their component parts. As illustrated in Figure 5.5, storage of central versions in the Development Warehouse helps maintain consistent component versions on different client machines.

In addition to source code SQL and client script listings, the Development Warehouse database stores executable versions of each component and Component Case. The data structure components contain a set of standard test data that is used by the executable components providing working usage examples. These working examples are used in the following ways:

- To distribute standard versions to client machines as needed
- To guide Success Circles in their development and benchmarking activities
- To test new versions.

The Warehouse Showroom interface is shown in Figure 6.7. Individual components are shown alongside their standard costs, the standard labor allowance for their use. Selecting a Component Case makes available its entity-relationship diagrams and state transition diagrams. Selecting the picture of any component activates a usage example demo, which shows the component's behavior and how it is used. Usage examples illustrate how Component Cases are used in workflows. The examples include client and server components working on standard test data—a compact "starter kit" working model to demonstrate the components in action.

Text fields: Cost = 2 hours
  Edit text field
  Large text field
  Large text field 2
  Text append field

List fields: Cost = 4 hours
  Spreadsheet
  Formatted spreadsheet

Other fields
  Check box: Cost = 1 hour
  Messenger check box: Cost = 1 hour
  Three-state check box: Cost = 2 hours
  Three-state messenger check box: 2 hours
  Radio button: Cost = 1 hour
  Popup menu: Cost = 2.5 hours
  Messenger popup menu: Cost = 2.5 hours
  State popup menu: Cost = 3 hours
  Messenger-state popup menu: Cost = 3 hours
  Picture: Cost = 1.5 hours

Clusters: Cost = 4 hours
  Container
  Adjusta view
  Layout cluster
  Hidden cluster
  Dimmed cluster
  Moving hidden cluster
  Gray cluster
  Plain cluster
  Messenger cluster

Buttons: Cost = 1.5 hours
  Push button
  List push button
  Outlining icon
  List outlining icon

Static items: Cost = 1.5 hours
  Static text field
  Icon
  Picture
  Smart picture

  Scrollers

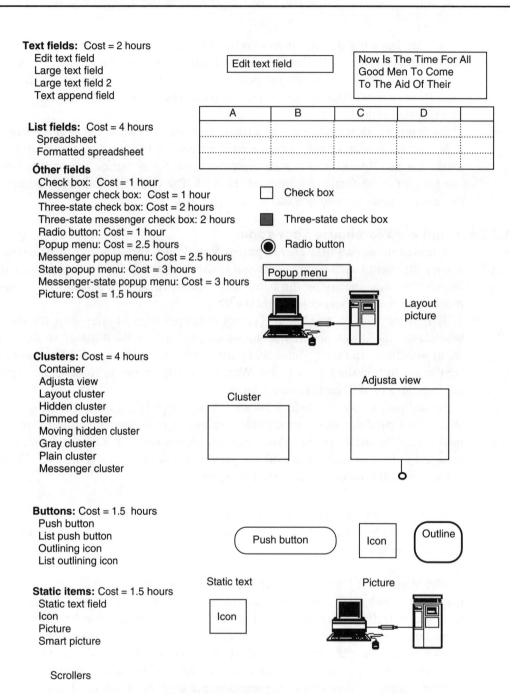

Figure 6.7 Warehouse showroom

6.4.4 Development Warehouse TQM Benchmarking

Modern manufacturing aims for "zero defects" by means of

- Automated production (through mistake proofing built into automatic operations)
- Automated tracking (through identification, monitoring, and CSF metrics)
- TQM (through continuous quality control and waste prevention).

In active client/server information systems, the database server uses event management to provide automated information production. An active database also provides automated tracking of both normal and exception processing.

Consider the following quality assurance metadata table:

```
CREATE TABLE qa
     component_name    varchar(26),
     component_type    char(6),      /*e.g., b_i_trigger*/
     circle_id         char(6),      /*responsible Circle */
     version           float,
     failures_cum      int,          /*cumulative to date*/
     last_failure      datetime,     /*when latest occurred/
     state             int )         /*0 = "invalid"    */
```

The version number has an integer portion that reflects the current design iteration and a decimal portion that indicates the number of revisions within that iteration.

A component failure is detected by the occurrence of an *undefined exception* on an operation involving the component. An undefined exception is one without a specific exception handler. Undefined exceptions cause a halt in the activation path short of the goal (in other words, a failure).

Quality assurance supports such metrics as

- Cumulative component usage for comparison against failures
- Mean time between failures
- Mean time to repair (that is, time in an exception state).

The benefit of component-usage tracking is that it enables TQM. The TQM approach keeps repair and maintenance costs low by isolating failures as soon as possible and at the finest possible level of detail. As shown in Figure 6.8, active database applications support TQM by tracking component usage in all operations, detecting failures and providing exception handlers for all defined excep-

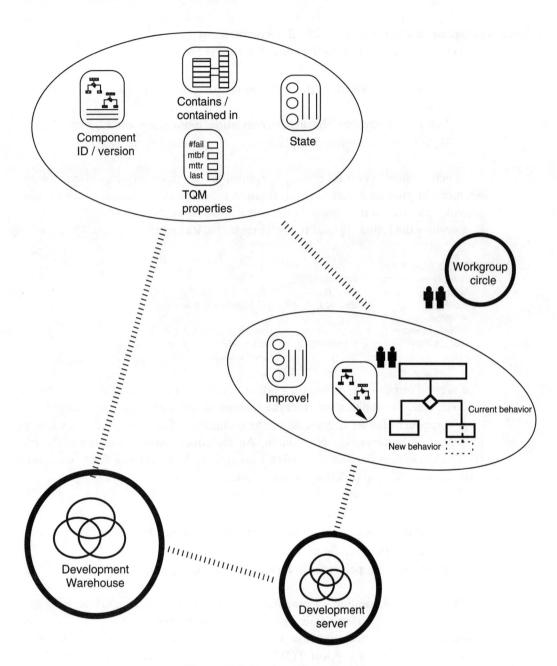

Figure 6.8 Total quality management

tions. These exception handlers update the quality assurance table to enter the base data for quality management metrics.

High counts of undefined exceptions do not necessarily indicate that a marginal component is low-grade software. Instead, the failures might be caused by a change in business conditions that the behavior of the Component Case is unable to match. If so, the Success Circle that is the logical client of the workflow in question must fine-tune the workflow to make it more responsive to business conditions.

Component improvement is the result of a *benchmarking process*. The benchmarking process has two activities: selecting the best behavior and then applying that behavior as a standard.

As shown in Figure 6.8, a Component Case is checked out of the Development Warehouse. The technical facilitators analyze its metadata and pinpoint the cause(s) of the exceptions. The Success Circle participants compare the workflow's behavior with other Component Case assemblies. They compare the Component Case under study with the workflow operations of their trading partners and competitors in order to decide whether and how to fine-tune the Component Case.

For example, a event handler might be modified to reclassify an exception event as a normal application event and behave accordingly. The modification is tested using the standard test data and then the Component Case is checked back into the Development Warehouse. When the new version of the Component Case is stored in the Development Warehouse, it becomes the standard behavior for the workflow.

State-based behavior simplifies the benchmarking process by associating the TQM properties of each component case with a traffic light. The metastate traffic light of a Component Case is similar in function to an indicator panel prominently displayed above a factory work area. Just as the indicator compares current production to goals, the traffic light icon displays one of three states: "OK," "Caution," or "Improve!" Changes in the TQM metadata affect the state of the traffic light. The Success Circle is alerted whenever a traffic light changes from "Caution" to "Improve!"

Classification of components by state reduces complexity by isolating the components that need improvement from the rest of the Component Case. Modifications are confined to specific properties/behavior within these components. The interface to these components is often unchanged, thus hiding the changes from other components. The modifications themselves and their impacts are confined. Chapter 7 discusses how state-based behavior is used to create responsive, self-adjusting, just-in-time information systems.

7

JUST-IN-TIME: STATE-BASED BEHAVIOR

This chapter explores the concept of state, the condition of a component with respect to its attributes. State classifies an active database and determines application behavior. An active database is "self adjusting" because its behavior varies with its state. To make the application efficient and explicit, the current state and past states are marked in the database. The metastate of a table is the composite state of its rows. Database programs structured in terms of state transitions take the place of rigid client programs. Control tables and events work with state-based behavior to configure just-in-time information systems.

■ 7.1 THE MEANING OF STATE

Active applications are controlled primarily from within the database server, so their adaptive control mechanisms utilize the server's event-management infrastructure. Figure 7.1 is a step-by-step illustration of self-adjustment. In this example, an application behavior change is triggered by a client transaction-processing request. At the top of the illustration, a client sends the server a request to execute a database procedure. The database procedure activates the server's SQL execution facility by using SQL commands stored in the database procedure.

The SQL commands change both data and metadata. Metadata updates reflect changes in the overall condition of the application data. At some point during the processing, facts and attributes represented by the data will reflect fundamentally

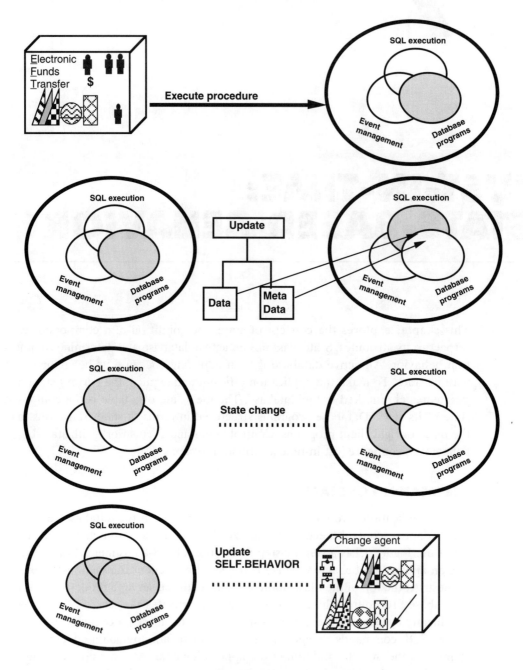

Figure 7.1 Self-adjustment

different business conditions. When this occurs, the application's behavior also must change to keep pace with new business conditions.

The server's event-management infrastructure dispatches signals to special utility programs called *database agents*. In Figure 7.1, an event alert is dispatched to a *change agent*, which changes the behavior of interface objects. Unlike a passive procedural application, an active database application is event-driven and, therefore, sensitive to state transitions.

The *state* of a row, table, or other database component is its condition with respect to its attribute values.

In relational design, each database table represents some *entity type,* or business concept. For example, the tables in the ER diagram shown in Figure 7.2 represent the concepts of parts, suppliers, and supplier orders. Each row in a table represents an *entity instance*, which is a specific instance of the business concept. The primary key column(s), which by definition can never hold null values, identify each specific instance of the table's business concept.

For example, the *Parts* table contains a row for part number 601053, another row for part number 402074, and no second or third row for either of these parts. The data value held by a primary key column in a given row marks the existence of the unique, specific instance identified by the primary key. This condition, known as entity integrity, is a prerequisite for the row having a state. For an entity instance to be in any state, it must first exist and be uniquely identifiable.

A foreign key is a column in a table (other than the table's primary key) that corresponds to the primary key of some other table. In Figure 7.2, the *Supplier* orders table contains the foreign keys *part_number* and *supplier_id*. A non-null foreign key value marks the existence of a relationship between a row or rows in one table and the row of the foreign table whose primary key holds a value equal to that of the foreign key.

For example, all the rows in the *Suppliers* orders table having a value of 402074 in the column row with a foreign key column *part_number* participate in a relationship with the row in the *Parts* table identified by the value 402074 in its primary key. This condition is known as referential integrity because the foreign key in the *Supplier* orders table refers to the primary key of the *Parts* table. The application's behavior with regard to the relationship depends on the state of the rows (in both tables) that participate in the relationship, and the state of the workflows that carry out the relationship.

The tables shown in Figure 7.2 are normalized. Therefore, no two rows are identical. Each of the nonkey columns in a normalized table represents an attribute pertaining to that table's main concept. The state of a row is comprised of its nonprimary key attribute values. The data value in each nonkey column of a row rep-

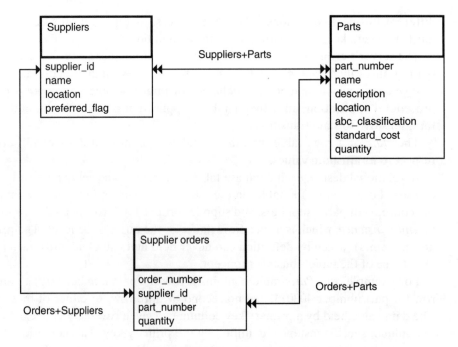

Figure 7.2 Parts supply (take 1)

resents the condition of the column within the row. The set of all the data values in a row defines the state of the row.

For example, the rows of the *Parts* table in Figure 7.2 are either in an *unconfirmed*, *standard_confirmed,* or *special_confirmed* state. This state is determined by the values of the columns *abc_classification*, *standard_cost*, and *quantity*. Depending on the state, the workflows involved in processing parts will differ. The following pseudocode evaluates the conditions that categorize the *supplier_order* placement relationship:

```
if lower(left(supplier_orders.order_number, 1)) = "f" or
    lower(left(supplier_orders.order_number, 1)) = "q"
    /* order number prefixes for forecasts and quotations */
  then the_state := "unconfirmed"
else
if lower(left(supplier_orders.order_number, 1)) = "c"  and
    supplier.preferred_flag = "p"    and parts.abc_classification = "a" or "b"
    then the_state := "standard_confirmed"
else
    the_state := "special_confirmed".
```

This simple example is typical of passive application design. The procedural logic evaluates conditions represented by data, an evaluation that categorizes the relationship. This categorization determines conditional processing.

Unfortunately, procedural conditional logic mixes workflow control and program flow control. This often leads to ambiguous conclusions that cannot be explained other than by re-evaluation of procedural program code. For example, the relationship *Orders + Suppliers* could be in a state of *special_confirmed* for an order that was placed with a nonpreferred supplier. The relationship would also hold a state of *special_confirmed* when a part had been ordered while its quantity was still above its reorder point, or because both of these conditions applied.

Without re-evaluating these conditions, it would be impossible to explain why a *special_confirmed* supplier order was placed. Furthermore, the changing business environment may enlarge the set of conditions that determine the state of a supplier order. The possible conditions in the business entity would then extend beyond the set of conditions evaluated in the procedural code.

For example, if the company decided to negotiate annual *blanket* orders with preferred suppliers, a new state of *blanket_confirmed* might be needed. In a passive database design, this new state would require its own set of procedural evaluation logic. The set-up time for this new type of *supplier_order* placement relationship would include the time required for procedural coding, which is likely to be greater than the time required for nonprocedural coding.

Figure 7.3 shows a modified version of the same database design. In this version, a provision has been made in the table structures explicitly to mark the state of each row in the database. This structural enhancement permits the evaluation to be shifted from the time a relationship is executed in a business workflow to the time the data enters the relationship.

The state serves as an active application's way of classifying entity and relationship instances into logical cases. The application's behavior can then be made specific to each logical case. This simplifies programming because complex condition evaluation code can be replaced by simple flow-of-control statements that are dependent on the logical case. The contrasting approach used by passive applications is to classify instances implicitly at run-time through procedural code similar to the pseudocode shown previously.

The behavior of a relationship in a workflow is (or should be) the same whether the state is explicitly marked when entries are made, or implicitly derived when entries are retrieved. Both procedural and state-based methods should achieve the same results. However, the degree of programming effort, the quality of the data model's alignment with the process model, and the performance characteristics of the application differ markedly.

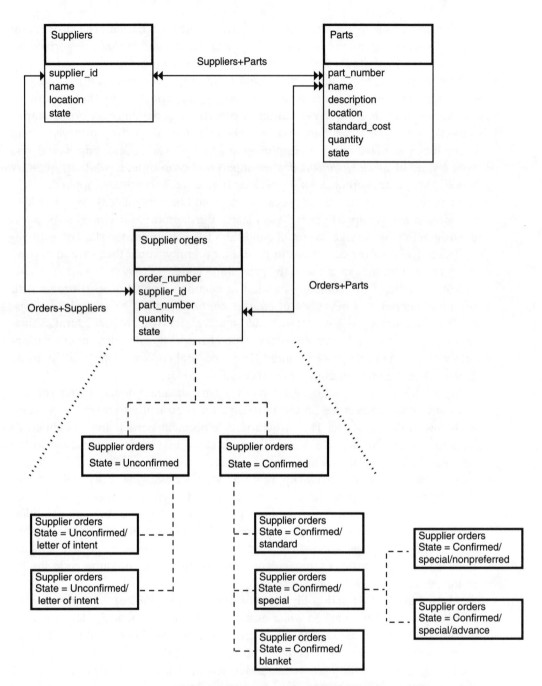

Figure 7.3 Parts supply (take 2)

As shown in Figure 7.3, the abstract concept of an order must be normalized (decomposed into lower levels of abstraction) for the *supplier_order* placement workflows to operate correctly. The first step in normalizing the relationship would be to define the state of a *supplier_order* in two broad categories, *unconfirmed* or *confirmed*.

Because broad categories are too diffuse for real-world business workflows, the *confirmed* state is further normalized to include substates, such as *special_confirmed*, *special_confirmed/nonpreferred* (the next level down), and *special_confirmed/advance*. The least abstract view of state is the condition of a row in a database table, as determined by a set of data values in the row.

The set of all possible values for a column in a relational database is known as its domain. If the actual state is narrowly defined as simply the value in a column, then the set of potential states for any row is the full set (what logic programmers call the "bag") of the domains of the columns. In practice, the universe of potential states would approach infinity in a database of any size, so the narrow definition of state as synonymous with column values is a degenerate case. Using state to categorize the database poses no practical advantage unless the number of state categories is finite.

The state of a row can be broken down further into a *vector* (that is, a one-dimensional array) of substates. Since repeating group columns are contrary to the relational notion of "first normal form," storing a state vector within each row would appear to violate the laws of relational purity. However, it can be done. Certain extended relational database products such as Interbase, which includes an array datatype, support state vector storage. A more "relationally pure" solution is to represent complex states by means of state codes, thus subsuming the repeating group.

■ 7.2 STATE REPRESENTATION

The state of a row in the database can be determined in the following two ways:

- **Late binding.** The state is derived from data values when needed.
- **Early binding.** The state is explicitly marked in the row itself.

Consider the case of an accounts receivable application that needs to classify customer accounts. For the purposes of this application, each customer balance is in one of the following five states:

1. *credit_balance.* The account is prepaid, overpaid, or credited.

2. *paid_in_full*. The account is fully paid up.

3. *payment_due*. The customer balance is due in less than 30 days.

4. *past_due*. The customer balance is unpaid between 31 and 90 days.

5. *delinquent*. The customer balance is unpaid in more than 90 days.

Having defined the universe of customer account states, these states can be either explicitly marked in the database or implicitly derived during processing.

7.2.1 Implicit State Computation

If the current state of a row is not stored in the database, it can be derived from the values of nonkey columns. For an application whose data is updated much more frequently than it is accessed, calculating the state at run-time may be preferable to storing it explicitly.

In an accounts receivable application, for example, the data may updated daily, but accessed only monthly when the accounts are aged. The procedure for deriving the state of an account might compare the payment due dates with the system date, and compare payment amounts with the customer balance. These processing steps may be implemented within a client program, or within a database procedure.

Because the state of a customer account entry is derived at run-time, evaluation logic may cause slow performance at such peak load times as the close of the customer billing period. By comparison, explicit state representation computes the state when the data is first entered, and recomputes it with each update. On retrieval, the application needs less "think time" for information processing because the state has been precomputed and stored.

7.2.2 Explicit State Representation

Explicit state representation consists of evaluating (or re-evaluating) the state of a row, and then marking that state in the database. Marking the state in each row requires an additional column to store the state value, two columns if a prior state value also is stored.

The examples in this chapter so far have represented the state as a name. However, simply naming the state usually is not enough. More detailed methods such as code representation and conditional array representation are more adequate to the needs of large-volume commercial applications.

Code representation treats the state value as a foreign key identifier. The unique code identifies the specific set of conditions that determine the state. As shown in Figure 7.4, a state code entry actually is a foreign key referencing a state table. Each row in the state table entry describes a unique state.

Data tables   Control tables

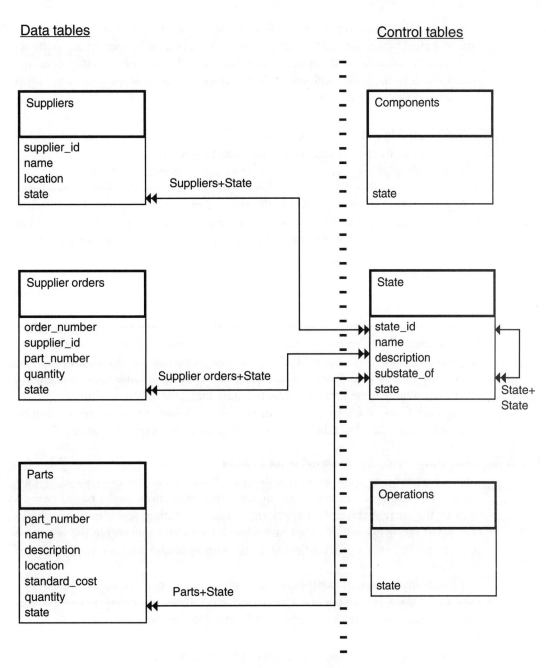

Figure 7.4 State table

A state table is an application control table that is shared by multiple applications. Control tables such as the state table are part of a global enterprise architecture, as opposed to a local application architecture. The benefit of integrating the state table into the global enterprise architecture is that its scope can be enlarged to represent such metadata as

- Compatible states for relationships
- Whether the state is a normal or an exception state
- The default next normal state or next exception state.

In *condition array representation*, the state of each row is encoded as a vector. Each element in the state array maps to one or more conditions. The head element in a state vector represents the overall state of the row, and the following elements represent substates, as shown in the top portion of Figure 7.5.

The individual substate conditions evaluate as true, false, or irrelevant. If true, the condition value of this substate element in the array is set to 1. If false or irrelevant, it is set to zero.

Each unique set of condition vector values identifies a unique substate combination. Because irrelevant conditions are set to zero, some combinations of condition vector values never will occur. The distinct sets of condition vector values can be assembled into a two-dimensional array, as shown in the middle portion of Figure 7.5. Each column in the array represents a state and its substate conditions.

Each state has an appropriate set of behaviors. A state array, therefore, can be represented as a decision table, as shown in the bottom portion of Figure 7.5.

7.2.3 Representing Prior States and Past Events

The behavior of an application is influenced both by current events and by past events. For example, an insurance underwriting workflow might be influenced both by the current state of an applicant's insurance rating, and also by the applicant's past rating history. An applicant who had a major claim within the last three years might fall into a different category than an applicant whose record is free of any claims.

To simplify state representation, past states may be considered as substates of the current state. For an applicant with a current satisfactory rating, prior substates might influence the rate calculation in different ways, as shown here:

- None, one, or multiple *past_claims*: substate 1, weight 16
- Small, average, or large *past_claims*: substate 1.1, weight 08
- *past_claims* within 2, 5, or 7 years: substate 1.2, weight 04.

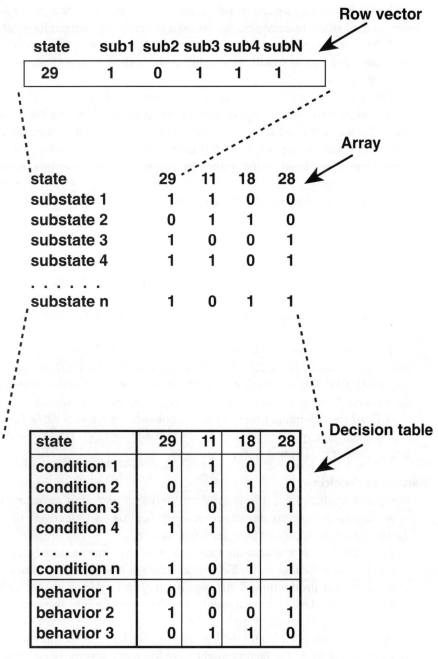

Figure 7.5 State arrays

The *past_claims* substate is rolled into the applicant's state of eligibility. The *past_claims* substate encompasses its own severity and chronology substates. At each level in the consolidation, substates are given a weighting. Multiplying the substate value by the condition weighting yields the weighted state value for each applicant's row.

The state calculations are performed in a top-down manner. If the value of substate 1 were zero (which implies zero claims multiplied by 16), then substates 1.1 and 1.2 would not need to be computed. The eligibility of an applicant depends on the overall state of the other insured members in the rating pool. The application design can avoid hard-coded values by comparing the state of one or more instances with the metastate (overall state) of the rating pool. Using weighted state values in this way helps in the design of self-adjusting applications.

■ 7.3 METASTATE

The metastate is the collective state of all individual row states in a database table (that is, the overall condition of the concept represented by the table). The metastate of a table or a relationship helps active database applications modify their own behavior. The metastate is utilized to monitor and vary the global behavior of an application.

To illustrate metastate, consider the parts table in Figure 7.3. All parts are in one of four states: *ON_ORDER*, *AVAILABLE*, *RESERVED,* or (the final state) *CONSUMED*. The proportion of parts in each of these states fluctuates during operations. During a plant shutdown, relatively more components are *AVAILABLE*. At peak demand times, most components are *RESERVED*. If some supply problem exists, more components than usual will be *ON_ORDER* and the metastate of the parts table will shift accordingly.

7.3.1 Metastate Tracking

For many applications, it is possible to define a *preferred metastate* or a *target metastate*. As a business entity succeeds in meeting its objectives, the associated database entities approach their target metastate.

For example, a manufacturing facility uses just-in-time inventory replenishment. The objective is to have available only as many components as are needed for two days of current production. With a daily build/test cycle, the number of components in *AVAILABLE* state should be roughly equivalent to those in *RESERVED* state. Assuming a five-day supply in the orders pipeline, the target metastate of the *component_parts* table would tilt toward *ON_ORDER*. If the prevailing metastate were *AVAILABLE*, the facility might have too much inventory on hand.

After the application adjusts its behavior, database procedures and client procedures act differently to bring the metastate back toward the target. In a broadcasting application, for example, the target metastate of the *commercial_bookings* entity might be 94%. In other words, on an ongoing basis, only an average of 6% of the time allotted for commercial breaks should remain available as air time approaches. The unsold time is used for public service announcements, as required by the regulatory authority.

In mission-critical applications, the metastate is tracked minute-by-minute. If the average metastate should drift below a threshold, then the application's behavior changes to allow a discount on the unbooked commercial time. When the metastate falls below 86%, for example, sales representatives may begin to offer discounts to bring the metastate value up to target.

In a real-world application, the threshold value would not be a fixed value. Instead, the threshold varies within a range, with the current threshold value depending on the rate of change (the *metastate volatility*). Otherwise, a volatile metastate oscillating immediately above and immediately below the threshold would cause arbitrary discounting behavior in the application. Averaging or some other method smoothes the metastate so that the application's behavior responds to trends, not transient fluctuations. Like the application itself, the application control infrastructure is self-adjusting.

7.3.2 Metastate Computation

Like state, metastate can be represented implicitly or explicitly. *Implicit metastates* are computed as needed. An SQL view with an aggregate such as COUNT, SUM, or AVG on the base table might suffice for a small table. A database procedure could be used to perform a more complex implicit metastate computation.

A stored procedure executing frequently—perhaps at one-minute intervals—and storing the computed metastate in a control table would be functionally equivalent to *explicit metastate* representation. The SQL commands are used frequently enough to remain in the server's execution shared buffer memory area. The control table itself is compact enough to be cached, residing in shared memory during execution. Because access to memory is more rapid than access to disk, explicit metastate representation does not slow the application.

Design decisions regarding implicit versus explicit metastate representation depend on the required persistence of the metastate. When only one database program occasionally needs to know the metastate, implicit representation is sufficient. When multiple database programs have an ongoing need to know the metastates of multiple entities, then explicit representation works best.

7.3.3 Discrete versus Fuzzy Metastates

The state of a row is always a discrete value, a member of the set of possible state values for the concept the table represents. The metastate of a table represents the overall condition of the table's concept. Depending on the needs of the application, the metastate might belong to a discrete set or a "fuzzy" set.

Discrete metastate sets are similar to sets of potential state values. One of the possible metastate values (such as the one shared by the most rows in the table) is chosen to represent the overall state of the table. This is sufficient for many applications, but it involves some approximation. The rounding process that calculates a discrete metastate filters out minority state values.

In situations where the application must be sensitive to metastate gradations, *fuzzy metastate* representation is in order. Fuzzy metastate representation notes the degree to which a given metastate applies to a table. For example, the metastate of the *portfolio* table in a financial services application might be ".85 above index AND .15 below index."

■ 7.4 STATE-BASED PROCESSING

State serves several purposes in application design, including the following:

- Simplified conditional logic and simplified database programming
- Localized behavior for specific state categories
- Collaborative behavior by entities in compatible states
- Application self-modification to reach target metastate.

The state acts as a shorthand for its determinant conditions. These conditions are stored as metadata and applied consistently, so they do not need to be re-evaluated outside the database with every retrieval.

For example, manufacturing inventory data is distributed among production facilities in Texas, Ireland, and Singapore. A headquarters application must know the condition of inventory in all locations. Retrieving all the details for headquarters evaluation would cause communications and processing bottlenecks, which are avoided by simply retrieving the state. This use of the state as a pointer to the determinant conditions facilitates structured database programming. The conditional logic is stored centrally in the database, and is applied universally and consistently.

State-specific behavior is helpful in designing structured database programs. The implementation details of specific behaviors are hidden. Specific interfaces to specific behaviors, including those that notify others of state transitions, are restricted to the components and states to which they are appropriate. The hidden implementation details can change as needed without altering the interface or the state definitions.

Changes to behavior are controlled by flow-of-control logic within database programs. These database programs respond to the server's event-management infrastructure. Changes in application behavior are directed to specific goals, such as attaining a target metastate.

7.4.1 Classification by State

Classification by state offers a number of advantages over classification by structure, by data attribute, or by procedural language code.

Classification by state allows a single parts table classified into logical categories by distinct states such as *RECEIVED*, *AVAILABLE*, and *RESERVED*. Classification by structure requires additional data tables in the database such as a *receiving_stock* table, a *production_stock* table, and a *work_in_process* stock table. To know the total number of particular parts in stock, a three-way join would be required, as shown here:

```
SELECT recv.qty + prod.qty + wip.qty = total_qty
   FROM recv, prod, wip
   WHERE recv.partno = prod.partno AND
      prod.partno = wip.partno AND
      recv.partno = 1057;
```

A single table with three state categories is equivalent to three tables, each dedicated to a single category. The single table equivalent is simpler and faster to process, as shown here:

```
SELECT qty
   FROM component_parts
   WHERE partno = 1057;
```

Classification by attribute approximates classification by state. Consider the substitution of a *station* column for the state column in the *component_parts* table. Assume station 110 stands for receiving inspection and station 120 is production inventory. It follows that when a component moves from station 110 to station 120, it implicitly changes state from *INSPECTED* to *AVAILABLE*. However, classification by attribute has its limitations. The fact that a component is at station 120 does not necessarily mean that it came from station 110. It could have come from state 220 (repair), in which case it must have failed testing. If the application must track defects by serial number, but classifies by attribute rather than by state, then other structures are needed to track component movements and failures.

Not all the components at station 120 are available, because some have already been reserved for current production. If the state is not marked, another way to tell which components are available is to examine the *assembly_serial* column. This column will hold a null value if and only if the component has not been reserved for an assembly, which, in turn, implies that it is available.

Where the state is determined by multiple conditions, the evaluation of attributes becomes sufficiently complex to degenerate into classification by procedure. The main benefit of classifying entries in the database is to simplify the procedural logic connected with information retrieval, not to move code from one location to another. For this benefit to be realized, the procedural code that classifies database entries should be executed in conjunction with database events prior to data retrieval. Otherwise, data access is slowed by the computational delay of executing the classification routine.

7.4.2 Workflow Coordination

Any binary relationship involves a logical client, a logical server, and a means of placing the relationship in a workflow. Consider the manufacturing workflow shown in Figure 7.6. Including a part in manufacturing-in-process assembly is an example of a relationship. Clearly, the assembly must be in a state that allows one part to be included and the part must be in an available state so it is eligible to be included. The state of the assembly and that of the component must be compatible.

Normal workflows assure compatible states. Production inventory components are in an *available* state and assemblies on the line are in a compatible *build/in_process* state. But what if some disruption leads to a component shortage? Work-in-process assemblies are sidelined to a *build/delayed* state while components in shortage arrive in an *in_transit/rush* state. These are compatible exception states. The relationship holds, but its state changes.

When the state of the relationship changes, the workflows realizing the relationship also must change. Specifically, the parts that have a substate of *rush* are expedited through receiving inspection and the shop floor is alerted. The assembly changes back to a normal state of *build/in_process* and the component changes to a normal *reserved* state. As Figure 7.6 shows, entities in compatible exception states coordinate their workflows to attain compatible normal states.

7.4.3 State-Based Workflows

From its initial entry until its deletion or archival, a row in a database table changes state. The row may change state repeatedly without any lasting effect on

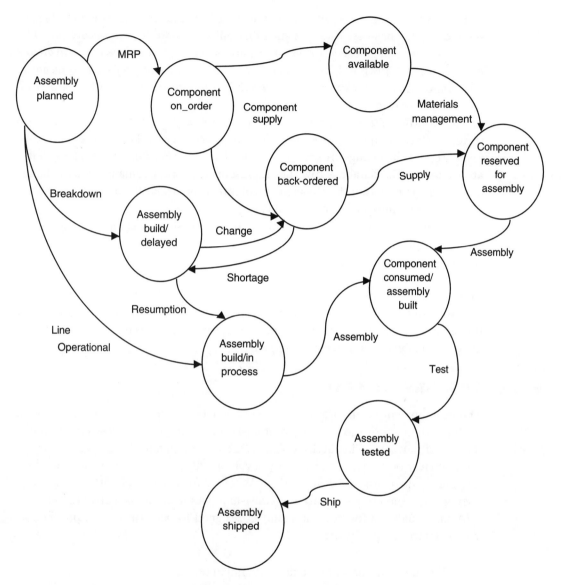

Figure 7.6 Compatible states

the row itself, or on the application. In fact, such fluctuation is the basic premise of on-line transaction processing. For example, a purchased part might change state from *ordered* to *back-ordered* to shipped without any persistent effect.

Each state has a finite set of states to which a state transition is possible. In some cases, the business rules are such that only two state transitions are possible: a normal state and an exception state. A part can change from *received* to *available* or *defective*, as shown in Figure 7.7. It can change back from *defective* to *received*, but cannot change backward from *received* to *in_transit,* or jump forward from *received* to *reserved* without violating business rules.

The workflow associated with a state transition adjusts its behavior to the substate. A state change from *in_transit/rush* to *received* calls for an expeditious response, but the change from *in_transit/normal* to *received* does not. These states are transient. The database row that represents this order remains free to change again and again (within the change control infrastructure of the active application) until it changes into a final, persistent state.

Once an entity instance changes into a persistent state, it cannot change again. In many applications, entities have a life cycle of transient states. A state transition can be normal (for example, the change from *ordered* to *received* in Figure 7.7). In a well-designed workflow, a transition to an exception state, such as the change from *ordered* to *back-ordered*, will lead back to a normal state (such as *in_transit*) in a subsequent transition. Changes to a persistent state mark the end of a state transition cycle. The persistent normal state in this example is *out_of_warranty* and the persistent exception state is *scrapped*.

■ 7.5 JUST-IN-TIME APPLICATIONS

The development of an information system is labor-intensive. The longer it takes to develop an application, the more it costs. In a changing business environment, the risk of failure also increases with increased development time. Even if a design is completely on-target at the start of development, the design may become obsolete during the course of development. Whether for reasons of cost or risk, minimizing application time-to-market is consistent with maintaining software quality.

A high-quality software component is designed to perform well in production. The hallmarks of quality are

- **Zero defects.** The software does not fail in service.
- **Minimal setup cost.** The software requires little or no extra work to integrate.
- **Low maintenance burden.** The software does not need much periodic rework.

Active database environments enable high quality at moderate cost. The initial database architecture investment is amortized over the lifetime of all components

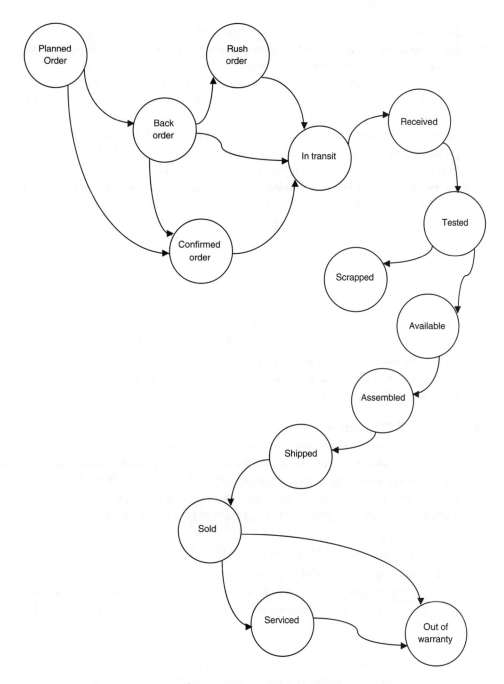

Figure 7.7 State transitions

based on that architecture. Active components lend themselves to sharing and to reuse, so those components that figure in a new application are likely to have been stress-tested in an existing application.

The scope of development within an active component architecture is confined to modifying fine-grained components as opposed to coding and debugging the complex, coarse-grained programs of passive environments. This enables active database workflows to have a lower maintenance cost than passive procedural programming applications. The scope of maintenance is confined to the implementation behavior or to a small database program, not a large COBOL or C program.

Integration of database components in active environments takes place within the database infrastructure. This is the opposite of passive environments in which it is necessary for multiple programs to coordinate their work through program calls and interface files with little or no support from the database infrastructure.

For all these reasons, active database components offer higher reliability than passive programs.

Database programming allows rapid time-to-market. Extended SQL languages for database programming, such as Transact-SQL or PL/SQL, add procedural constructs to standard SQL. Using an in-house or vendor-supplied Development Warehouse environment, SQL commands are rapidly built and quickly tested. The SQL commands are then structured within database procedures. Once the SQL is tested within a database program, the software component is ready to enter the production environment.

7.5.1 Event-Driven Operations

Unlike passive database operations that are driven by external program code, active applications are driven by application events. Events are predefined conditions that coincide with a state transition. Prior to the occurrence of the event, part of the database is in a given state, and afterward it is assigned another state. The steps in event-driven operations are as follows (see Figure 7.8):

1. An event is defined in terms of database conditions.
2. Client-based and database programs subscribe to the event.
3. The event is set and the database infrastructure is sensitive to the event.
4. The event occurs and the server becomes aware of a state (or metastate) transition.
5. An alert is transmitted and subscribers are notified.
6. Subscribers direct control to their event handlers.
7. Optionally, the event is reset.

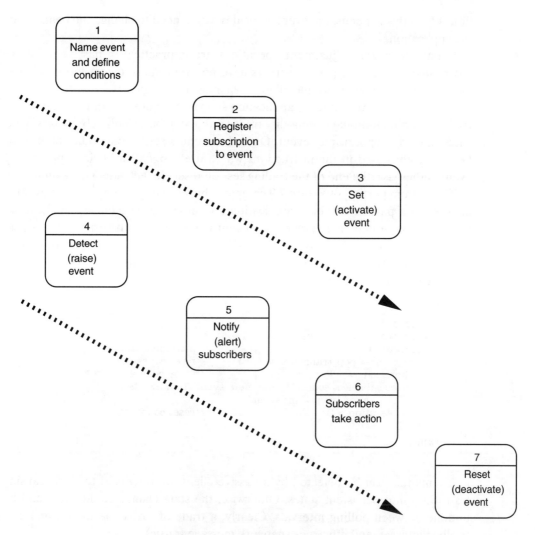

Figure 7.8 Event-driven operations

The concept of events and the concept of state are related. An event is marked by a state transition. The defining condition of an event is false prior to the event having occurred, meaning the entity under observation is in its prior state. When the condition of the event becomes true, the associated state change triggers the event.

When an event is defined in terms of an aggregate operation (such as a count) on an application table, the state transition marking the event is a metastate transition. When this happens, the event coincides with a need to change the behavior of the application.

Event-driven self-adjustment operations are impractical in passive database environments. Because passive servers have no event-management infrastructure, the client is tasked with any and all event-management logic.

Consider the option trading application shown in Figure 7.9. In this example, a trader enters conditional commodity trades into a database. This activity sets (activates) a buying opportunity event. Once the event is set, a commodity offer at or below the threshold in the instructions will "raise" (signal) a buying opportunity event. Otherwise, the end of the trading session resets (deactivates) the event.

The bottom portion of Figure 7.9 compares how the buying opportunity event is handled in a passive database application and in an active database application. Because passive database servers lack event-management infrastructure, the passive application simulates this functionality through procedural programming. Between transactions, the client program executes a polling loop. The following pseudocode represents the loop logic:

```
int PollingLoop (*myevent)
     while not(new_trans or new_event) do
         iteration++                              /*increment counter*/
         new_trans = pop_transtack(self_id)       /*new transaction? */
         if (iteration >= 99)                      /*force polling  delay */
            exec sql select count(*)...into new_event from events
                    where event = myevent
                iteration = 0                      /*reset counter*/
         endif
     endwhile
```

Events that can be detected by a passive client are restricted to those causing transitions into persistent states. Otherwise, the state change could occur and be undone between polling intervals. Clearly, a trade-off exists between timeliness (polling interval) and efficiency (network message traffic).

The active database application in the lower portion of Figure 7.9 delegates event-management tasks to the database server, where event-handling logic is shared and standardized. When a buying opportunity event occurs, all interested clients receive an event alert. While the active client continues processing other transactions, the client's event-handling logic changes the state of the conditional buy instructions from *enabled* to *placed*. At the same time, the back office receives an electronic mail message to execute the trade within a 15-minute "processing window."

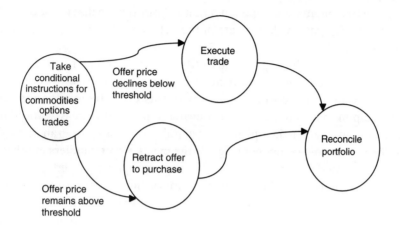

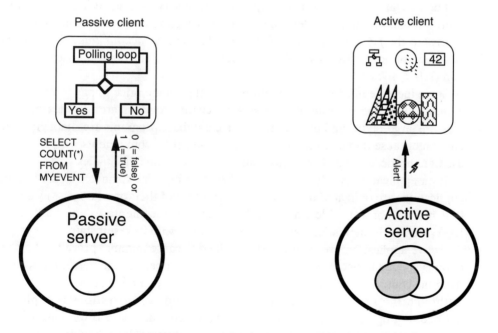

Figure 7.9 Event notification: Passive versus active

7.5.2 Just-in-Time Database Applications

Because active database components adjust both their behavior and their activation path to keep pace with the state of the data, an active application has inherent flexibility.

Server-based database programs utilize event-handler routines to vary the application in response to application events. A database program does not require procedural logic to evaluate any events other than those for which it is directly responsible. Indeed, any such evaluation would increase procedural complexity and go against the spirit of structured database programming. Instead, when the responsible component signals the event, event handlers in other components are activated and transfer control to the appropriate procedural block.

Figure 7.10 illustrates the dynamic nature of the activation path, which passes control from one component to the next. The figure shows an active programmed trading application that changes its activation path in response to preemptive *buy_signal* events by backing out of in-process trades pending settlement. In this sample application (but obviously not in all financial services applications), the 15-minute window between the time the trade is placed and the time it is executed is treated as a logical transaction. Until a trade is executed (committed), it may be backed out (rolled back).

The activation path in this example follows a server-based Bill of Operations control table. The Bill of Operations changes in response to a buy-signal, directing control to the *preempt_operation* (which in this case is *backout_trades*). Following the preemption, control reverts to the operation at the start of the logical transaction (*select_invest*).

Some increase in complexity might be expected as the price to pay for such flexibility. In fact, the opposite is true. Passive client programs are complex because they are large, static, and procedural. Active database programs are simple in comparison because they are built of small, single-purpose components with extensive use of nonprocedural code and close interaction with database tables.

If an application is self-adjusting, it also must be self-explanatory. Just-in-time applications are obligated to maintain an audit trail of their operations. Any events that modify control table (metadata) entries are documented in an audit trail. Every step in the activation path is logged together with its result state.

Active application processing is streamlined because minimal procedural evaluation is needed to decide what to do next. The next operation to perform is known from the control table, and that table's contents are updated in response to events. Although the flow of operations varies, the scope of operations is explicitly defined. An operation applies only to those specific database rows that are in a state eligible to participate in the relationship. Evaluating the conditions pertaining

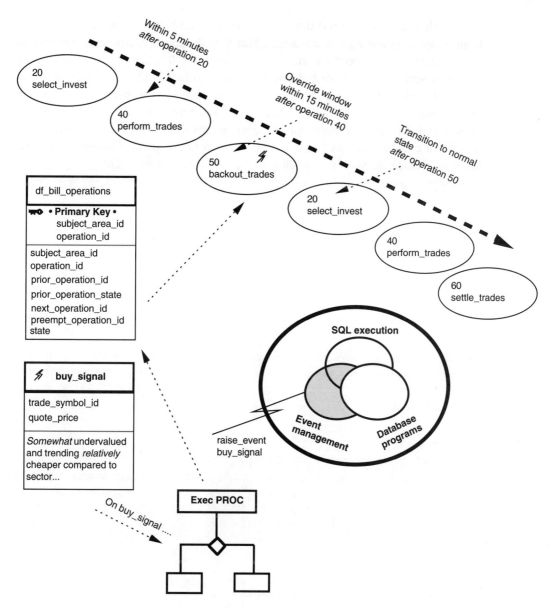

Figure 7.10 Just-in-time application

to these rows is unnecessary because their state (or substate) is a shorthand for those conditions.

This chapter has explored the ways in which state-based, event-driven applications adapt to changing circumstances. But how do active components coordinate their behavior throughout the client, server, and middleware environments? How can the client be capable of behavioral change without becoming all-encompassing? If the client were programmed with conditional logic to handle all eventualities, it might become just as large, complex, and unwieldy as a passive database application. If server-resident database programs had to be complex enough to handle all eventualities, SQL execution speed would degrade. Chapter 8 explores the role of database agents in synchronizing application components.

8

MACHINE TOOLS: DATABASE AGENTS

Coordination, essential in any client/server computing environment, is critical for an active database. Active server-based components adjust themselves to events. Client and middleware components must keep pace with changes in server-based components. However, client and middleware components extend beyond the server's effective control. Agents, utility programs that work on behalf of the database server, keep an active database synchronized.

In the business world, an agent is a third-party representative. Commercial agents act on behalf of some other person or business entity. For instance, a customs agent facilitates the transfer of goods from an exporter to an importer. A database agent performs a role that is similar to that of a business agent, working on behalf of the database server to synchronize operations. The server retains ultimate responsibility for the state of the application, but delegates coordination tasks to agents. The tasks that are best delegated to agents are those that might degrade server performance and those that extend beyond the server's normal sphere of control.

■ 8.1 SHOP FLOOR CONTROL FOR THE DATABASE FACTORY

Shop floor control, the coordination of production facilities to avoid waste, is a major challenge in industrial manufacturing. Production resources must be attuned to current demand to avoid overproduction. The time required to retool the production line, however, must be kept minimal to prevent production backlogs.

Information production in the Database Factory faces a challenge that resembles the problem of balancing responsiveness with efficiency in industrial manufacturing. The various client, server, and middleware components in an active application must align their behavior to the state of the entities and relationships in the database. In contrast to a passive database server, active application control emanates outward from the database server.

8.1.1 The Problem: Coordination and Control

In passive client/server computing, the server confines its activity to responding to client requests. This narrow role presents an architectural problem for a passive database application. The data is centralized in the database, but the processing logic is distributed to remote clients. Data-manipulation operations are controlled by the procedural logic of individual client programs (which is wrongly assumed to be meticulous) and coordinated by the database server.

Active database servers centralize both shared data and shared procedures within the database. Centralizing shared data-manipulation operations solves the architectural problem inherent in passive operations, but introduces a behavior coordination problem. Various components of the application, such as the user interface objects introduced in Figure 4.4, remain distributed on client machines. These interface objects act according to *scripts,* the small code modules governing their behavior.

In an active application, interface objects vary their behavior according to state changes in the application. However, script code size must remain small for the sake of code reuse and maintainability, which limits the range of their behavior. The application designer must narrow the behavior in individual scripts to the main responsibilities of a component. However, the designer can specialize the application's behavior with alternative scripts, which are appropriate to an exception states or special events.

Major transitions or uncommon events in an application may exceed a given script's repertoire of behavior. When a script is no longer appropriate to the current metastate of the database, it is exchanged for an alternative version that is appropriate to the new metastate.

Because behavior is controlled by the state of data and the state of data relationships, the database server is ultimately responsible for controlling application behavior. However, the direct exercise of control by the server is likely to have a negative performance impact. Even if the server had the capability to control behavior on a client machine (by RPCs to initiate script changes, for instance), frequently exerting control would take the server away from its primary data-management tasks and degrade its performance.

Like client components, middleware components must balance autonomous operation with responsiveness. Middleware performs diverse tasks that range from managing the client/server connection to controlling workflow routing.

As an example, workflow routing tables associate individuals and workgroups with the workflow operations for which they are responsible. In an active application, these routing tables must adjust themselves to shifts in workload and priority. Because middleware is more communications-oriented than database-oriented, the middleware tables usually are stored in system files used by the operating system and communications software. This means the middleware tables that extend the database application to workgroup servers are not directly accessible from the database server.

Similarly, remote database servers must be able to run their applications autonomously and securely. They cannot be slaves of a central database server. Nonetheless, remote servers must be able to coordinate their behavior in order to collaborate with an enterprise database server, as well as with one another.

Within the database server itself, coordination tasks must be balanced against the high priority of mission-critical transaction-processing tasks. For example, application control tables such as a Bill of Operations table must remain synchronized with the current overall state of database entities and relationships. Just as major state changes may call for an exchange of interface object scripts, a metastate change may cause database programs to enter or leave the activation path. Furthermore, the next operation in the Bill of Operations must be known prior to activation to prevent execution delays when the current operation transfers control. However, the server should not have to neglect mission-critical transaction-processing tasks to perform relatively low-priority administrative tasks.

Wherever application components reside, their coordination presents both a performance challenge and a control challenge. Remote components may be beyond the server's effective control. Even when the server has a means of controlling external components, exercising direct control might degrade performance. Delegating coordination tasks to database agents provides a means to meet the challenges of both performance and control.

8.1.2 The Solution: Database Agents

A database agent is a special-purpose utility program responsible for client/server component coordination. In a perfect world of standard interoperable software components, database vendors and other software houses would provide customizable agents, agent source code, and agent templates. Off-the-shelf products such as

Lotus Notes, Business Objects' BusinessObjects and OpenVision's Event Manager are among the initial software offerings that will lead to customizable agents. However, today's client/server developers cannot rely strictly on third-party products to coordinate active applications. Developers must devise their own coordination infrastructures, and must make choices regarding their integration strategies.

Client/server coordination may be achieved in a number of ways. As an alternative to agents, client software could have embedded intelligence to interrogate the state of server components and take appropriate action. However, this approach has the disadvantage of complexity. The client code would contain both transaction-processing SQL code and the complex conditional code needed to determine the state of the server-based components and to decide on appropriate action. Furthermore, sharing or reusing custom code that combines application logic with coordination logic is a difficult task. This sharing and reuse is facilitated when the coordination logic is isolated from the application logic. Database agents isolate, share, and simplify client/server coordination functions.

The database agents illustrated in Figure 8.1 are built from two subassemblies: an *agency* subassembly and an *agent* subassembly. The agent is encased within its agency, and is activated exclusively by messages sent to or forwarded by the agency. An agency is designed for a specific platform, meaning a machine and its operating software. The agency may reside on a client machine, on the database server machine, or on a middleware server.

Database agents are layered in the same general manner as client programs.

- The network interface comprises the lowest layer of the agency platform.
- The database API sits on top of the network interface.
- The agent, isolated within the agency in the top layer, performs coordination tasks.

■ 8.2 AGENT ADVANTAGES

Dividing functionality between the agent and the agency provides the main benefits of specialization and isolation. Agency components are specialized for a specific agency platform, while agent components focus on specific coordination tasks. The agency isolates its agent from platform-dependent implementation details.

Agents communicate with the external world exclusively through the agency. The agency relays messages (such as event alerts) to the agent. The agent's response is a message that is forwarded to an external component. Because the agent is isolated from platform dependencies, agent components are sharable

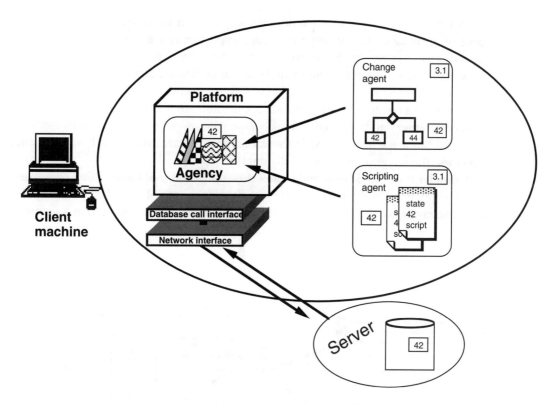

Figure 8.1 Agents and agency

among similar agents residing on different machines and on disparate communications networks. Isolation has the further benefit of reducing the time and effort to maintain agent software. Because an agency and its agent appear as a single unit to external components, the following sections refer to these two subassemblies somewhat interchangeably.

■ 8.3 ASSURING SAFE INTEGRATION

Not only are monolithic software environments inflexible, they are also relatively unreliable. Production errors in monolithic applications, the inevitable result of procedural programming, can corrupt corporate data in ways that are detected only after they bring down mission-critical applications. Prior to the final breakdown, programmatic data corruption grows rapidly as a by-product of transaction processing. However, corrections can only be applied and verified manually.

Whenever errors grow faster than corrections can be made, a company loses control of its data. This is why monolithic applications are unsafe. When companies downsize computer hardware to save operating costs, they sometimes overlook software downsizing. The result is an unreliable monolithic application running on a downsized platform. The savings from downsizing are limited, but unanticipated costs resulting from an unsafe application are unlimited.

Client/server database applications balance their workload among client, server, and middleware components. If these components are haphazardly connected, however, the integration is potentially unsafe.

Consider the electric plug and socket shown in the top of Figure 8.2. The socket has no apparent means by which we can determine its polarity. The positive and negative prongs of the plug are identical, so the plug could be inserted in a manner

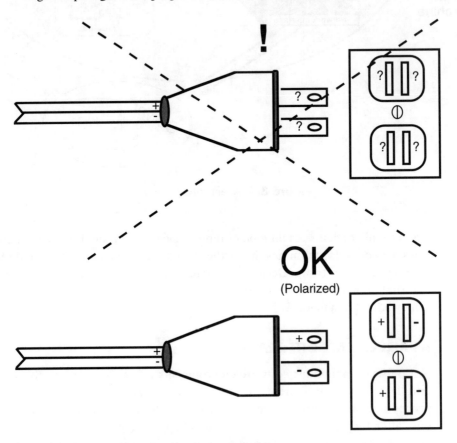

Figure 8.2 Unsafe and safe connections

that is both harmful to the appliance and dangerous for the operator. By contrast, the plug and socket shown in the bottom of Figure 8.2 are polarized, meaning the negative terminal cannot fit into the positive socket. When a polarized plug is inserted into a polarized socket, the operation of connecting the electric appliance is self-protecting.

Similarly, client/server operations are rendered self-protecting when all components are coordinated in compatible states. The specific tasks needed to achieve coordination are delegated to various database agent types.

■ 8.4 AGENT TYPES

The purpose of an agent is to simplify component coordination. Because the state of the data managed by the database server determines the state of the relationships in which the data participates, the server is the focal point for coordination. The state of these data relationships determines the permissible operations on the data. These operational conditions, in turn, determine the state of the components performing those operations.

The server is the point of origin for component coordination, which could create problems if the database server directly controlled the properties and behavior of every component. The server would have to be omniscient, aware of the location and condition of each external component. Also, the server would need to be omnipotent, capable of executing concurrent database and coordination operations with no significant loss of effectiveness. Omniscience and omnipotence are unrealistic expectations for any software product.

The goal of coordination is more easily reached through such basic client/server capabilities as *message dispatching*. Both client requests and server responses are communicated as messages. Most client/server database products include the additional capability of sending a message (or a command) to the operating system of the server machine. Active servers send event alert messages to their remote subscribers. The transmission and control of these messages and alerts is automated within the server's database programming and event-management infrastructure. Database agents are the key to this automation.

In a real-world factory, assembly line workers would not use hand tools to achieve high-volume production. Modern factories use automated lathes instead of hand lathes. When a different shape is needed, the lathe is reprogrammed with a new sequence of operations to produce the required shape. The new program is not manually keyed into the lathe, but instead a preassembled, pretested program is loaded into the lathe from a tape or cartridge.

The automated lathe is a programmable machine tool, or a machine that makes machines. An agency is software that modifies software. This is the Database Factory equivalent of a machine tool. The equivalent of the program that controls the operations of the machine tool is the agent. Just as a factory has a variety of machine tools, various agent types perform different specialized roles in coordinating client/server information production.

8.4.1 Change Agents

Change agents are responsible for activating and monitoring change activities, such as component exchanges. Exaggerated expectations of the database server's capabilities are unrealistic, it would be incorrect to expect omniscience from an agent coordinating component exchanges on behalf of the server. Transferring the change-management function from a multipurpose server to a single-purpose change agent is a good start, but further delegation is needed to distribute specific change-management functionality to the correct location on the Database Factory's assembly line.

Figure 8.3 shows how delegation simplifies the complex task of component exchange. At the bottom of Figure 8.3, a metastate transition occurs from state 44 to state 42, which has been detected by the server in the course of its normal transaction-processing operations. This state transition activates the server's event-management infrastructure. The new state requires a retooling of the activation path, including the exchange of client, server, and middleware components. Coordinating these exchanges is the responsibility of the change agent. However, as the figure illustrates, a change agent delegates platform-specific execution details to remote change agents, in order to keep its code small and manageable.

When the database server detects a major state transition, it activates the associated event alerter. The event alerter mechanism transmits an event alert that is received by the subscriber, which, in this example, is the main change agent.

The main change agent forwards the event alert to its platform-specific subordinates. A client change agent takes charge of coordinating client component changes. A middleware change agent handles middleware component exchange, and the server change agent is responsible for exchanging server-based components such as control tables.

Although the distributed change control in Figure 8.3 may appear complicated, it works rapidly and leverages client/server resources. The client and middleware change agents reside on the same local network as the components on which they operate. Likewise, the server change agent runs on the server machine. These change agents respond to terse messages, which they rapidly transform into the commands controlling the operations of other special-purpose agents.

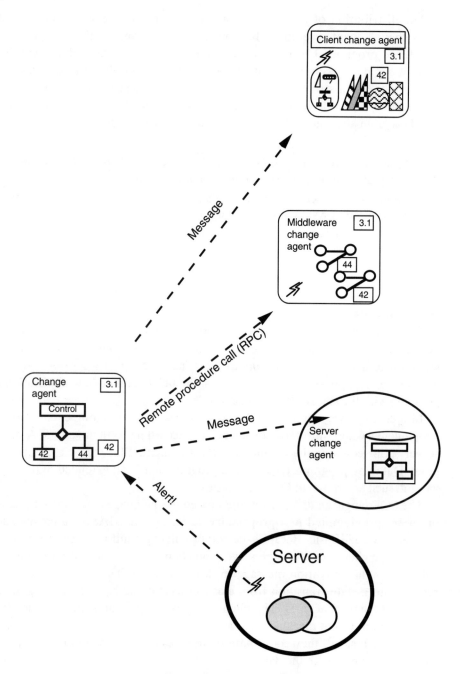

Figure 8.3 Change agent

The distribution of functionality among specialized agents working under a main change agent resembles the division of labor among the subroutines of a structured program. The routines at the top of the program's hierarchy have a wide, general scope and delegate detail work to subordinate routines. Like the main routine of a structured program, the main change agent delegates specific coordination details to its subordinate agents. Notable differences between a structured program and a group of agents include the following:

- Program routines are confined to a single executable program, but agents are distributed among several agencies on multiple platforms.
- Program code is custom-made, but agents leverage the network, database, and operating system infrastructure.
- Program routines are monolithic, but agents are separate programs integrated by message-passing for ease of disassembly or reassembly.

8.4.2 Scripting Agents

When a database state transition necessitates component exchanges, the change agents initiate these changes. However, the actual exchanges are coordinated by subordinate agents called *scripting agents*. The function of a scripting agent is to coordinate an application's scripts (that is, the behavioral code in application components) with the state of the application.

In a client/server application, behavior is distributed among client and server components. Client interface objects behave according to their scripts. A database server script contains the extended SQL statements that create a database program. Database programs typically are programmed in an extended SQL language variant, such as Transact SQL or PL/SQL.

The SQL language differs from the procedural languages of client scripts, which often are programmed in a proprietary variant of the BASIC language such as Microsoft Visual Basic. Because the server language and architecture differ from those of the client platform, the server and client scripting agents shown in Figure 8.4 process the activation message in different ways. The client scripting agent responds to a state transition from state 44 to state 42 by broadcasting an event alert to all client machines. The client then exchanges the state 42 script for the state 44 script. Client machines that are not connected at the time of the event are not alerted. Instead, they coordinate themselves with the state of the application when they connect with the database.

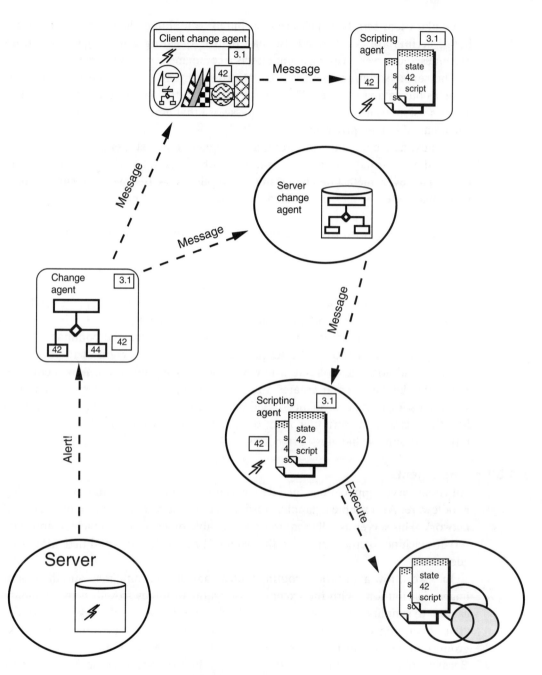

Figure 8.4 Scripting agent

Unlike client scripts, which are distributed to multiple client machines, server-based scripts are centralized. Instead of broadcasting a message to multiple machines, the server scripting agent directs a command script to the database server.

The server scripting agent is a client program that executes on the same machine as the database server. The agent connects to the database server in an interactive session, using a "logon ID" and password that grants it the authority to drop and create database programs.

Because active database programs are designed to adjust themselves to the state of the data, normal operations do not require constant revision by a scripting agent. However, metastate changes in the application—the overall result of many individual state changes in the data—sometimes create a need to exchange database programs.

As discussed previously, a change agent responding to an event alert triggered by a metastate change activates specialized agents, such as the scripting agent. When activated by a message, the scripting agent retrieves from the Bill of Operations table the names of the database programs affected by the change. For each database program affected, the scripting agent sends the server a batch file known as a script, which contains change control commands.

The database server processes this script file as though the commands were being typed in by a DBA. The script drops the existing version of the database program and goes on to create a new version appropriate to the new metastate. When the database server creates a new database program, it optimizes the SQL statements for best performance based on current conditions in the physical database. This is why the scripting agent drops and re-creates the database procedure, rather than simply changing parameters.

8.4.3 Routing Agents

All client/server applications include a certain amount of communications-routing middleware. As a simple example, consider a client/server application on a TCP/IP network. This server usually requires a hosts table on each client machine and each server machine to cross-reference the names of network nodes and their IP device addresses.

In a workflow application, routing tables control electronic mail and document image distribution. With the exception of synonym tables stored in the database catalog to simplify references to remote tables, middleware tables take the form of "flat" operating system files. A complex environment with electronic mail, workgroup databases, and remote servers is likely to have many middleware tables. Because middleware tables are external to the database server, synchronizing their entries to database server events presents a problem.

Figure 8.5 illustrates the use of a *routing agent* to synchronize middleware tables. In this example, various middleware tables have been converted to database format and are stored in one central location, a passive database on a middleware server.

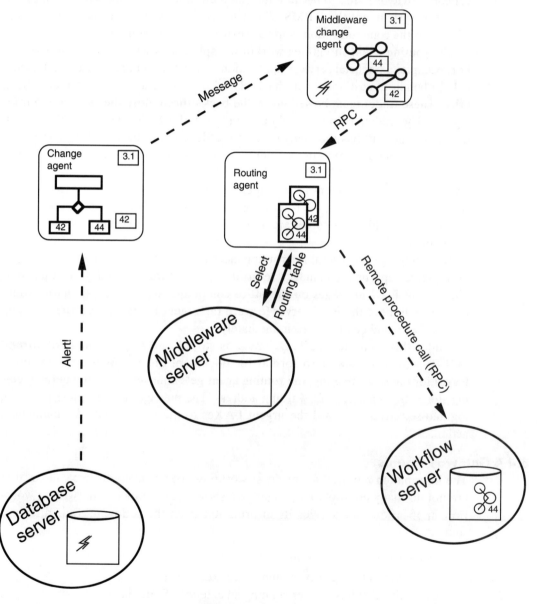

Figure 8.5 Routing agent

The database is useful for storing and updating a central copy of each of the middleware tables. The routing agent executes on the middleware server machine, updating the middleware database and converting data as needed to flat files. This conversion activity is required because the communications software is managed by the operating system, not the DBMS. The database is convenient for updating routing tables, but the communications software expects to work with flat files.

The routing agent integrates workflow applications with the database server. For example, a financial services application places trades in response to a buy signal, on behalf of customers who have placed orders for a certain stock at a given price. These trades must be settled by the back office before the close of the trading day. The trading volume is volatile, but the staff level is relatively stable. When the brokerage staff has too many trades to settle, cross-trained staff from the institutional trading and trust departments handle the overflow. The routing agent updates the routing tables to distribute trade settlements as needed to level the workflow. When settlement traffic tapers off, the workflow goes back to a normal state. When this happens, the routing agent receives a message to revert to normal routing. The middleware tables are updated, converted to flat files, and distributed to remote machines.

A routing agent is useful for routing electronic paperwork to mobile staff. For example, a department manager returning from a three-day sales meeting finds nine urgent FAX messages on the office computer. A preferable scenario would have been to have the FAX server forward the urgent FAXes to the sales meeting so that they could be processed immediately.

Under this scenario, the FAX image is stored in a *tagged image file format* (TIFF), which is a standard format for document images. When the manager leaves for the sales meeting, the routing agent gets a message specifying the meeting site as the manager's forwarding address. The manager can examine the FAX log and selectively forward the urgent FAXes to the meeting site for immediate action.

8.4.4 Gateway Agents

The information required for business workflows comes from diverse sources that are not normally interoperable. Figure 8.6 shows an insurance underwriting workflow application that derives its information from the following four different sources:

- A departmental file server
- A passive database server running a SQL dialect
- An active database server running an extended SQL dialect
- A mainframe at a rating service running a legacy database under CICS.

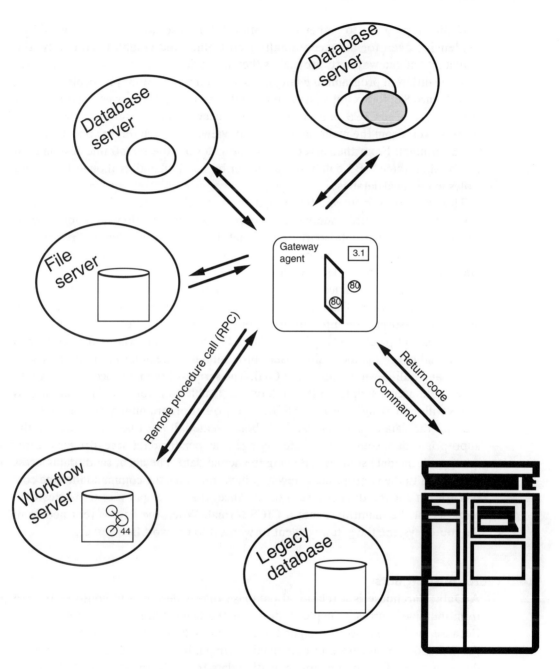

Figure 8.6 Gateway agent

Coding a program to gather information from these diverse sources would be challenging even for an exceptionally well-trained individual. Fortunately, the availability of gateway software makes the task easier. *Gateway software* translates between different programming languages and communications protocols.

In Figure 8.6, for example, a database gateway translates between two different SQL dialects. The CICS gateway makes the legacy database interoperable with the active server. From the mainframe's point of view, the active server appears to be a CICS terminal. From the server side of the gateway, the mainframe responds to RPCs. Mainframe DB2 database tables can be manipulated as though they were tables in the local database.

This example uses three different gateways, which highlights the need for coordination. The insurance underwriter who processes the workflow does not know in advance from which data source additional data may be needed and, therefore, which gateway(s) will be employed. In fact, the underwriter does not need to know the details of the remote data sources.

The *gateway agent* hides the complexity of the communications environment from the underwriter. The underwriting workflow application maintains database tables that associate required information with its source. For each data item, a data access script obtains additional data. The underwriter varies the script in a "point-and-click" manner using visual programming, meaning the buttons, check boxes, and pull-down menus of the GUI. The scripts of the interface objects modify the data-access scripts, so the underwriter is able to meet changing data-access needs without having to learn the SQL or any other programming language.

Once the data-access command has been created, it must be transmitted to the appropriate data source. The gateway agent associates data-access request categories with the data sources supplying the actual data. The agent sends data-access commands to the appropriate gateway, which translates the command into the correct format for the data source. For instance, the CICS gateway translates data requests for the mainframe into a CICS format. When the data is returned from the source system, the gateway agent forwards it to the workflow server.

8.4.5 Warehouse Agents

A Data Warehouse is a relational database that is designed to consolidate data from multiple sources. (Chapter 9 discusses the Data Warehouse in more detail.) Because the Warehouse is designed to facilitate data access, manipulating data in the Warehouse is much easier than manipulating it in the source systems where the data originates. By the same token, getting data from the source to the Warehouse can be challenging. Many legacy applications organize their data in flat files, permitting duplicate records that are not allowed in the Warehouse database because duplicate rows would violate data integrity.

Relational data sources present a different challenge. Relational source data in transaction-processing applications is normalized for storage economy and processing convenience. For rapid data transfers and for ease of access, data tables in the Data Warehouse have minimal normalization. Intermediate data transformations are necessary between normalized data sources and the Warehouse.

During extraction and Warehouse load operations, data undergoes transformation and repackaging. Each operation is a potential point of failure, usually because of some inconsistency in the data. Taking erroneous data off-line as soon as possible makes sense, just as removing defective work-in-process from a manufacturing assembly line at the earliest possible time to avoid waste also makes sense. Making Warehouse load operations consistent with the data to prevent failures makes even more sense. In manufacturing, mistake proofing is a term used to describe this approach.

A *Warehouse agent* applies mistake proofing to Data Warehouse extract operations. As shown in Figure 8.7, the external data-distribution infrastructure of a Data Warehouse is as diverse as the production applications that it integrates.

In this example, the Warehouse integrates legacy data from a mainframe, shared files from a LAN file server, and data from a passive database server. If the Data Warehouse had to pull in data from these disparate sources under central Warehouse control, the Warehouse procedures would become complex. As is the case when any database server is expected to control the external environment, errors would be likely.

Instead, the Warehouse server controls the operations of the Warehouse agent. The agent performs data-extract tasks, and confirms the results by making consignment entries in the Warehouse schedule. The operations of the Warehouse agent, such as *extract* or *upload*, are controlled by the Schedule of Operations, which is a control table in the Warehouse database. The results of each operation, including the time and the result state, are registered in the schedule by the agent.

This is when mistake proofing kicks in. When the agent registers results, a database trigger on the Schedule of Operations propagates an update to another control table in the Warehouse database. Unless the agent registers a result state of *consigned*, downstream operations will not be attempted. Furthermore, the Schedule of Operations is modified to spare the agent wasted effort.

For example, imagine that the Warehouse combines purchasing data from the passive database server with inventory data from the mainframe. If the purchasing

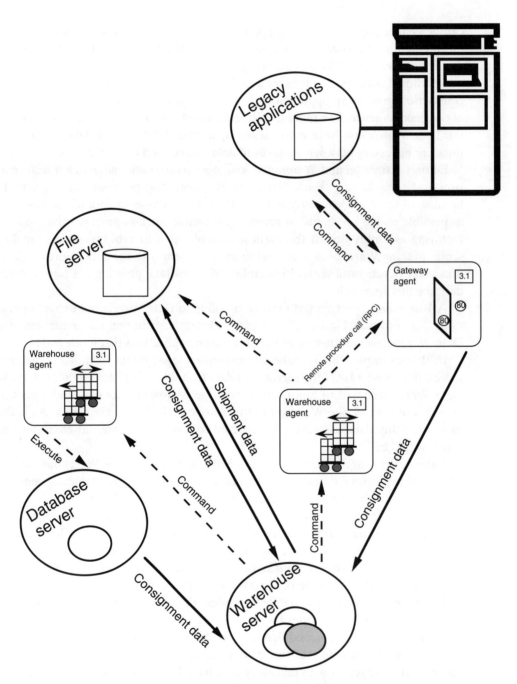

Figure 8.7 Warehouse agent

data is unavailable, mainframe and communications resources would be wasted if the agent requested the inventory data extract. When the purchasing data *upload* operation fails to produce a consignment, mistake proofing prevents the mainframe data extract from taking place in vain.

The Warehouse agent in this example does not attempt to directly control the extract and consignment of mainframe data to the Warehouse. Just as the Warehouse server delegates consignment tasks to the Warehouse agent to bring its workload within scope, the Warehouse agent delegates open systems data-distribution tasks to a gateway agent—much as any other active application would.

In the case of server-to-server data consignments, the agent acts as a client of the source database server. The goal of the agent's operations on the source server is to place data into *shipping pallet* data tables that are identical in format to the *receiving pallet* data tables in the Warehouse database. The use of identical structures is part of the mistake-proofing approach. If the load to the *shipping pallet* table in the source database is successful, the data transfer to the identical structure in the Warehouse database using the same command probably will also succeed.

■ 8.5 AGENT MANAGEMENT

The agents that extend the range of the server to distributed application components are themselves distributed to the client, server, and middleware platforms where they do their work. Just as changing conditions require retooling of the components on which an agent operates, the agents themselves must evolve with the application.

All components should be thoroughly tested before use. Central versions and quality metrics are required for effective component asset management. These considerations apply to all components, but are especially important for agents because they are part of the control infrastructure. Agent maintenance work must take place in a central, secure environment, such as in the Development Warehouse.

Figure 8.8 illustrates the use of the Development Warehouse agent area for agent maintenance. The various types of agents represented on the right reside and execute in different parts of the client/server environment. The agents are tested in the areas where they execute. However, the standard versions of all agents and the standard versions of the test data and any test scripts are stored centrally in the Development Warehouse agent area.

The agent-related metadata shown in the top portion of the illustration also is stored in the Development Warehouse. An agent's metadata includes quality management metrics such as the number of failures and mean time between failures,

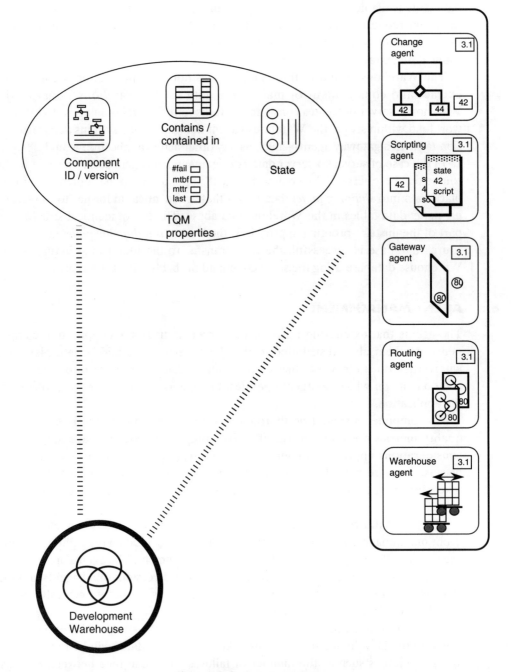

Figure 8.8 Agent maintenance

the agent version, its Bill of Materials, and its current state (that is, *active*, *suspended*, or *under development*).

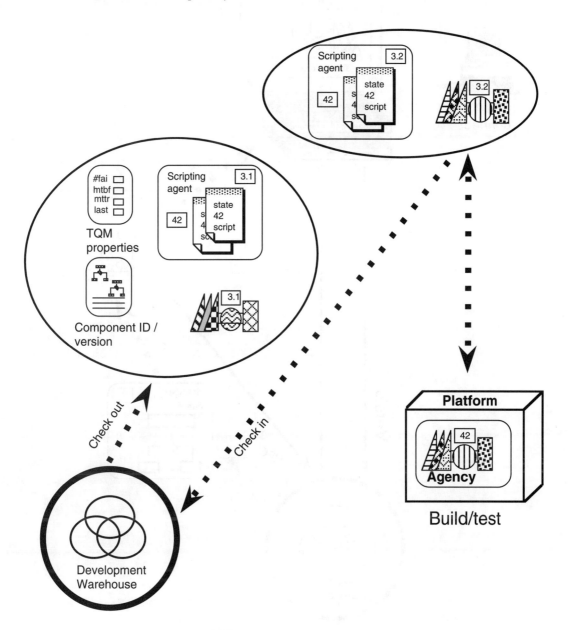

Figure 8.9 Agent versions

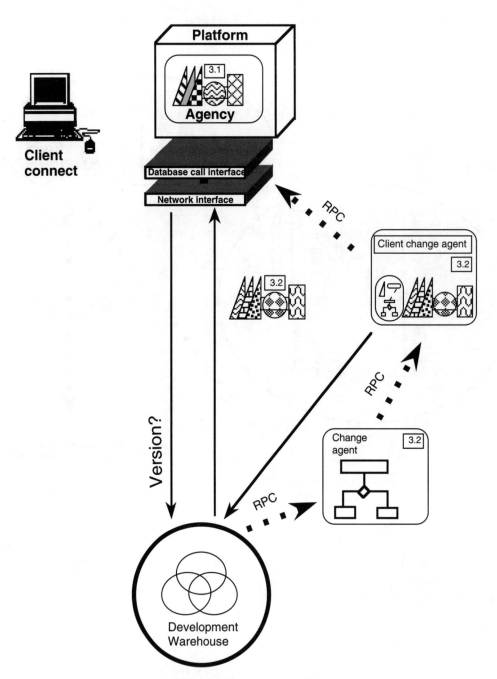

Figure 8.10 Agent distribution

Because agents are the part of the control infrastructure that coordinates other components, access to agent source code must be restricted in order to prevent widespread accidental damage. One common-sense security precaution is to store agents in a different area of the Development Warehouse than that used for general-application components. Except for those developers who are responsible for maintaining the control infrastructure, the development staff should not be able to access the agent source code. Since this staff has no need to deal with the agent code, the agent area should be off-limits to most developers.

Within the agent area, access requirements for agent code differ from those for agency code. As discussed previously, the agent code is function-specific, while the agency code is platform-specific. A software developer working on a UNIX Data Warehouse agency code may be a different individual than a Data Warehouse administrator responsible for maintaining a Warehouse agent. The control tables used by the agent might be assigned to a third individual. Clearly, all three team members must coordinate their efforts and work together. However, because the components that each developer needs to modify are in different categories, the access privileges appropriate for the team members working on these components are different.

Figure 8.9 shows agent version control for a scripting agent. As shown, the current version of the agent source code and metadata is checked out of the Development Warehouse. After the agent and its documentation are modified, the agent is tested on the agency platform(s) where it will execute. Next, the new agent version goes through the check-in process. During check-in, the version number is incremented and the quality management metadata entries are reset. The former metadata and documentation are archived, and form part of the audit trail.

The check-in process triggers the distribution of the new version to the appropriate agencies. As shown in Figure 8.10, an alert is sent to the change agent to complete the change-control process. Because the version of an agent must match the version of the components on which it operates, agent version control is important for keeping the client/server environment synchronized. Mistake-proofing ensures that the change control is effective.

When the agent in Figure 8.10 is activated, it sends a query to the Development Warehouse to retrieve its correct version number. If the version numbers do not match (for example, because the agency platform was off-line when the new version was initially distributed), the agent "raises" an event. The change agent has an event handler for this event, which re-applies change control on the specific agent platform.

9

THE DATA WAREHOUSE

A Data Warehouse is a consolidated database that is designed to facilitate data access from multiple data sources, including both current technology applications and legacy applications. Many of the information systems in production today are legacy applications, which means they use programmatic data access to produce private data, not shared information. Reprogramming legacy applications for shared data access is expensive and risky. The alternatives to reprogramming legacy applications include supplementing them with a 4GL application generator, a workgroup database, or workflow software. None of these offers a complete solution, but all of them may be integrated with relational database software to build a shared Data Warehouse. A generic Data Warehouse design includes data tables, control tables, and state transition tasks. Warehouse data loading can use a "push" system, a "pull" system, or a hybrid "push-pull" system. Distributed warehouse applications, a high performance solution for multisite companies, make use of RDBMS data-replication technology.

■ 9.1 THE CHALLENGE OF LEGACY APPLICATIONS

Information is a perishable commodity that is valuable only while it remains useful. Information must be in the right place at the right time in the right form to be used for commercial advantage. Otherwise, information reverts to ordinary data.

Most commercial applications in production today produce low-value data, and not information. This data is produced as a by-product of automating departmental operations. To derive information from departmental data, the following three operations must take place:

1. The categories of useful data are projected from the mass of data.
2. Specific data of interest is selected on a basis of key data values.
3. The results are joined together to form a coherent whole.

In conventional software development, these operations are performed by separate procedural routines within application programs. Existing commercial applications often are characterized by private data organization and exclusive programmatic data access—the hallmarks of "handcrafted" information systems. Because such applications are a legacy of older software development technologies, they are often called legacy applications. For consistency, that term is used in this discussion.

Many legacy applications were written years ago for implementation on mainframe computers. However, neither the vintage of the program nor the hardware platform on which it executes define it as a legacy application. The defining characteristics of a legacy application are its private data organization and its programmatic data interface. A mature application that has been downsized from a mainframe to a PC without re-engineering for shared data access remains a legacy application. Even today, new legacy applications continue to be built on PCs and on UNIX platforms.

Legacy applications include both proprietary packages and custom programs written in such languages as COBOL, C, or BASIC. A company can find itself with a mismatched collection of legacy applications programmed in different languages and implemented on diverse hardware platforms (see Figure 9.1). Often, the only common characteristic of a company's legacy applications is the lack of interoperability—the inability of the applications to "talk" to one another.

9.1.1 Legacy Packages

Application packages, preprogrammed applications that are proprietary to a third-party vendor, often use private file-organization methods and programmatic access. Such packages clearly fall into the legacy category. Like all legacy applications, they present an impediment to information sharing.

To keep their proprietary application logic secret, many vendors sell their packages without the source code. Lacking the source code, customers cannot modify the package. Some package vendors make their source code available, but are

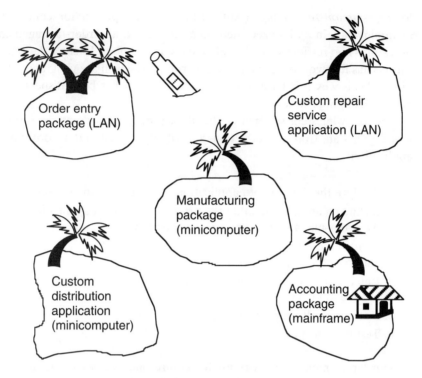

Figure 9.1 Islands of information

unwilling to support the package after the source code has been modified. With or without source code, re-engineering legacy packages for shared data access is very difficult for anyone other than the package's vendor.

9.1.2 Interfacing Legacy Applications

Unlike relational database applications, legacy applications never were designed to exchange information. Without a central access directory, it is often difficult to even know where the data resides. Once the data location is ascertained, it is hard to gain access. The data may be dispersed to remote sites. Rigid all-or-nothing security often impedes access. Once access obstacles are overcome, slow access speed may present problems. Many legacy transaction-processing applications were designed to provide fast response for short transactions such as account balance updates. Such applications may provide unacceptably slow performance for concurrent, large-volume data access during normal business hours.

Each legacy application has its own private data-storage organization. For example, a procurement application stores its data in sequential *American Standard Code for Information Interchange* (ASCII) files, while a production-control application maintains data in an indexed file organization, and an order-management application stores and retrieves data by relative record number. Each of these legacy applications has its own storage and retrieval routines, which are programmatic by definition. This is why it is hard to join legacy data that has been dispersed among disparate legacy applications.

The following steps summarize the tasks a programmer must perform in order to join legacy data from a production-control application and an order-management application:

1. Analyze the data in both applications to assure it can be integrated.
2. Define an interface file that the production-control application can write and the order-management application can read.
3. Change the source code of two or more programs, possibly using two different programming languages.
4. Enhance the order-management application's file descriptions to include the production-control data.
5. Recompile all programs using the interface.
6. Test the interface.

This labor-intensive activity might require one full day to create a single point of interface. If the legacy data is not well-behaved, extra time may be needed to fix corrupt data or to decode overloaded fields. Even orderly legacy data often needs sorting, filtering, and reformatting if it is to make sense. In a real-world integration effort, reprogramming applications to build interfaces and clean up legacy data may take longer than the project schedule allows.

9.1.3 Interfacing Relational Applications

All SQL-based relational database applications fall outside the legacy category—even embedded SQL applications. Relational applications have a common, tabular data organization and nonprocedural data-access capability. When granted access by the DBA, any user can share RDBMS data by using interactive SQL. Data from one relational application is shareable with other relational applications, which is in contrast to legacy applications. Data from different RDBMS servers (such as Ingres, Oracle, and Sybase) can be integrated through database gateways that translate SQL dialects, or by means of multiple-driver clients.

In contrast to the time and effort required to interface legacy applications, a programmer might spend less than one hour using SQL to join two client/server relational database applications.

The three operations required to derive information from data (projection, selection, and joining) are built into the relational model. As illustrated in Figure 9.2, all three operations can be performed in a single SQL statement. Projection picks columns from a table, such as part number, serial number, and reason. The projected columns become members of the result set. Selection picks rows from the table on the basis of their data values. In this example, CLAIM and REPAIR rows have been selected. The join operation puts together data from various tables based on their data values. In this example, the Shipments and Returns tables are joined on the basis of equal values in the serial number column.

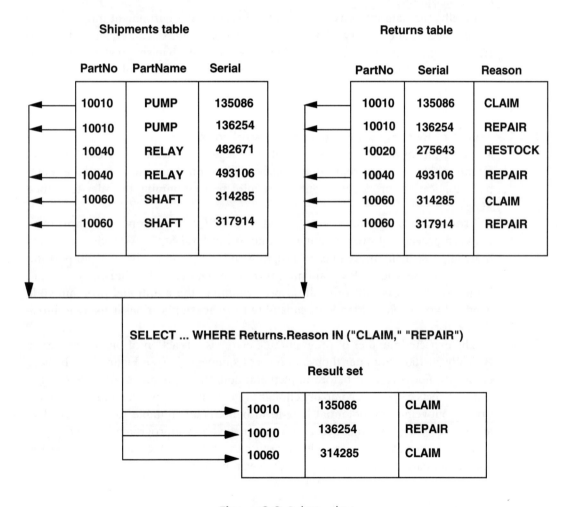

Figure 9.2 Relational join

In relational database environments, nonprocedural set-oriented operations derive information from data. This is why RDBMS software provides a means of integrating disparate data that is simpler than procedural programming. However, relational applications do not automatically lend themselves to data integration. Relational applications that were designed for rapid data capture may not facilitate fast data access.

Relational design methodologies encourage normalization, the decomposition of complex tables into simple ones to avoid data redundancy and repeating groups. For coherent data access, data from multiple tables must be joined to achieve denormalization.

Finally, the data-integrity barriers of the relational environment might need to be disabled to allow entry of noncompliant legacy data. Because legacy data and RDBMS data exist in separate environments, some mechanism must transfer legacy data into the relational environment without harming the nonlegacy data maintained in relational systems of record.

9.1.4 The Risks of Reprogramming Legacy Applications

The only means of data access available to a legacy application is procedural programming. In order to reprogram legacy application data into a relational database application, procedural routines require reprogramming in order to embed SQL code.

Procedural programming with embedded SQL represents a compromise between procedural programming and nonprocedural SQL. As such, embedded SQL requires many more lines of program code than interactive SQL to perform equivalent operations. Programming this additional code is labor-intensive and prone to error. Like all procedural programming, the additional program code needed to bring embedded SQL capability to legacy applications is likely to introduce errors.

The expected number of programming errors is a function of the lines of code, typically 50-100 errors per thousand lines of source code (see Figure 9.3). If these errors are not corrected before implementation, they remain as software defects. These defects can cost a company enough short-term lost revenue and lost production to outweigh any potential long-term benefits attributable to improved data access. In view of the time, cost, and risk involved in reprogramming legacy programs, it is worthwhile to consider alternatives such as 4GLs, workgroup software, and consolidation databases (such as data warehouses).

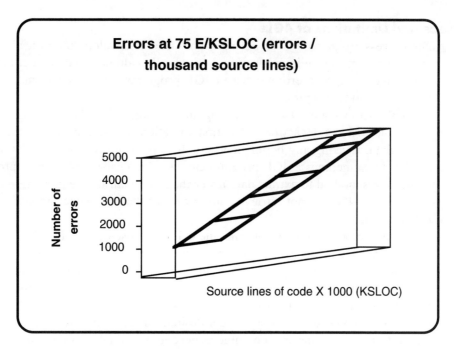

Figure 9.3 More code means more errors

9.1.5 The Standalone 4GL Alternative

The 4GL alternative bypasses legacy programs to extract data directly from their files. No defining 4GL standard is comparable to the SQL standard. However, many 4GL products have the same characteristics as SQL, including

- Nonprocedural (that is, behavior specified by results, not processing details)
- Generative (that is, enhanced through regenerating, not reprogramming)
- Integrated (that is, integrated user interface, data access, and reporting).

These characteristics help minimize the expense of developing 4GL applications.

The 4GL products are nonprocedural and have a more concise syntax than procedural languages. Like SQL, a single 4GL statement can perform a complete application function. Because fewer lines of code are required to perform application functions, fewer errors are expected per function. Line-by-line testing proceeds rapidly because each statement produces complete function results. Because 4GL errors are easier to detect and simpler to fix than procedural programming errors, they are less likely to remain as post-production defects.

9.1.6 Uses and Limitations of 4GLs

Data-access programs in 4GL normally are faster to develop than procedural language programs. Once in production, however, they do not hold any performance advantage. In fact, interpreter-based 4GL programs often execute more slowly than compiled legacy programs.

As shown in Figure 9.4, a 4GL program performs a number of programmatic operations to access legacy data. The first operation is to search a file to extract the target data. Lacking any better means, a 4GL program searches legacy files sequentially. Sometimes a 4GL program can use the legacy application's programmatic access method to extract data faster than by exhaustive sequential search. In any case, the 4GL cannot retrieve data any faster than the legacy application that owns the data.

While searching a legacy data file, the 4GL uses a selection procedure to select data for extraction. Since 4GLs are proprietary, each 4GL product has its own nonstandard syntax to perform the selection. In general, the syntax is similar to the WHERE clause in SQL. As records are selected during the search, the selected records are reformatted and written to an extract file. The extract file is then sorted one or more times to put it in the order desired for reporting. After sorting, subtotals and summary totals are computed as needed. In a final operation, the completed report file is directed to a printer, or retained on disk for future reference.

Multiple 4GL report programs provide an alternative to reporting from a relational database, but one that is resource-intensive and imposes operational limits. Each 4GL program creates its own extract file of selected legacy data. The disk capacity may not be sufficient to store the redundant data. The hardware may be too slow to perform all of the daily 4GL reports within a 24-hour day, forcing a dif-

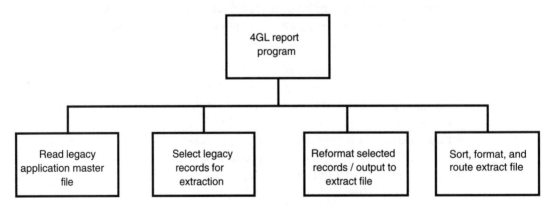

Figure 9.4 4GL legacy data processing

ficult choice between expensive upgrades and data gridlock. If legacy applications are allowed to continue processing at the same time as the 4GL extraction (a requirement for round-the-clock operations), different 4GL reports will be based on inconsistent sets of "moving target" legacy data.

4GLs do not provide the performance, optimization, or concurrency features of client/server database products, so they offer only a partial solution to legacy data reporting problems. Nonetheless, 4GL programs offer a viable alternative to reprogramming legacy applications to meet changing data-access needs. They are particularly useful for extracting predefined legacy data for transfer into a relational database.

9.1.7 The Workgroup Software Alternative

Workgroup applications, small multiuser applications implemented on departmental PC LANs, represent a downsized alternative to mainframe legacy applications. A workgroup application uses inexpensive PC software to meet the needs of a department or a workgroup.

Because their data cannot be shared outside the workgroup, standalone workgroup applications are legacy applications. To overcome this limitation, communications links connect workgroup applications with central corporate applications.

Data retrieval from a corporate data center to a workgroup application is known as a *download*. Downloads make it possible for workgroup applications to supplement legacy applications by working off the same base data. The workgroup PC software provides a rapid development environment. Workgroup file servers offer cheaper mass storage than proprietary mainframe or minicomputer disks, so departmental reports can be run in parallel with central reports from the legacy application.

Downloads are sequential file-transfer operations. With downloads, data traffic jams arise when one download has to wait for another. Even if the target data is at the beginning of the file, the whole file must be transferred. File transfer is therefore slower and more cumbersome than message-based strategies such as client/server integration.

9.1.8 Workflow Integration

In recent years, versatile communications technologies such as internetwork bridges and routers have become increasingly advantageous. These technologies interconnect LANs and *wide area networks* (WANs), enabling workgroup database products to take on a new role in workflow applications including electronic mail/notes, document images, and voicemail. Workgroup database products, upgraded versions of single-user desktop database products, act as servers of workgroup clients.

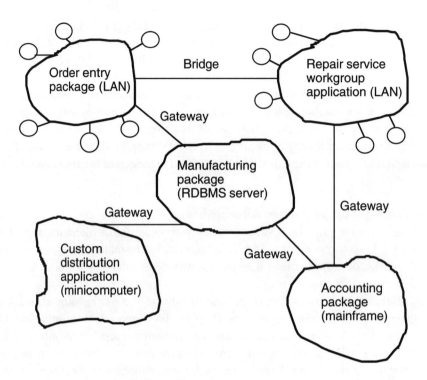

Figure 9.5 Workflow integration

Through the use of SQL connectivity middleware, workgroup applications can act as clients of other servers.

In the *workflow integration* illustrated in Figure 9.5, multiple clients share access to a workgroup database. This integration includes a gateway to interface the workgroup database with legacy applications on a mainframe. The gateway program impersonates a mainframe terminal, translating commands from the workgroup application into mainframe syntax.

Because it is message-based, workflow integration offers more flexibility than file transfers. Incorporating a scheduler and routing tables adds the capability to automate the workflow. However, workflow integration falls short of a complete solution to the problems of legacy data integration. The user interface cannot provide better information and, therefore, the functionality of the mainframe legacy application is not truly improved.

Even though legacy application programs need not be reprogrammed for a workflow integration to work, the workgroup application and its gateway do require programming. The workgroup application must be programmed to make the appropriate calls to the legacy application at the proper point in processing. The gateway software must be programmed in the screen and transaction formats of the legacy application.

Given the complexity of workflow integration and the difficulty of programming the connectivity, workgroup applications and mainframe applications tend to remain disjointed islands of information. As long as corporate data and workgroup data remain disjointed, problems such as inconsistent, redundant, and contradictory data will stand in the way of informed decision-making.

Taken in isolation, workflow integration falls short of a complete solution to the problem of consolidating and reporting legacy application data. However, the prospects improve when the workflow application connects with a database server. When 4GLs, gateways, and workgroup databases all are clients of a relational database server, the RDBMS becomes a data consolidation resource. The Data Warehouse is a popular term used to describe this means of achieving cost-effective legacy data integration.

9.1.9 Purpose of the Data Warehouse

A Data Warehouse is a relational database application for data sharing and data distribution. A principal goal of a Data Warehouse is to consolidate legacy data, thus integrating applications that might otherwise be incapable of shared data access. If the Warehouse can meet the stringent access requirements of legacy applications, integrating client/server applications should be comparatively easy.

In a metaphor based on industrial manufacturing and distribution, all information systems can be classified as either Factory applications or Warehouse applications. *Factory applications*, the systems of record for the enterprise, produce data. By comparison, *Warehouse applications* store, repackage, and distribute data to meet the needs of information consumers. Because a company's Factory applications are its central systems of record, a Data Warehouse cannot be allowed to update Factory data. Combining and repackaging the data are legitimate Warehouse activities, but updates are disallowed.

As shown in Figure 9.6, the Data Warehouse distributes data to information consumers in several forms: database download files, database reports, and SQL query results.

Factory applications fall into various categories, including

- "Old plant" custom legacy applications
- Legacy packages with no source code
- Workgroup subject-area applications

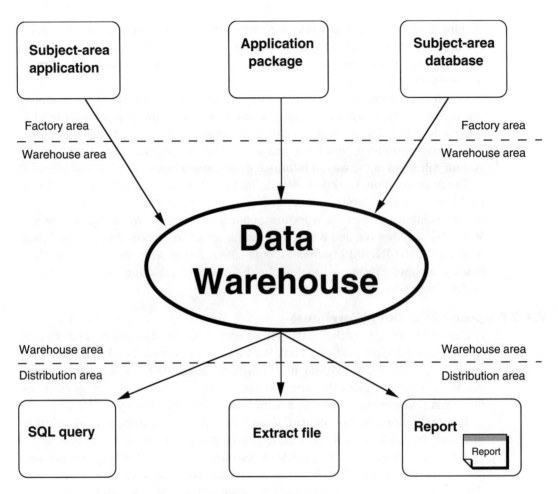

Figure 9.6 Data Warehouse areas

- Remote applications (EDI and time-sharing services).

Whatever the category of a Factory application, selected data can be consigned to the Data Warehouse on a regular, automated basis. In turn, any RDBMS software used to build a Warehouse application can receive data consignments in the form of flat ASCII files extracted from the various Factory applications.

In order to promote in-depth understanding of the Warehouse concept, the following section presents a generic Data Warehouse design. This generic specification is suitable for implementation with most RDBMS software, such as Oracle, Sybase, or Informix. Generic designs such as the one presented here are useful for comparing the data-access features of competing RDBMS products as part of the software selection process.

■ 9.2   A GENERIC DATA WAREHOUSE DESIGN

The generic Warehouse database includes control tables and data tables, the two types of tables found in active database implementations. The Data Warehouse control tables contain the metadata needed to control Warehouse operations. The Warehouse ER diagram shown in Figure 9.7 represents the control tables. It shows the control table attributes and depicts the relationships that allow the control tables to work together. Because data tables hold variable, application-dependent data and not metadata, they are not included in Figure 9.7.

The Warehouse data tables fall into two functional categories: long-term storage and short-term storage. The tables designed for long-term data storage are called *Warehouse bins*. These bins are organized in categories of data called *subject areas of information*. The name of a bin table is formed by the standard bin prefix (*dw_b_*) followed by a subject-area identifier. The *dw_bin* control table contains a row describing each bin. This entry is used as a logical pointer to the actual data table. The names of the procedures used to load and unload bins are stored in the *dw_bin_method* table. Bin tables are indexed for rapid data retrieval, and use the full range of data types supported by the RDBMS.

The data tables that provide temporary storage for consignment and shipment files are called *Warehouse pallets*. Pallets hold data for only one period, and are recycled after use. The two types of pallets are receiving pallets and shipping pallets. These are used for temporary storage of inbound (receiving) and outbound (shipping) data. To simplify load and unload operations, pallet tables use only the character datatype. Receiving pallet tables have the same length and form as their corresponding extract file records, while shipment pallets correspond to character-format outputs such as report detail lines.

Pallet table names are prefixed *dw_p_*, followed by the full subject-area identifier. The full identifier is made up of the subject-area identifier of the bin with which the pallet is associated suffixed by a code identifying the pallet's subarea. This identifier is further qualified by the move direction ("i" for inbound or "o" for outbound) to distinguish receiving pallets from shipping pallets in the same subject area.

Each pallet has a row in the control table *dw_pallet*. Just as *dw_bin* maintains logical pointers to the actual bin tables in the Warehouse, *dw_pallet* maintains logical pointers to the Warehouse pallet tables. For pull method consignment loading, where loading is actively controlled by the Warehouse, the *dw_io_method* table

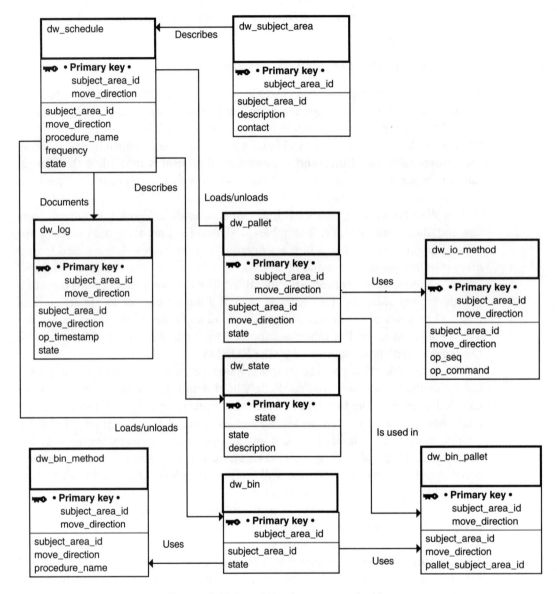

Figure 9.7 Data Warehouse control tables

stores the RDBMS command used to load the pallet (or the name of a load procedure that can be invoked to perform the function).

A bin may be fed by several receiving pallets, and a shipping pallet may be filled from several bins. For example, an *orders* bin is replenished daily from the *sales orders*, *blanket orders,* and *service orders* pallets. The *dw_bin_pallet* table cross-references bins to pallets.

The Warehouse Schedule (*dw_schedule*) drives data-transfer operations. The Warehouse Schedule is organized by subject area, and stores the result state of operations.

9.2.1 Warehouse State Transitions

On the route from a Factory application to the Warehouse, and from the Warehouse to the information consumer, data-transfer operations undergo a series of state transitions. These are shown in the Warehouse state transition diagram in Figure 9.8.

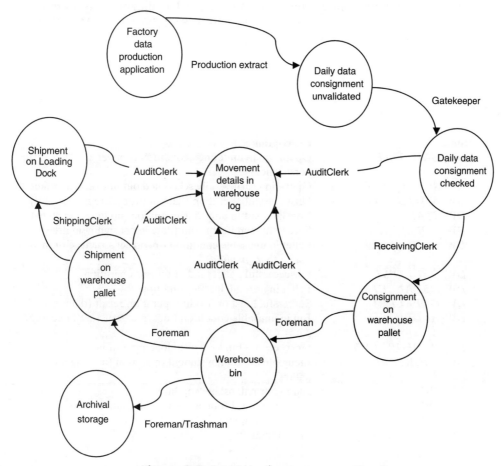

Figure 9.8 Data Warehouse state transitions

The first state transition results in a data-extract file, known as a *consignment* in this generic Warehouse design. Once a consignment is inspected and received, it is loaded onto a Warehouse pallet. State transitions occur in conjunction with the following data movements:

- From a Factory application to a consignment file
- From a consignment to an inbound pallet
- From an inbound pallet to a bin
- From a bin to an outbound pallet
- From an outbound pallet to a shipment.

The Warehouse state table (*dw_state* in the ER diagram) lists the possible states. The result of the SQL query SELECT *STATE_ID*, *NAME*, *DESCRIPTION* FROM *DW_STATE* is shown in Table 9.1.

Table 9.1 Warehouse States

	State	Description
0	DW_UNDEFINED	Operation in undefined condition (not yet available or lost persistence)
2	DW_SCHEDULED	Operation successfully scheduled but not yet performed
4	DW_NOTFOUND	Unsuccessful operation (data or procedure not located)
6	DW_STALE	Consignment in unusable condition (no longer current)
10	DW_CONSIGNED	Successful manifest result (data in consignment area)
12	DW_BADPALLET	Pallet in unusable condition (incorrect structure or incorrect match to *io_method*)
14	DW_BADHOIST	Unsuccessful pallet load or unload operation
18	DW_OKPALLET	Pallet in normal, usable condition
20	DW_ONPALLET	Successful hoist or forklift operation result (data on pallet)
22	DW_BADBIN	Bin in unusable condition (incorrect structure or corrupt data)
24	DW_BADFORKLIFT	Unsuccessful bin load or unload operation
26	DW_SHORTPALLET	Ineligible bin replenishment operation (missing pallet or pallets)
28	DW_OKBIN	Bin in normal, usable condition
30	DW_INBIN	Successful forklift operation result (data in bin)
35	DW_DISTRESSED	Damaged shipment
37	DW_LOST_GOODS	Lost shipment

The normal result states for scheduled operations are *DW_CONSIGNED*, *DW_ONPALLET*, and *DW_INBIN*. These are coded as multiples of 10 for ease of recognition, so that the exception states stand out when reviewing the log. The normal states for a pallet and a bin are *DW_OKPALLET* and *DW_OKBIN*. The other states in the list are exception states. For a scheduled operation to be in a normal state, Warehouse integrity requires that its pallet or bin must also be in a normal state.

The text inside each bubble on the state transition diagram of Figure 9.8 describes the state of data after a Warehouse operation. The arrows connecting the bubbles are labeled with the names of the tasks that perform the state-transition operations. To promote understanding by nontechnical participants, the Data Warehouse task names resemble job titles in a real-world warehouse.

9.2.2 Data Warehouse Consignments: Production Extract

In an initial transformation, data is extracted from a Factory production application into a flat ASCII file. Every RDBMS product includes a utility capable of loading a flat file into the database, so flat files are the generic medium of choice for consignment extract files.

The specific data-extraction process that creates the extract file depends on the data-access possibilities available within the Factory application. A 4GL program usually is the most cost-effective way to produce the extract, because it copies selected legacy data without the need to reprogram legacy applications. For the 4GL approach to work, the legacy file layout must be known and access must be straightforward. Complex selection logic and proprietary data organizations may be beyond the capabilities of a 4GL.

In the case of an application package, data may only be accessible through access routines internal to the package's programs. Clearly, if the package's source code is not available, reprogramming it to change access routine calls is impossible. Reports produced by the package provide a solution to this impenetrability problem.

A package sold without source code often will provide its customers with a report-generator facility. The generated report is run with its output directed to a file instead of to the printer. Next, a utility program strips the report file of headers, footers, white space, unwanted data, and unwanted totals. The result of this report-stripping is a data consignment.

9.2.3 Consignment Control: Push versus Pull

Consignment production can be controlled either from the Factory applications or from the Data Warehouse. In a *push system*, the Warehouse is passive and the

Factory applications control both consignment production and pallet loading. In a pull system, an active Warehouse controls the extraction process and pallet loading. In a *push-pull system*, the Factory applications control consignment production, but the Warehouse controls pallet loading.

If the Data Warehouse had direct access to Factory applications, it would be possible for the Warehouse to pull in consignments directly from the Factory applications. However, if the Factory applications had easy data access, they would not be legacy applications and the Data Warehouse would not be needed to integrate their data. Although it is usually impossible to pull consignment extracts directly from legacy Factory applications, the Warehouse Schedule can still drive an indirect pull system.

In one type of indirect pull system, Warehouse control programs use the Schedule (stored in the *dw_schedule* table) to initiate extraction programs. As each extract terminates in a normal or exception state, it updates a Bill of Operations file. After all the scheduled extract programs have finished execution, the Bill of Operations file is loaded onto an empty pallet table. This pallet is then used to update the Warehouse Schedule with result state data.

The Warehouse agents discussed in Chapter 8 are useful for both the push system and indirect pull Warehouse loading, especially when the Factory applications use the same RDBMS technology as the Warehouse. A *consignment agent* works with the Warehouse Schedule and the consignment control table *dw_io_method*. To produce scheduled consignments, commands comparable to those stored in *dw_io_method* are created.

The data moves in the opposite direction, from the Factory database to the consignment file or table. As the consignment agent works down its schedule, it connects to different Factory applications. One advantage of this approach is that responsibility for consignment creation is delegated to the consignment agent, so the Factory application requires only minimal enhancement to accommodate Data Warehouse operations.

Warehouse agents have the benefit of mistake proofing. If the agent discovers a mistake in the data, such as a *duplicate key condition*, it marks its extract operation in an exception state. Unless the agent marks the consignment in the normal state of *consigned*, no attempt will be made to load the consignment.

9.2.4 The Gatekeeper

Data validation is one of the thorny issues in Data Warehouse design. Redundant, incomplete, and inconsistent data can be expected from legacy applications. If the Data Warehouse is a relational database environment, to what extent should it take advantage of RDBMS capabilities to repair faulty legacy data?

For example, referential integrity between two legacy applications only can be maintained by procedural programming. The SQL92 standard includes declarative referential integrity in the SQL CREATE TABLE statement, so the Warehouse data tables can be used to detect or disallow referential integrity violations that slip between the cracks in the Factory applications. Validation can take place against consignment files, inbound pallets, pallet-to-bin loads, or against loaded bins.

One school of thought in Warehouse design maximizes relational capabilities to assure data integrity in corporate reporting. The contrasting "minimalist" point of view is based on the premise that the Data Warehouse is a distribution utility for data derived from Factory applications. The minimalist school of thought holds that corrupt data in systems of record must be repaired in those applications, and not in the Warehouse.

In a middle-ground approach to consignment validation, the *Gatekeeper* repairs inbound data by using default values as required to protect Warehouse operations. For example, a missing data item in a consignment extract can cause the downstream pallet-to-bin transition operation to fail when it encounters an illegal null value. Substituting a default value for the null value would prevent this error. Similarly, replacing an illegal date with the system date will prevent problems during a subsequent character-field-to-date column conversion.

The difference between these two validations is that the default value substitution is declarative, but the date validation is programmatic. Provided the default value is declared when the pallet's CREATE TABLE statement is coded, subsequent missing value replacement is automatic. On the other hand, the date validation routine must be explicitly invoked.

The Gatekeeper validates consignments by executing any optional validation procedures. These are associated with the consignment by its subject-area identifier. For example, the validation procedure associated with consignment file *dw_c_wpli* would be named *dw_v_wpli*.

Beyond simple tests, validations require procedural code. A tradeoff exists between the speed of consignment loading and the rigor of validation. The level of validation assigned to the Gatekeeper is greatest in the "relational purity" approach. If Warehouse data is to be deemed pure, it must be extensively tested before entry, and this slows consignment loading. With the minimalist approach, consignment loading proceeds rapidly, but subsequent operations may fail.

The middle-ground approach assumes that some bad data will be allowed into the Warehouse. The few "clock-stopper" errors are repaired on entry so as to avoid the extra work of resubmitting rejected consignments. For example, replacing an invalid date value with a Warehouse-generated date is a typical repair. The

Factory application subsequently corrects the date value and reconsigns the corrected record to the Warehouse.

Runaway extracts from legacy applications are detected by the Gatekeeper when the size of a consignment file exceeds a "load limit." The load limit is stored in the *dw_pallet* table, so each individual subject area can have a different limit value.

9.2.5 The Receiving Clerk

The *Receiving Clerk* has the task of loading validated consignment files onto Warehouse pallet work tables. In the push-pull load process shown in Figure 9.9, the Receiving Clerk controls the interface between Factory push applications and Warehouse pull operations.

The Receiving Clerk uses the Data Warehouse Schedule together (in pull systems) with a table called the Receiving Manifest (*w_manifest*). The Manifest is actually a pallet table, the first one loaded. In a pull Warehouse, the Receiving Clerk calls the operating system to request the Manifest of all current consignments on the receiving dock. Consignment files are identified by the prefix *dw_c_*, followed by the identifier of their subject area.

The Manifest is delivered in the form of a file of subject-area names, with one record for each current consignment. The Manifest file is loaded onto an empty pallet (*w_manifest*) and compared with the Schedule to avoid attempts to load false consignments. This comparison is necessary to avoid any possibility of loading bogus (unscheduled) consignments. Scheduled consignments that are not listed on the Manifest take on a state of *not found*. The Receiving Clerk assigns the others a state of *consigned*. The states are marked in the Schedule with their integer codes from the *dw_state* table.

The Manifest is not used in a push Warehouse. In a push system, the consignments to be loaded are tagged by an agent before the Receiving Clerk commences operations.

9.2.6 The Hoist

The Receiving Clerk runs a utility procedure called the *Hoist*, which is the bulk-copy command in the database utility appropriate to the Warehouse RDBMS: ODL for Oracle, bcp for Sybase, or copy for Ingres.

The bulk copy command is stored in the *dw_io_method* table. The *seq* column in this table is used to build multiline commands. The Receiving Clerk selects current consignments in a predetermined order. The pallet for the current subject area is recycled (truncated) immediately before the bulk copy command is dispatched. To facilitate recovery from failure, receiving pallets are recycled at the last possible

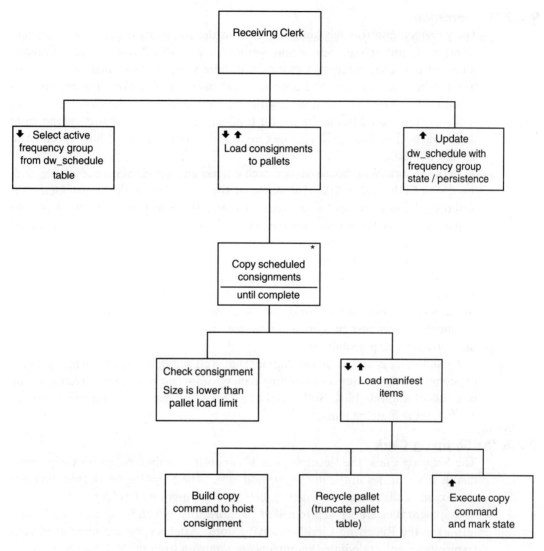

Figure 9.9 Receiving Clerk structure

moment, just before they are needed for the next consignment load. The Receiving Clerk retrieves the load command from *dw_io_method*, then passes it to the Hoist for execution. The load operation changes state to *DW_ONPALLET* if the bulk-copy operation succeeds. Otherwise, the state is set to *DW_BADHOIST*

9.2.7 The Foreman

The *Foreman* controls the bin operations in the following order: space management, load, and unload. Space management is performed first in order to make room for new consignments. Obviously, if there were no space management control, the bins eventually would approach disk capacity. The Foreman dispatches a procedure named the *Trashman*, which visits every bin in the Warehouse and removes stale-dated items. Items are time-stamped when they are loaded from their pallets. The Trashman removes items older than the "shelf life" specified in the *dw_bin* table.

In the generic Warehouse design, each bin has an associated procedure for loading current inbound pallets. The name of the procedure is the prefix *load_* followed by the bin's subject area. Before running the load procedure, the Foreman dispatches a procedure (the *Tallyman*) to make sure that all of the pallets needed for the load are present and in a normal state.

A bin may have one or several optional unload procedures to copy selected data to shipment pallets. A shipment pallet is a copy of the selected contents of a bin or multiple bins, intended for distribution from the Warehouse to those information consumers who cannot have or do not want on-line access. Aside from scheduled shipments, Warehouse bins are available for on-line inquiries, but this falls outside the Foreman's responsibilities.

Repackaging is an option on shipments as well as bin loads. *Bin-load repackaging* combines the contents of multiple pallets. *Shipment repackaging* combines the contents of multiple bins. Both types of repackaging make use of database stored procedures containing joins.

9.2.8 The Shipping Clerk

The *Shipping Clerk,* the Receiving Clerk's opposite number, builds bulk copy commands from entries in the *dw_io_method* table. The Shipping Clerk then executes these commands to copy shipment pallets into Shipment ASCII files.

Shipment files are written to a *Will Call directory*, which is the outbound counterpart to the Receiving Clerk's receiving dock. After a specified number of days (typically seven), stale-dated shipments are removed from the Will Call area.

9.2.9 The Audit Clerk

Although all operations run according to the Warehouse Schedule, not all scheduled operations run normally. For example, a missing consignment file will prevent a scheduled load operation from taking place. A data exception during a pallet-to-bin load will result in a *bad forklift* state on that particular operation, although Warehouse processing continues for other operations.

The job of the *Audit Clerk* is to log all operations in the *dw_log* control table. Operations for the current period are reported in the audit trail file *dw_audit*, which the Audit Clerk writes to the Will Call directory.

■ 9.3 DISTRIBUTED DATA WAREHOUSES

The generic Warehouse design of the previous section describes a central corporate application fed by distributed data sources. In a business environment characterized by growth, mergers, and acquisitions, data often is distributed among standalone legacy applications at multiple sites. Achieving enterprise integration by replacing legacy applications with a single RDBMS application is difficult at a single site, and perhaps impossible in multisite operations. As the generic design demonstrates, the Data Warehouse concept is a cost-effective way to integrate single-site legacy data. However, distributed data introduces additional challenges.

9.3.1 The Challenge of Distributed Operations

Central operations on distributed data are inherently more difficult than single-site operations. To achieve enterprise integration, the Data Warehouse must solve the following remote distributed data challenges:

- Synchronized consignments (that is, equally current consignments everywhere)
- Precise replication (that is, the same query results for all locations)
- Equal response time (that is, the same response time for the same query anywhere).

These challenges can be met programmatically by enhancing the Warehouse application with distributed-processing or file-replication functionality. The alternative, automatic approach to distributed-data challenges makes use of the distributed-data features of the RDBMS.

9.3.2 Programmatic Approaches to Distributed Data

The programmatic approaches to distributed data operations are used mainly on proprietary platforms that do not support automatic distributed RDBMS features. An RPC is the mechanism whereby a process executing on one computer can invoke another process on a different computer. An RPC permits a central pull system Warehouse to initiate consignment file-production and file-transfer operations from remote sites. Of course, each RPC must be individually coded and tested.

In a distributed push system Warehouse, applications in remote sites are programmed to produce consignment files. These consignment files are then transferred to one or several Warehouse servers. The transfer operations are initiated by the remote sites using a *point-to-point file-transfer protocol*.

Multisite file transfers to distributed Warehouse servers do not guarantee precise replication. Any of the transfer operations may fail, so the Warehouse must compare consignment manifests. To assure the same query results for all locations, only those consignments that are present on all Warehouse servers can be loaded. The missing consignment files can be sent from one Warehouse server to another, or simply not loaded on any server. However the missing consignment problem is tackled, the solution involves sophisticated programming.

In contrast to programmatic approaches to distributed data, automatic approaches are based on RDBMS features and do not require additional application code.

9.3.3 Distributed Warehouse Queries

Distributed queries enable a central Warehouse server to access data on remote servers, provided the remote data is accessible to the Warehouse RDBMS. The relational join operation shown in Figure 9.2 would be feasible on distributed data only if the RDBMS supports the feature—not all do. Assuming that the Warehouse RDBMS supports distributed joins, joining remote data usually takes longer than a single-site join because of bandwidth and transmission delays inherent in the communications link connecting the two servers.

If a failure occurs on the remote server, or if the network goes down, the join will not work. Furthermore, the remote data may reside in legacy systems whose proprietary data organization is incompatible with the RDBMS. In short, a central Data Warehouse does not work well with distributed data because it cannot shield itself from sluggish networks, remote data unavailability, or the proprietary data-access methods of legacy applications.

9.3.4 Data Replication

Replication is the propagation of data copies from a primary (master) table on one server to a set of replicas residing on remote servers. These copies may be entire tables or partial tables (called *fragments*). Automatic data replication is a database server feature, and, as such, provides an active and vendor-supported method of distributed data integration. By comparison, programmatic data replication is passive. It requires a substantial custom programming effort.

Figure 9.10 illustrates *store-and-forward data replication*, the most appropriate form of data replication technology for a Data Warehouse. Because they are orient-

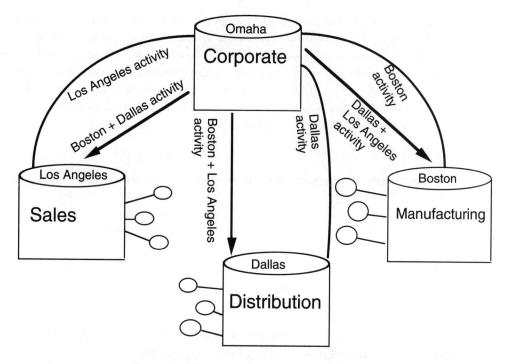

Figure 9.10 Data Warehouse table replication

ed toward transaction processing and rely on distributed update mechanisms (such as 2PC), the contrasting *real-time data replication* and *near real-time data replication* technologies are not as well-suited to distributed Warehouse applications. Instead, real-time and near real-time data replication are most useful in distributed transaction-processing applications.

In the store-and-forward data replication example, disjointed sets of legacy applications are located alongside Warehouse servers in Boston, Dallas, and Los Angeles. Each Warehouse server loads consignments from subject-area applications that are located at its site, so there are no remote consignment files. Once a Warehouse server's pallet tables are loaded locally, the RDBMS automatically forwards copies of its updated pallet tables to the other two Warehouse servers.

All three servers then load the full set of pallets (including both local originals and replicas) to their respective bin tables as part of their normal operations. These load operations result in identical Warehouse bins. Identical queries will thus obtain identical responses, no matter which Warehouse server responds to the query.

Only the pallet data is replicated in this design. Pallets are smaller than bin tables because they are entirely recycled with each load. Pallet recycling is part of the generic Warehouse design, and does not concern the replication facility. Data replication services are proprietary and vendor-specific. However, every vendor's replication facility is capable of transmitting incremental changes to primary tables, without sending a copy of the entire table. The advantages of pallet replication in a distributed Warehouse include

Benefit	*Justification*
• Faster data storage and retrieval	Local pallet-to-bin loads, no telecommunications delay
• Consistent query results	All Warehouse servers store identical bin data
• Reduced communications cost	Data transfer at off-peak tariff
• Minimal network traffic	Only new data is replicated
• Automatic synchronization	Replication is an RDBMS function.

With the exception of automatic synchronization, these benefits could be obtained with custom programming. However, the onus of supporting programmatic solutions such as file-replication programs falls on the customer's development staff, not on the RDBMS vendor.

Data synchronization and recovery tasks such as file-transfer retransmissions after a network failure must be coded into programmatic distributed Warehouse applications. When these routines fail in service, it is MIS and not vendor staff who must perform emergency repairs.

Problem determination for faults in communications software (middleware) can be more time-consuming for in-house staff than for vendor staff, who often have more complete diagnostic tools. Furthermore, RDBMS data-replication products are utilized by a large customer base. Problems experienced at one customer site probably have been seen and solved previously at other customer sites, so data replication glitches are fixed relatively quickly.

The disadvantages of data replication are redundant data storage and proprietary implementations. The redundant storage is a not a major issue, for the same reason that storing copies of legacy data in the Warehouse is a nonissue. The cost of storage is less than the cost of programming legacy applications.

The lack of standards for data replication is a more substantial issue. Each RDBMS vendor supporting data replication does it differently. The risk of vendor dependence must be weighed against the benefits of replication.

10

THE INSTRUMENT PANEL: ACTIVE DATABASE FOR COMPETITIVE ADVANTAGE

Computers, communications networks, and software run the Database Factory. Senior technical staff serve as the line managers, and software engineers are the production engineers. Data is the production inventory and information is the product—but how good is that product? Does the production process add value or just add cost? Is the Database Factory competitive? This chapter discusses ways in which the Database Factory pays back its investment and contributes to the success of the enterprise.

■ 10.1 SURVIVAL THROUGH ACTIVE TECHNOLOGY

In an increasingly interdependent and competitive business environment, narrow-focus information systems make it difficult for those who rely on them to thrive. Passive database applications force data along rigid paths and often conceal information when it is most needed.

If passive database applications are part of the problem, then active database applications could be part of the solution. The specific active database traits that foster competitive advantage include

- Agility (that is, rapid creation, deployment, and reassembly of information system components)
- Compatibility (that is, external data integration for rapid, accurate response)

- Flexibility (that is, sharable and reusable components, self-modification)
- Quality (that is, high service level, minimal downtime, defect prevention).

A passive database is controlled from the outside (by its client application), so its behavior is simply reactive. Because it is incapable of adapting itself to the constantly changing business environment, a passive application rarely supports competitiveness. A passive client can only offer a programmatic response to predefined stimuli.

A passive program only changes when someone reprograms it, so any adaptation to meet new needs is manual and labor-intensive. With every line of code added or changed, enhancing a passive application increases the risk of functional error. During the time required to code and test new behavior, ever-changing business conditions will have brought about new requirements that differ from those addressed by the program enhancements. When cost and staffing are considerations, a passive application seldom can be reprogrammed quickly enough to keep pace with changing business conditions.

Pre-relational legacy applications present an extreme case of completely passive, procedural programming technology. The Data Warehouse makes it possible for even the most inflexible of these legacy applications to share existing data. However, reprogramming is necessary for any new data that is not produced by a legacy application and is not a by-product of legacy data.

In a volatile business environment, the useful life of programmed enhancements to a legacy system can be shorter than the time required to develop them. Given the cost and benefit figures summarized in Table 10.1, a set of enhancements requiring 20 work days to program will not pay back its development cost within a 3-week implementation horizon. If the development time were reduced to 11 days, then the enhancements would pay back their cost within the 3-week period. Automated code generation builds procedural code from nonprocedural 4GL code. However, 4GL code generation does nothing to prolong the useful implementation life of the program. When the code no longer meets business needs, it must be replaced.

The 4GL code-generation process is automated, but the 4GL coding activity remains manual, albeit nonprocedural. Nonprocedural coding increases programmer productivity, but not to the point where rework cost is immaterial. If maintenance programmers are fully occupied writing 4GL code, the labor utilization is optimal but (assuming comparable wages) the labor cost of maintaining applications is constant. When enhancement requests arrive faster than they can be serviced by 4GL programmers, a backlog accumulates. The decision must then be

Table 10.1 Costs and Benefits of Programmed Enhancements

Development Work Days	Development Cost @ $50/Hour	Useful Life (Weeks)	Benefit @ $2,000/Week
1	400	1	2,000
2	800	2	4,000
3	1,200	3	6,000
4	1,600	4	8,000
5	2,000	5	10,000
10	4,000	10	20,000
20	8,000	20	40,000

made whether to increase the staff (and the labor cost) or to keep software maintenance costs level and let the backlog build.

The decision to do nothing may save effort on those requests that eventually become obsolete when fresh requirements enter the backlog, but doing nothing does nothing to make the company competitive. A more balanced approach to software cost containment is to make a one-time investment in an active database application architecture. Self-adjusting applications prolong the service life of their components and defer maintenance programming, so the investment is paid back over time.

RDBMS technology combines flexible structure with nonprocedural operations, which are the criteria for event-driven applications. However, as shown in Figure 10.1, passive database applications require procedural programming to supplement SQL statements with flow-of-control logic. Passive applications require their client programs to be recoded for even the slightest modification, so they cannot fully exploit the inherent flexibility of the relational model.

Multiple client programs and workgroup servers compete for control of the passive server in Figure 10.1. Potentially, each of these must be modified correctly in conjunction with database enhancements to meet new business needs. By contrast, the components in an active application often can accommodate shifting business requirements within their existing control logic. When component modification is finally necessary, new or modified components can inherit much of their behavior from existing components.

Active database applications incorporate control structures within database programs. These control structures, stored and executed in the RDBMS, enable active components to change their behaviors in response to events. Adaptation to ongoing changes is achieved by a number of active design techniques, such as

- Varying the activation path

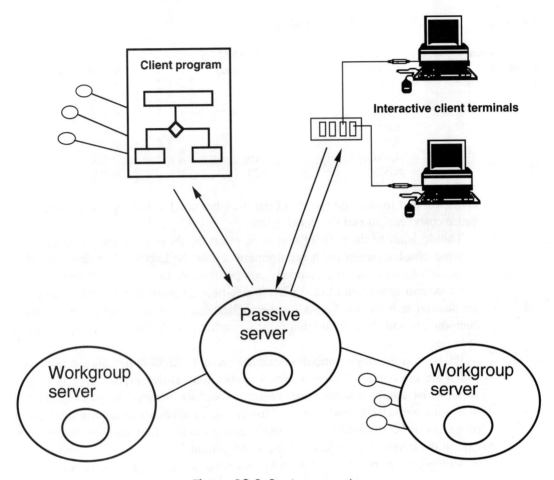

Figure 10.1 Passive aggressive

- Relating behavior to the metastate (aggregate state) of the data
- Designing event handlers that respond to events.

The database programs of an active server are a shared database resource like the data itself and allow the reuse of existing procedural code.

Corporate necessity is the main justification for responsive applications, but an investment in active components reduces overall costs. Maintaining and enhancing active components takes less time than is needed to maintain a collection of passive client programs because fewer steps are required. Table 10.2 compares quality metrics and programming costs (based on a labor cost of $50/hour) among legacy,

Table 10.2 Programming Costs versus Quality Metrics

OLTP Study 100 Transaction Application	COBOL with Indexed File	Passive SQL Database	Active SQL Database
Lines per transaction	240	240	80
Days per transaction	15	2	3
Days per change	5	2	1
Development cost per transaction	6,000	800	1,200
Program cost per change	2,000	800	400
Defects per transaction	3	2	0
Average days per repair	2	1	0
Average cost per repair	800	400	0

passive database, and active database approaches to a hypothetical transaction-processing application.

The figures in Table 10.2 are purely indicative. The actual costs vary with the ease of development on the implementation platform. For instance, the legacy application might cost $700,000 in skilled labor to develop on a mainframe computer, as compared with $600,000 to develop on a minicomputer, or $450,000 to develop on a workgroup LAN.

The skill and experience of the developers also affect the cost. The skill level required to develop active components depends on the component platform. Designing client interface objects using visual programming and a Development Warehouse, for instance, calls for less skill than designing a set of database programs. Component reuse has a lower technical skill requirement than initial component design.

Organizations willing to invest in a disciplined implementation can take advantage of the high quality of pretested code and the low overall costs of component reuse. This Development Warehouse approach makes it possible to focus information technology resources on commercial opportunities, not maintenance programming.

10.1.1 The Advantages of Agility

Business agility is characterized by rapid, nimble adaptation to new and changing opportunities. Similarly, an agile information system is rapidly created and quickly modified. The keys to rapid creation, quick change, and fast operations are automation, prefabrication, and concurrent processing.

All computer information systems automate data production, but turning the data they produce into useful information is too often accomplished by means of slow manual processing. Consider two competing supermarket chains, Company X and Company Y. Company X uses reports to analyze corporate data. Its com-

Table 10.3 Manual versus Automatic Processing

Data Sifting	Semiautomated (Company X)	Automated (Company Y)
Distribute output (minutes)	60	5
Find patterns (minutes)	120	10
Annotate results (minutes)	60	2
Accuracy (percent)	98	100
Concurrent searches (processes)	1	5

petitor, Company Y, has automated the data-sifting process. Company Y detects patterns in point-of-sale data and formats the results into a *database publishing* report. Automation has three advantages in this example: speed, accuracy, and completeness.

As Table 10.3 indicates, Company X needs four hours of manual processing before it can begin to decide how to allocate soft drink shipments from the distribution warehouse to individual stores. Company Y has accurate point-of-sale information within 20 minutes, which allows it to bypass the distribution warehouse by using FAX transmission to vendor trucks for direct store delivery of soft drinks. The automated competitor clearly enjoys the benefits of faster distribution and lower handling cost, but what are the factors that make this possible?

Company X, the semiautomated competitor, has a data-processing philosophy that views report production as the goal of an information system, rather than as an intermediate point in processing. In this example, manual report analysis absorbs two hours of skilled labor, as opposed to 10 minutes of computer time for automated analysis procedures.

The less-agile competitor must wait one hour for the reports to be distributed before analysis can begin. Much of the data contained in the report is irrelevant, and any significant information discovered during analysis must be reprocessed. Data is manually re-entered from reports into spreadsheets, and from the spreadsheets into word processing documents.

At each step, manual processing leaves openings for mistakes. By contrast, Company Y uses database output-filter routines to distribute results electronically in a paperless database publishing format. When the automated analysis routines detect marketing opportunities, the supporting data is distributed as an enclosure within a "Heads up!" electronic mail message to the marketing department.

Figure 10.2 illustrates *agile information distribution*. The output-filter drivers shown in Figure 10.2 repackage analysis results into spreadsheet, electronic memo, or database publishing file formats. The routing of output depends on the result state of analysis. For instance, an analysis report normally might be sent to

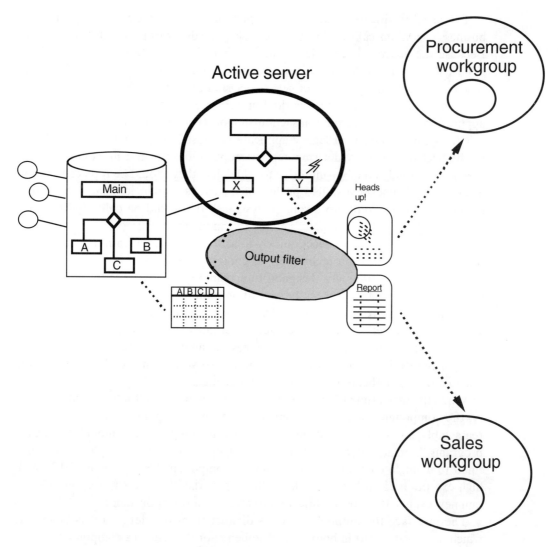

Figure 10.2 Agile distribution

the production control department alone. However, if the analysis gives rise to a "potential business opportunity" alert, additional output is distributed with a "Heads up!" message to the sales and procurement workgroup servers. An agile information system automates output distribution to provide these departments with early notice of a surge in demand.

The usual justification for manual report analysis is that constantly changing business conditions call for different analysis procedures from one day to the next. Because the analysis is completely *ad hoc*, it resists automation. This argument makes some sense in legacy decision-support environments because of the long time needed for coding. However, legacy decision-support technology is no longer a valid option in today's business world. Furthermore, decision-support (Warehouse) applications are distinct from transaction-support (Factory) applications.

Clearly, mission-critical legacy applications must be replaced in a disciplined, methodical way. Legacy decision-support applications are not mission-critical. If they are too rigid and labor-intensive to add value, they should be replaced as soon as possible. Whenever a skilled professional such as a financial analyst or a sales manager is sidetracked into a rote analysis task that could be delegated to automated components, the company's ability to compete is impaired.

In a company that must react quickly to survive, self-modification makes active database the information technology of choice. As shown in Figure 10.3, active component applications are designed to accommodate changing business conditions. Within the active server, the activation path changes in response to events, switching control from component "X" to component "Y." In conjunction with server-based processing, a change agent alternates control among client components "A," "B," and "C." This synchronizes the analysis method with the current state of the decision-support database on the server. Both the client and server portions of this application are designed for change.

When the magnitude of change exceeds a component's self-adjustment capability, the component must be re-engineered. Active components are designed for reassembly, so the cost of enhancement is low in comparison to monolithic legacy programs. In many cases, an enhancement to an active database application is confined to a single component. For example, component "Y" in Figure 10.3 has a high exception count because it lacks the appropriate behavior to respond to certain new events. It needs modification to meet its new responsibilities.

The interface to component "Y" is distinct from the details of its behavior, which are isolated within body "Y." The behavior that enables component "Y" to fulfill its new responsibilities is contained in "shadow" body "Y prime," which supersedes body "Y." Interface "Y" and the call to component "Y" from the main routine of the database program remain unchanged.

Decision-support client components "A," "B," and "C" of Figure 10.3 are parameterized, which makes it easy to fine-tune the analysis queries at execution time. Control over the analysis process is just as comprehensive as with manual processing, but automation makes the analysis process faster and more powerful. Skilled

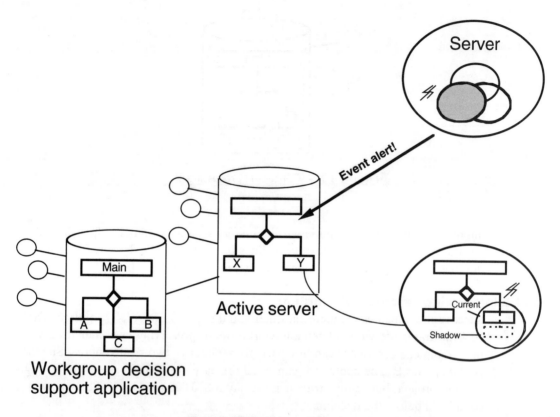

Figure 10.3 Designed for change

staff, no longer preoccupied with the mechanics of analysis, apply the results to formulate competitive strategies.

Conventional data-processing reports proceed in a linear fashion, presenting a single view of the data. This view may be partial or misleading. The contrasting approach, *concurrent execution* of multiple analysis procedures, applies a goal-directed framework to different lines of inquiry.

For example, the goal of the framework shown in Figure 10.4 is to analyze international investment opportunities. Procedure "A" examines stock prices, while procedure "B" looks at bond yields and procedure "C" monitors currency markets. The individual result states of each analysis activity are fed back to the framework's main analysis routine. The main routine then re-executes routines "A," "B," and "C" by using different parameters based on prior analysis results.

For example, if procedure "C" indicates downward movement on the dollar, and procedure "B" identifies an upward trend in bond prices, then procedure "A"

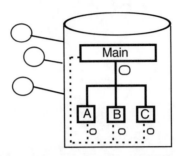

Figure 10.4 Concurrent processing

might seek buying opportunities in the energy sector. Automated focusing based on interim results among interrelated lines of inquiry yields deeper, faster insight into business opportunities than manual extrapolation from reports.

10.1.2 Integrating External Information

Successful companies compete on quality and service, not solely on price. Table 10.4 illustrates the value of reliable workflows in preserving customer loyalty. In this example, a contractor can buy parts from either of two rival vendors, Supplier A or Supplier B. The contractor can resell the parts for $33,600 as part of an engineering project, but the contractor must pay a $20,000 penalty if the work is not completed before the deadline.

Supplier A and the contractor utilize EDI for order entry, so the contractor's order is entered into the system only once. In this example, EDI order entry is 99.9% accurate. Supplier B relies on its order-entry clerks to rekey all customer orders with an accuracy of 92.5%. The contractor's gross margin is greater from

Table 10.4 Reliable Workflows

EDI Case Study	Supplier A	Supplier B
Item price	$24.85	$23.40
Items in lot	1,000	1,000
Lot price	$24,850.00	$23,400.00
Sales price	$33,600.00	$33,600.00
Gross margin	$8,750.00	$10,200.00
Late penalty	$20,000.00	$20,000.00
Error rate	0.1%	7.5%
Error cost	$20	$1,500.00
Net margin	$8,730.00	$8,700.00

Supplier B. However, the estimated error cost is $1,500 (which results from the 7.5% probability of having to pay a $20,000 penalty), and this sways the contractor toward Supplier A.

Looking at this simplified example from the viewpoint of Supplier A, the EDI link offers sufficient convenience and accuracy to act as a barrier to customer exit. Because customers enter their orders directly, EDI enables Supplier A to offer a higher service level than Supplier B, with fewer order-entry clerks and less overtime during busy periods.

Combined with workflow automation, EDI helps a company take advantage of profit-making opportunities that might not otherwise be exploited. For example, a bank maintains a settlement fund. When a customer account is closed, the accrued interest usually includes a fraction of a cent that cannot be paid out. Therefore, the settlement payments are rounded down, with the remainder going into the settlement fund.

These fractional cents add up to tens of thousands of dollars every week. The settlement fund database works with a foreign-exchange server. At any hour of the day or night, either the London, New York, or Tokyo foreign-exchange market will be open. Depending on the time and current market conditions, the settlement fund database routes foreign-exchange transactions for execution on the appropriate currency exchange. The workflow routing infrastructure helps the bank put its "found money" to work.

Used in conjunction with an inventory database, EDI streamlines procurement operations. The EDI message in Figure 10.5 contains 114 data elements, which is more data than the maximum of 30 data elements that fit on the data entry screen used by Supplier B. The additional data elements in the EDI message carry data regarding the manufacturing history and the quality assurance metrics of the parts supplied. This data is used by the customer to comply with a contractual requirement to maintain source and quality data for all parts.

The goal of semiautomated order entry as used by Supplier B is to enter as many orders as possible as quickly as possible with as small a staff as possible. Supplier A has exactly the same goal, but uses automation to harmonize this departmental goal with the broader goal of superior customer service. To attain the narrow departmental goal, Supplier B restricts the information content of the workflow. By contrast, Supplier A automates the workflow to provide more information and better service at lower cost.

As summarized in Table 10.5, the investment in external data integration pays for itself within a two-year period. After the payback period, the bottom line for Supplier A shows a higher profit margin with a lower cost of sales. Staff levels and hours are less closely tied to order volume than with semiautomated order entry,

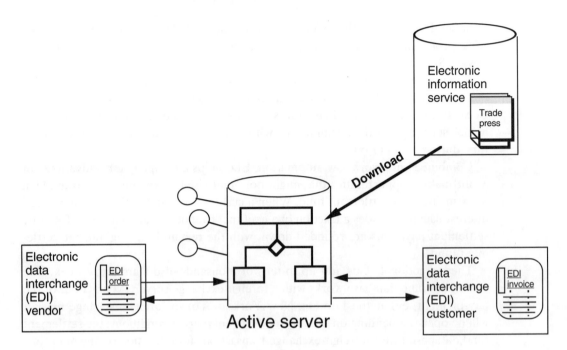

Figure 10.5 External data integration

so the order-management department can devote more attention to the qualitative aspects of customer service.

Short of making a capital-intensive investment in EDI, what can a medium-size company do to automate its order-entry operation? A semiautomated company

Table 10.5 Investment in External Data Integration

External Data	One-time Costs	Annual Costs	Annual Savings	12 Months	24 Months
RDBMS Server	$80,000			$–80,000	$–80,000
Server hardware	$150,000			$–150,000	$–150,000
Network	$130,000			$–130,000	$–130,000
EDI software	$35,000	$3,500		$–38,500	$–42,000
Development	$300,000			$–300,000	$–300,000
Staff training		$22,000	$31,000	$9,000	$18,000
Mainframe lease			$125,000	$125,000	$250,000
Clerical labor			$50,000	$50,000	$100,000
Programmers			$250,000	$250,000	$500,000
Total	$695,000	$25,500	$456,000	$–264,500	$166,000

like Supplier B relies on verbal communication for feedback and control during order processing. Time spent confirming the line items on an order reduces the inevitable misunderstandings, but the confirmation need not be verbal.

For example, Supplier B might integrate a FAX server with the order-entry application. The FAX server fills in the blanks on the electronic image of an order confirmation, combining the order data entered by the sales representative with inventory data from the database. FAX transmission enables Supplier B to confirm orders faster than by mailing hardcopy. The paperless confirmation of the FAX contains as much additional information as Supplier A includes in its EDI confirmation message. Because order data effectively enters the system twice prior to confirmation, the FAX solution is less reliable than the EDI link. However, if Supplier B holds its low prices, the relatively "low-tech" FAX solution raises the service level enough to keep the firm competitive.

10.1.3 Competitive Intelligence

Successful companies move quickly to take advantage of business opportunities by keeping ahead of the competition. Because no company can act on opportunities that go undiscovered, automated methods of detecting opportunities boost competitiveness.

For example, the company in Figure 10.5 subscribes to an electronic information service. During off-peak hours, a Data Warehouse search agent logs on to the information service and performs keyword searches of government digests and industry publications. The results of the search, which include articles mentioning the competition as well as news reports indicating potential business opportunities, are downloaded into the Data Warehouse. Within the Warehouse, the downloads are categorized. The Warehouse database maintains a subscription list organized by download category. Subscribers receive current downloads as enclosures in electronic mail "Heads up!" messages, so they are alerted in time to take prompt action.

10.1.4 Active Workflow

Legacy information systems segregate data flows from the other constituent parts of the workflows that they partially automate. Legacy report data flows up the corporate hierarchy to reach executive decision-makers. Masses of data converging at the apex of the hierarchy amount to *information glut,* a data overload that management cannot be expected to handle efficiently. Information glut constitutes an upward delegation mechanism in which workgroup-level decisions are "kicked upstairs." The implicit assumption is that information ought to flow upward because decisions are made at the top. By removing decision-enabling information from the departmental workflows, legacy applications undercut the goal of empowerment.

The results of *hierarchical information flow* are bureaucracy, delay, and lost opportunity. Imagine a company whose sales representatives were forced to wait for executive approval for every purchase order, no matter how small. Obviously, such a company would lose sales to a competitor that permits sales representatives and their supervisors to make local decisions. Few companies would intentionally set up a counterproductive policy, but the delays associated with rigid workflows have the same effect of lost sales.

The rigid workflow shown in the top of Figure 10.6 runs 10 minutes longer than the flexible workflow illustrated in the bottom portion, and 15 minutes more for new customers. The rigid workflow takes longer because each step in its processing sequence must complete before the next step can begin. This sequence of data-processing operations forces staff to wait for the computer application. The contrasting flexible workflow allows concurrent operations, so the workflow processing does not keep customers waiting. The sequential processing of the rigid workflow resembles a job stream in a legacy application. By contrast, the flexible workflow takes advantage of client/server database technology to facilitate concurrent processing.

In an active workflow system, the component that is responsible for an overall task collaborates with other components in a client/server relationship. The client component delegates subtasks to operations components, but retains overall responsibility for the workflow. Server components are responsible for operations such as document image retrieval or annotated FAXes routing.

In a build-to-order workflow based on work orders, for example, a data inquiry component might act as the client of a document image server. On the other hand, the image of a work order could be the client of a database server in a change-management workflow. In the first case, the client component initiates an inquiry and the server responds with the document image. In the second case, the image itself is the client. Scanning an image of the work order triggers a request message for the server to store the image of the work order.

The components of an active workflow collaborate to maintain a high service level. They work together to route data, distribute document images, and enforce work guidelines.

For example, a bank that competes on service is committed to respond to customer requests within a half hour. Service requests fall into various categories, such as financial transactions, account inquiries, and marketing information requests. Each request is routed to the appropriate workgroup.

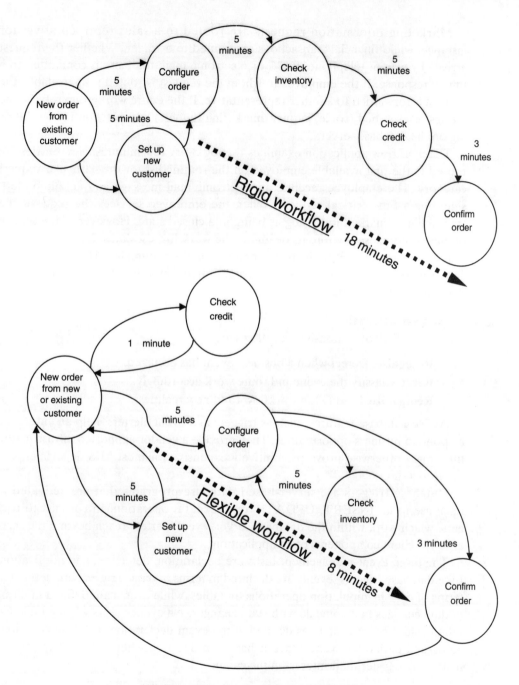

Figure 10.6 Rigid versus flexible workflow

Marketing information requests are routed to a sales representative, for instance, while financial transactions are routed to a trader. Whether the request arrives by way of telephone, FAX, or electronic mail, the bank is committed to a timely response. If the employee to whom the request is routed is unavailable, the request is forwarded to another representative. If the entire workgroup is busy, the request is classified (trade, inquiry, marketing request) and noted in the workflow log on the database server.

The workflow application examines the log every few minutes. New entries are routed to the first available employee on the routing list for the particular request category. The employee receives an electronic mail message and an audio alert, signaling a time-critical request. When the employee services the request, the transaction is marked in the log as being in a closed state. However, if the service request is not closed before its deadline, the workflow escalates the priority of the request and forwards it to the next employee on the routing list. The bank uses the active workflow to meet its service commitment, monitor its service level, and maximize its staff productivity.

10.1.5 Responsive Activation

The "three R's" of responsive workflows are

- **Recognize**. Detect when a business event has occurred.
- **React**. Classify the event and route work accordingly.
- **Reorganize**. Modify the workflow to fit new realities.

Active database features, such as triggers and event alerters, help an enterprise respond to business opportunities. They provide a vendor-supported infrastructure that might otherwise prove prohibitively expensive for most MIS departments to develop in-house.

Database triggers are server-based database programs that are activated in response to an INSERT, UPDATE, or DELETE operation. In contrast to triggers, which work within the database server, event alerters reach beyond the server to the client components of an application.

The three event-management tasks are declaration, detection, and notification. Like database triggers, events are declared in terms of data. Triggers are defined in terms of data-manipulation operations on tables, while events are defined in terms of data changes that coincide with state changes. An event occurs when a table (or relationship) changes state as defined in the event declaration. Event declarations name and define an event. Once it has been declared, client and server components may register their interest in the event.

An event often is defined by an SQL condition that initially is false. When the condition turns from false to true, the database server detects the event. In some database servers, the condition is evaluated by a database program. Other RDBMS products utilize a trigger to evaluate the condition.

In the notification activity, which begins when the server detects (or is informed of) an event, the registered subscribers to the event are alerted. These subscribers include database programs on the same or a collaborating database server. Additional subscribers may include client applications and agents.

In a mechanism known as *synchronous event management*, the subscriber suspends execution until the event occurs. The alternative mechanism, *asynchronous event management*, enables subscriber processes to continue working on other tasks while they await an expected event. The subscriber's flow of control is interrupted by an event alerter from the RDBMS server. Both synchronous and asynchronous events reduce application complexity. Event alerters spare the application (and its developers) from the effort of continuously polling the database in order to detect events.

Figure 10.7 illustrates how triggers and events build responsiveness into a discount retail store operation. The discount chain marks up merchandise 12% over the price it pays its vendors. Whenever the price paid by the discount chain for an item fluctuates, a trigger recalculates the retail price. Any price variance at reorder time activates the trigger. The reorder activity is itself activated in response to a "low-inventory" event. When customer purchases deplete the overall inventory of an item group to a level equivalent to one week's current demand, a low-inventory event occurs.

To meet the goal of purchasing efficiency, the condition for the reorder event is an overall metastate transition on all the items supplied by the same vendor in all stores, not a local state transition for a single item in a single store. This goal of cost reduction through purchasing efficiency potentially conflicts with the goal of revenue maximization by preventing lost sales at individual stores. To reconcile these goals, local replenishment events occur at the individual store level, as shown in Figure 10.7.

In response to these events, inventory flows through a distribution hub to the points of greatest demand. These local replenishment events smooth imbalances in the existing inventory, so reorder events are deferred until they become unavoidable. In the case of high-volume, low-cost items such as beverages, event-driven replenishment with direct store delivery reduces the load on the distribution hub and lowers the handling cost.

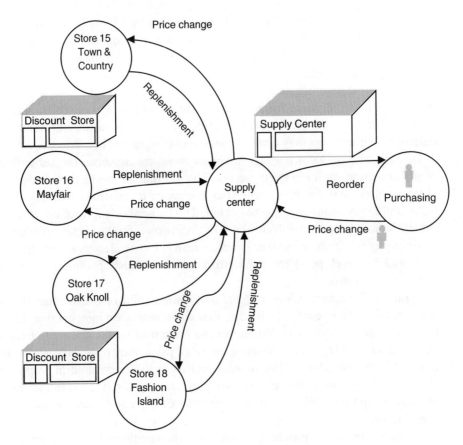

Figure 10.7 Event-driven responsiveness

Event management provides a framework for workflow components to adjust themselves to changes in circumstances. When the components that subscribe to an event receive an alert, they adjust themselves to collaborate in new ways.

For example, retail price changes occur in conjunction with reorder events. A significant price shift involving multiple items is defined as a supplier reorder event to which the store scheduling components are subscribers. When the event signals lower prices, the labor-scheduling component adds part-time staff to meet the expected surge in customer demand. The delivery-scheduling component is alerted and adjusts itself to avoid stock-outs.

These components collaborate to enhance the company's competitiveness by reducing its cost of operations. The response is coordinated by components working with the event-management infrastructure of the database server, not by some massive and complex external program.

10.1.6 Quality and Reliability

Passive application code is driven by programmatic control logic, not by events. Even small changes in application behavior require program modifications. When the behavior is distributed between two or more programs, each of these must be reprogrammed and tested. In the best (and most unlikely) outcome, in which all these program changes function correctly, the programming effort is a recurring drain on profitability. It is more likely that the code of a passive application contains errors. Some of these remain as defects that cause failure in the production application after testing.

When a run-time failure hits a distributed passive application, the source code that contains the error must be reprogrammed and redistributed to each client machine. Source code repairs can force a mission-critical application to remain offline for hours. The more client nodes, the greater the cost per repair.

For example, fixing a single error in a distributed retail application could force each store to shut down. Table 10.6 calculates an indicative downtime cost for a 20-store implementation with 10 checkout registers per store and 100 updates in the application.

The cost per outage decreases if the failure is localized at a single location, the database server. Because the defect can be isolated in one place and in one set of application components—those in the activation path at the point of failure—downtime is minimized.

Defect prevention is even more cost-effective than rapid repair. The keys to defect prevention are simplification, automation, and continuous improvement. Replacing large, complex programs with small, single-purpose components does not in itself yield simplification. In fact, a diverse collection of client and server components can prove to be a complex, unwieldy mess. Focusing on the much smaller set of components belonging to a Component Case reduces the complexity.

Table 10.6 Indicative Downtime Costs

Key Statistics	Cost per Outage
45 minutes average downtime per store	$60 per outage cost of lost labor per store
$8 per hour labor cost per checkout clerk	+ $6,000 per outage cost of lost sales
$8,000 per hour sales volume per store	= $6,060 per store total cost of outage
	× 20 stores
Total cost per outage	= $121,200

Further simplification results from limiting behavior to that appropriate to the goals and responsibilities of the Component Case.

Business process automation substitutes automatic controls and programmed operations for manual processing. Automated processing is more consistent and predictable than manual processing, hence less prone to error. When paper files are replaced by a database application, information storage and retrieval are partially automated. When paper documents and routing slips are replaced by electronic images and computerized routing, workflow automation increases the reach of database applications.

Procedural programming is a particularly expensive manual process. At some point, someone must code a program, so total automation currently remains out of reach. However, from the viewpoint of a company implementing an information system, substituting database server infrastructure for procedural program functions brings significant benefits.

For example, event management is expensive and unreliable when implemented with procedural programming. The program must poll the database at regular intervals to determine whether the event has occurred. The program is doing no other work while it is polling. Between polling intervals, the event might take place, hide its tracks by subsequent activity, and go unnoticed.

To prevent this, the programmer must allocate a program *flag* for each event. The program must correctly initialize, set, and reset these flags, which increases the complexity and maintenance cost of the application. By contrast, server-based event management automates event detection, event notification, and transfer of control. This eliminates the need for event flags and event polling in the application.

Of course, the staff of the RDBMS vendor must write and maintain the event-management program code. From the RDBMS customer's point of view, delegating the event-management functions to the server is equivalent to automation. Instead of having to write, test, and fix procedural code, the application developer specifies the event by using nonprocedural SQL. What would otherwise be a complex, error-prone piece of application code is replaced by an automatic feature of the database server. Unlike application code, RDBMS features are extensively tested, widely implemented at many customer sites, and supported by the database vendor. Any defects in the server code are likely to have been found and fixed before local implementation, either during beta testing or at another customer site.

Continuous change in the business environment requires ongoing adjustments to information systems. Depending on whether an *ad hoc* or a disciplined approach is taken, these adjustments may either cause or prevent defects. Continuous maintenance, the *ad hoc* approach, increases the likelihood of defects by adding more procedural code to applications. Continuous improvement, the disciplined approach, reuses existing code instead of adding new code. This is accomplished by deploying proven components in new roles.

Sometimes change can be accommodated simply by rearranging the activation path. Of course, new requirements often call for re-engineering existing components to add new responsibilities. Database control tables maintain quality data on each component, including downtime and repair data. If the repair history is beyond tolerance, the component is re-engineered to make it more reliable.

Adding new functionality to a component sometimes increases its complexity to the point that the component no longer performs a single function. If so, specific functions are delegated to a new component, which then enters the spiral of reuse and improvement.

■ 10.2 GETTING STARTED WITH THE DATABASE FACTORY

Given the need to align information system resources toward corporate survival, what constitutes a realistic action plan? Just as no enterprise instantly switches from leadership to complacency, no complacent company becomes competitive overnight. A complacent organization must first realize that its survival is threatened. Next, it must reach consensus on how to proceed. In the case of the information technology (MIS) department, the path forward includes the choice of a technology architecture. Once consensus is reached, re-engineering proceeds. Figure 10.8 illustrates the transitional states from complacency to competitiveness.

10.2.1 From Complacency to Competitiveness

While an organization remains complacent, the MIS department and corporate management remain in maintenance mode. As long as reports reach their recipients and the computer stays up, no need is perceived to disturb the MIS glass house. Because innovative uses of technology appear to be costly solutions chasing nonexistent problems, innovation is nearly impossible in a complacent corporate culture. However, this complacent phase is an ideal time for systems professionals to gear up and become better informed. The subsequent, turbulent phases on the road to competitiveness may not allow time for reading books, attending seminars, or visiting trade shows.

Eventually, when business conditions change, the perception sets in that all is not well with the firm. During this phase, as an awareness grows that the enterprise is out of alignment with the marketplace, a parallel perception develops that the MIS department is out of alignment with the firm. This leads to feelings of dissatisfaction. For a company experiencing a downturn, MIS is seen as not delivering value for money. If the areas that MIS serves lose head count, why should the MIS

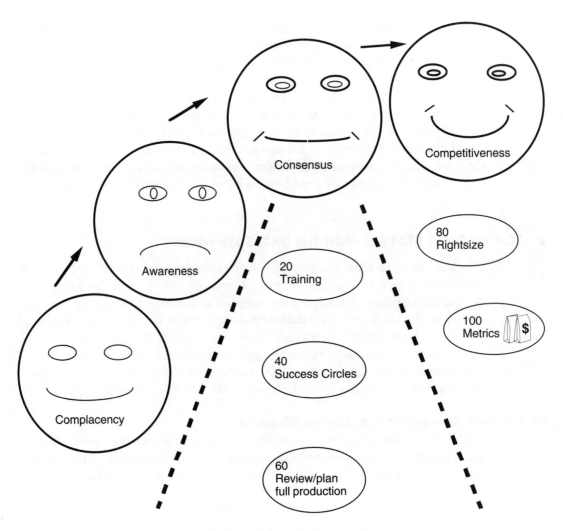

Figure 10.8 Power-up states

department not lose head count? Although information technology budget cuts occur at this point, it is also a good time to launch low-budget "easy win" initiatives.

When the firm emerges from a downturn along with a recovery in its marketplace, MIS is often considered a drag on performance. Obviously, the perception that MIS prevents profit centers from doing their best is unfair to a department that has been forced to operate a reduced service within a reduced budget. However, defensive posturing is no substitute for early visible results.

During the complacent phase, MIS organizations often lag so far behind current technology that they cannot produce quick results. During the awareness stage, the MIS department should improve its responsiveness. If not, internal customers may turn to outsourcing. They may slap together home-grown workgroup applications that lack important features such as data sharing, security, standards, and documentation.

Whether development proceeds in cooperation with or in spite of the MIS department, the development technology probably will differ from that of existing systems. The awareness phase is a good time for the MIS department to take the lead and try out alternative technologies. To minimize the disruptive political side effects of introducing new technology, a skunkworks is sometimes appropriate in this phase.

10.2.2 Skunkworks Development

A *skunkworks* is a small, unofficial development facility for limited-scope projects. Small size helps keep the skunkworks unobtrusive. If the skunkworks cannot be found, it cannot be sidetracked. The small scope of skunkworks activities is a self-imposed constraint, intended to assure success with limited resources.

Because a skunkworks project has a smaller scope and shorter duration than a large-scale legacy technology project, a spiral system development methodology is appropriate. Legacy project control uses large, discrete project phases. In the traditional waterfall method of project control, the phases often are called analysis, design, and implementation. Within these large phases are intermediate milestones and checkpoints. The waterfall method is too cumbersome for the rapid development activities of a skunkworks. For example, requirements analysis, database design, and communications interface testing may well be concurrent activities in a client/server skunkworks.

Two alternatives to the traditional waterfall method, which are suitable for skunkworks project control, are

- "Minicascades" (that is, parallel "miniwaterfalls" for each activity)
- Spiral development (that is, iterative requirements/design/coding in successive refinements).

One advantage of spiral development is that it allows for incomplete results at each cycle. If a prototype component is not fully functional, it will be improved in the next cycle. One note of caution is that the cycles must be brief and the scope of rework must be kept small for rapid protocycling to prove effective. Crawling out of a 1-meter hole is easier than leaping out of a 10-meter pit. Paradoxically, in the skunkworks failure breeds success. Alternative application behavior and alternative implementation technologies are quickly and quietly evaluated. Competing GUI client software, desktop hardware platforms, middleware, and even database servers can be installed, exchanged, or reconfigured without politics or embarrassment.

Skunkworks development is unencumbered by the perfectionism associated with traditional mainframe development. Historically, rigorous specification was cost-effective because the cost of rework associated with legacy technology is very high. Freezing the design, programming rigorously, and reviewing structured program code prior to system testing used to be important. Such activities have only one goal: to specify program behavior in great detail before committing expensive labor to the programming effort.

Although the goal of avoiding rework is understandable, labor-intensive traditional design easily can cost more in a client/server environment than the rework it is intended to avoid. In any event, the window of design in a volatile business environment is necessarily short. No matter how rigorous the specification, major shifts in business requirements within lead time may invalidate the design.

■ 10.3 THE POWER-UP SEQUENCE

Powering up the Database Factory, like other re-engineering activities in this book, is an evolutionary spiral with the following four phases:

- **Plan**. Organize Success Circles, train participants, and plan a pilot application.
- **Build**. Build a pilot plant, Component Case kits, and a Development Warehouse.
- **Test**. Test components in pilot workflows, refine, and then retest.
- **Review**. Evaluate initial results and review quality metrics.

The review phase leads into the planning phase of the next sweep through the spiral. Any point in the power-up spiral contains forward momentum and alignment with business goals.

The power-up spiral prevents "analysis paralysis" and avoids lengthy delays during coding. Weekly Success Circle reviews cut development risk and guide continuous improvement. Built-in Development Warehouse quality metrics provide a framework for benchmarking active components.

After the initial power-up iterations, as component sharing and reuse take hold, the technical facilitators shift their efforts to new workgroups entering the develop-

Table 10.7 Goals and Objectives

Broad Goal	Measurable Objective	Means of Attainment
Market-driven	Internal customer satisfaction	Success Circles
	Earn external customer loyalty	Data Warehouse, gateways
Asset management	Active component architecture	Database, workflows
	Shared and recyclable components	Development Warehouse
Enterprise environment	Connect information islands	Data Warehouse, agents
	Collaborative workflows	Event-driven components
Empower participants	Team environment	Success Circles
	Access to resources	Warehouse showroom
Focus on quality	Quality metrics	Control tables
	Continuous improvement	Component tracking and recycling
	Defect prevention	Agents, state-based processing

ment spiral. The skill requirement for ongoing initiatives shifts from technical to business expertise. The faster development takes on a business focus, the sooner the Database Factory pays back its cost. Advanced technology—especially products that support an active database—accelerate the development spiral. Fortunately, several database vendors now offer various active database features in their client/server products. However, technology alone cannot guarantee success.

Active database applications are successful when they foster competitive advantage by

- Increasing product and service quality
- Minimizing time-to-market while maximizing responsiveness
- Lowering operating costs and adding value with each operation.

Table 10.7 summarizes competitiveness goals, supporting objectives, and the Database Factory features that provide a means to attain those objectives.

■ 10.4 CALL TO ACTION

This book has presented the Database Factory, a framework for enterprise computing. Innovative companies will make use of this framework to take advantage of business opportunities that suddenly arise and abruptly disappear. The skill and dedication of individual employees and managers in these companies differentiates the competitive leaders of each industry from the less agile followers who spend more, but achieve much less. Information technology professionals owe it to themselves and their organizations to power up the Database Factory in order to help the enterprise survive and prosper.

GLOSSARY

active server Database server that incorporates its own control structure for SQL execution, event management, and database programming

agility Rapid resource creation, deployment, and reallocation to take advantage of new circumstances

alternation Command execution that is dependent on a condition or logical case (for example, *if* statement)

application log An application table that stores audit trail data

ASCII American Standard Code for Information Interchange, a character-encoding standard

assembly Software or manufactured products constructed from standard components

association Relationship whose behavior creates a persistent result set (associative entity)

associative entities Abstract entities storing data from a relationship between two main concepts

associative table Table holding data pertaining to associative entities

asynchronous event Event that occurs while an event subscriber continues its work

bandwidth Message-carrying capacity of the communications medium

Bill of Labor Breakdown of assemblies by per-operation labor cost

Bill of Materials Breakdown of assemblies by subassemblies and individual parts

Bill of Operations Breakdown of assemblies by build operations

bind variable Variable in an embedded SQL program for sending data to the database

blob Binary large object; massive binary data stored in the database

cascading delete Delete operation in which deletion of primary key item causes deletion of foreign key items

change agent Agent responsible for activating and monitoring change activities to synchronize component behavior to server metastate

check constraint A limitation on data-manipulation operations based on a validation check

client/server Message-based cooperative processing model in which server processes provide services to client processes

client Process that is eligible to request services from server process

commit Integrity feature that ensures a completed transaction is applied in its entirety

commit phase Second phase of two-phase commit protocol, in which a distributed update is committed

committed transaction Insert, update, or delete operation(s) that has made a persistent change to the physical database and is, therefore, eligible for recovery

component case A framework for standard component assemblies used in shared business functions

CAD Computer-aided design; graphical design environment for mechanical/electronic engineering

CASE Computer-aided software engineering; graphical design environment for software engineering

CSF   Critical Success Factor, behavior that is critical to an organization's success and can be measured

concurrency   The ability of multiple users to simultaneously read and update the database

concurrent engineering   Collaborative design method utilizing interdepartmental teams (for example, concurrent software engineering)

consignment agent   Warehouse agent responsible for consignment operations

DDL   Data Definition Language, the syntax for creating database structures and declaring key relationships

DML   Data Manipulation Language, the command syntax for database operations

data replication   Automatic propagation of updates from a primary table to a set of distributed replicas

database agent   Utility program that works on behalf of the database server to keep remote components synchronized

database publishing   Integration of desktop publishing software as the client of a database server to produce active documents

DBA   Database administrator, the individual responsible for database security and integrity

database cursor   Embedded SQL structure for row-by-row retrieval/navigation of a database table

DBMS   Database management system, software environment supporting DDL and DML execution

database procedure   A procedure that is stored and executes within the database server

database server   A software process that provides access to and performs operations on the database

database trigger   Code stored in the database that executes in conjunction with an INSERT, UPDATE, or DELETE command

declarative   Asserted (declared) in DDL statements (for example, declarative referential integrity)

demand-driven   Responsive to changes in external requirements (for example, demand-driven inventory)

Development Warehouse   Client/server repository for collaborative application development

distributed update   An update operation on data stored in different locations on different servers

domain   The set of distinct permissible values for a column of a relational database table

download   File-transfer operation from a central computer through a communications line to a local computer

downsizing   Migrating software applications to smaller implementation hardware (for example, mainframe to LAN)

duplicate key   Duplicate primary key, a violation of entity integrity

EDI   Electronic data interchange, a data interconnection convention for commercial transactions

embedded SQL   SQL commands that are incorporated in the source code of a procedural language program

enterprise computing   The alignment of information flows with workflows throughout an organization

ERD   Entity relationship diagram, a document used in database design

entity instance   A row in a database table representing a specific unique occurrence of the entity represented by the table

entity integrity   Condition where each row in a table is uniquely identifiable by the primary key

entity type   A concept, class, or category represented as a database table

event alerter   The message that notifies a subscriber process that an event has occurred

event definition   The act of naming an event and (optionally) defining its semantics

event detection   The means by which the server becomes aware of the occurrence of an event

event management   An active server's ability to define, detect, and respond to state transitions (events)

exception handler   Routine to which control passes automatically when an exception event occurs

exception state   State other than normal state; result state of an exception event

explanatory behavior   Deductive behavior demonstrating that operational objectives are being attained

file-transfer protocol   A convention for the transfer of copies of data among operating environments (for example, ftp in tcp/ip)

flexible factory   A factory that can vary production among different products with minimal setup time

foreign key   A column (or columns) in one database table that refers to the primary key of another table

fourth-generation language   4GL; a nonprocedural language in which high-level commands specify the results of operations

functional decomposition   The breakdown of a multipurpose program into single-purpose routines

fuzzy   Derived from multiple simultaneous membership values (for example, fuzzy metastate)

gateway   Software that translates one environment's protocol to another (for example, RDBMS CICS gateway)

gateway agent   Agent responsible for coordinating remote data sources and distribution points

GUI   Graphical user interface, usually incorporating windows, icons, and pull-down/pop-up menus

hierarchical modularity   Structured programming feature where high-level abstract modules delegate detail work to lower-level modules

history table   Table storing audit trail data reflecting the past condition of items in the database

horizontal scaling   The ability to incrementally improve performance by upgrading an existing server machine's disk, memory, or processors

host variables   Delimited program variables embedded in a SQL string for run-time value substitution

integrity constraint   DDL constraint syntax to protect entity integrity and referential integrity

iteration   Repeated execution of a sequence (for example, *do...while* loop)

just-in-time   Inventory replenishment coordinated with daily production requirements

locking   DBMS feature that prevents conflicting results from concurrent operations

logic table   Table storing control logic to govern the activation of application components

look-up table   Table that represents an abstract concept in the application (for example, *inventory_classification* table, *terms* table)

lower-CASE   CASE environment in which visual interface manipulation generates code

main table   Table that represents a main concept in the application (for example, part table, customer table)

metastate   The collective state comprised of all individual row states in a database table

MRP   Manufacturing resource planning; integrated production control and inventory management

middleware   Communications-oriented software between client and server

mistake proofing   Automatic mistake prevention

multiversioning   Mechanism that preserves the prior state of rows undergoing update to guarantee consistent data-access results

normal state   The correct, standard, or expected state resulting from a state transition

normalization   The breakdown of a complex table into multiple simple tables

notification   The process of informing subscribers that an event has occurred by sending an event alert message

OLTP   On-line transaction processing; characterized by high-volume interactive update activity

OSI Open systems interconnection

package Prepared code modules to perform specific application function(s)

passive server Server that is controlled by external commands and limited to SQL execution

pipe Infrastructure that treats the output of one program as the input to another

prepare phase The first phase of a two-phase commit, in which a distributed update is coordinated

primary key The column(s) that uniquely identifies individual rows in a relational database table

QBE Query-by-example; query construction using hypothetical examples for selection criteria

QBF Query-by-forms; query construction using display screen (form) manipulation for selection criteria

RMA Returned Merchandise Authorization; document allowing return of sold goods, usually for warrantee claim

R3 method Method of workflow definition by Roles, Relationships, and Responsibilities

RISC Reduced instruction set computer, a popular processor type for server machines

referential integrity Consistent key values between rows in two or more tables participating in a relationship

RDBMS Relational database management system, a DBMS supporting the relational model of data

relational model A data-representation model based on tables, nonprocedural operations, and predicate logic

RPC Remote procedure call; a command that executes across a communications interface

real-time Instantaneous processing; process that responds immediately to events (for example, real-time data replication)

replication The propagation of data copies from a primary table on one server to a set of replicas residing on remote servers

rightsizing Implementing on the most appropriate hardware for application tasks

rollback Integrity feature that ensures a canceled transaction is undone in its entirety

routing agent Agent responsible for synchronizing middleware behavior with the overall state of the application

rule A database trigger in the Ingres RDBMS

scaling The ability to move the DBMS to larger (smaller) hardware with corresponding linear performance increase (decrease)

schedule table Control table storing the schedule for time-based component activation

schema Metadata describing database structure; set of catalog entries describing database structures

script Procedural code for behavior (for example, interface object script)

scripting agent Agent responsible for synchronizing behavioral code in application components with the overall state of the application

sequence A set of commands that are executed in their order of appearance within the source code

server A software process that provides access to services (for example, database server)

server machine The computer on which a server resides and executes

server platform Integration of the server machine, its operating system, and its communications environment

server trigger Code stored in the database that executes in conjunction with an INSERT, UPDATE, or DELETE command

sneaker-net Manual file transfer using removable magnetic medium (for example, diskette) by individual wearing tennis shoes

SQL Structured Query Language, the main DDL/DML for database servers

SQLCA SQL communications area; embedded SQL program database interface structure

state The condition of an item with respect to the values of its attributes

state representation   The code utilized for persistent storage of a state; the value of a state as stored in the database

state table   Control table defining all possible states and substates in an application

structured programming   Design methodology that reduces program complexity through functional decomposition

Success Circle   Joint (user and MIS) development team for concurrent software engineering

successive refinement   The principle of improving product quality through continuous modification

SMP   Symmetric multiprocessor, a computer with two or more processors sharing memory and disk

synchronous event   Event that occurs while an event subscriber halts execution and waits

temporary table   Working table having very short persistence

3GL   Third-generation language, procedural programming language with detailed commands for individual operations

TIFF   Tagged Image File Format, a standard format for document images

TQM   Total Quality Management, data structures and behavior for tracking product quality in every operation

transaction   Logical unit of database application work that is either committed or rolled back

2PC   Two-phase commit, a protocol for distributed transaction integrity

upper-CASE   CASE environment in which visual interface manipulation generates design documents

vertical scaling   The ability to port the DBMS to a more (less) powerful machine with a corresponding performance increase (decrease)

visual programming   Programming by manipulating a graphical interface (GUI) instead of writing procedural code

volatile   Characterized by frequent or constant change (for example, volatile data, volatile behavior)

WAN   Wide area network; network connecting geographically remote sites

Warehouse agent   Agent responsible for remote data-access operations on behalf of a Data Warehouse

waterfall   Project control method that features discrete sequential project phases

workflow   Integration of voice, data, and image with automated routing in business procedures

working table   Table holding in-process data for incomplete application behavior

INDEX